W9-CHD-935

What Others ARE SAYING...

"Everyone must decide in his heart if he will live his life for *his own* success, or if he'll dedicate himself to the success *of* God—impacting the lives of others for the cause of Christ. The question we should ask ourselves is not, *'Will I leave a legacy?'* but *'What will be my legacy?'* Phil Downer and Chip MacGregor have done us all a favor, creating a book that helps us know how we can leave a legacy that makes an eternal impact."

~Dr. Joe Stowell
Former President of Moody Bible Institute

"As a nation, we are losing the notion that truth is something to be lived. Being a disciple, one who actually lives all of life under Christ's leadership, is becoming an increasingly radical idea. The man who helps another do the same is even more rare. But Phil Downer is a disciple who helps others. His life is marked by choices only a follower of Christ would make. He is leading his family and his colleagues down that same path, and his authority to write *Eternal Impact* comes out of his own life as a disciple."

~Jim Peterson
Author of Evangelism As A Lifestyle

"Anything written by Phil Downer has to be valuable simply on the basis of this man's life and the example of his family. We have much to learn from this close friend whom Jack and I deeply admire as a man of God, husband, and father."

~Kay Arthur
Precept Ministries

"If Phil Downer had lived at the time of King David, he would have been the leader of David's 'thirty mighty men.' This soldier's consuming passion is to walk with integrity before his Lord. He is a rock-solid, straight-shooting example we can all follow."

~Pat Morley
Author of The Man in the Mirror

"I can think of very few people who are as well qualified as Phil Downer to write a book on a vital topic such as discipleship. Phil has modeled being both a disciple and a discipler ever since the day he came to know Christ personally. This book will benefit the Kingdom, and I recommend it enthusiastically."

~Ron Blue
Founder, Ronald Blue & Company
President, Christian Financial Professionals Network

Eternal IMPACT

INVESTING IN THE LIVES OF OTHERS

PHIL DOWNER

with Chip MacGregor

ETERNAL IMPACT PUBLISHING
Signal Mountain, Tennessee

Scripture quotations in this book, except those noted, are taken from the New American Standard Bible.

New American Standard Bible, © 1960, 1962, 1963, 1968, 1971, 1972, 1973, 1975, 1977 by The Lockman Foundation. Used by permission.

New International Version, ®, Copyright © 1973, 1978, 1984 by the International Bible Society. Used by permission of Zondervan Publishing House. The "NIV" and "New International Version" trademarks are registered in the United States Patent and Trademark Office by International Bible Society.

The King James Version (KJV)

Scripture quotations marked NLT are taken from the Holy Bible, New Living Translation, copyright © 1996. Used by permission of Tyndale House Publishers, Inc., Wheaton, Illinois 60189. All rights reserved.

Cover design by Jessica Tucker Design, Signal Mountain, Tennessee

ETERNAL IMPACT

Copyright © 1997, 2005 by Phil Downer

Published by Eternal Impact Publishing
Signal Mountain, Tennessee 37377

Second Edition

Library of Congress Control Number   2004104171

ISBN 0-9742295-7-1

All rights reserved. No portion of this book may be reproduced in any form without the written permission of the publisher.

Printed in the United States of America

05 06 07 08 09 10 / DH / 10 9 8 7 6 5 4 3 2

Eternal Impact Publishing exists
to provide excellence in resources
for the passion of helping people grasp
and fulfill their God-given purpose
of living life to know, adore, enjoy,
and exalt Jesus Christ and reaching and
discipling others to do the same.

Paul Q. Downer, Managing Director
PaulDowner@DNAministries.org

Dedication

I am dedicating this book to all those men and women whom Susy and I have had the privilege of discipling over the last twenty-five years, including our children—Abigail, Paul, Matthew, Joshua, Anna, and Susanna. We pray they will stand in the gap, continue the fight, and finish well, winning and discipling others long after we have departed the scene.

~Phil Downer

For my son, Colin. May you make an eternal impact as you live for Him.

~Papa

Forword
by Susy Downer

To whom do you owe your life? Your marriage? Your children? Your ministry?

Of course it is the Lord, but if you could identify one person, wouldn't you want to thank that person? Model that person? Suppose you were like me and there was one person you had never met who was responsible (with our sovereign Lord) for a woman in your town coming to know Christ and reaching another woman who reached you in the depth of the despair from your destroyed marriage. Suppose it was through this same person, as it was with me, that a doctor was willing to disciple your husband who struggled with anger, unfaithfulness, and workaholism. Wouldn't you want to help others model that person, too?

Through the consequences of the faithfulness of a woman I had not met, I was given salvation, a spiritual mother, a changed husband, and a mended marriage. Flowing out of this miracle a few years later came our six children and a thrilling, fulfilling ministry in which all eight of us participate. I know you, like me, would want to meet that woman and learn the Scriptural principles that so dramatically changed so many people through the power of our Lord. In this book, Phil has given an account of the biblical principles and practical applications necessary not only to benefit from such a person, but to become such a person yourself. Don't miss reading this book. If you can't afford to buy it, let us know, and we will find a way to provide it to you.

Table of CONTENTS

A Soldier
on the
FRONT LINES

Two friends of mine went home to be with the Lord recently, and their passing started me thinking about eternal things. Both men loved the Lord, and both tried to serve Him, but as I thought about their lives, a vivid contrast became apparent. One had made an eternal impact, leaving a legacy of righteousness still felt in the lives of those left behind. The other had made a temporary impact, and though he was active in the faith, I don't know that he'll be remembered long because he left no one behind to continue the fight. Let me explain . . . .

I had been friends with Chuck for more than twenty years, and I was excited to finally see the factory he'd built up over his years in business. Chuck had encouraged my wife and me early in ministry, getting us to share our testimonies and operate as a couple, and he had stood with us through some difficult financial times. He had modeled integrity to his people, and had discipled many men into maturity in Christ. But Chuck had been diagnosed with cancer, and when he invited me into his office, I knew he didn't have long to live.

The secretary showed me through corridors reeking of success, the smell of machine oil wafting through the air of that hundred-million-dollar, privately owned business. Chuck greeted me halfway down the hallway of the executive suite, and I expected to be ushered toward the factory, so I could see the manufacturing process and perhaps gain some leadership insights from the man who had created it all. Instead, Chuck steered me into his office, its walls filled with awards and honors garnered through a lifetime of service. That's when I thought Chuck had invited me into his office to review his life and perhaps talk about his disease. But he didn't say a word about his awards. Instead, he pointed to two chairs pushed over toward one side of the room. Then, with hands raised as if presenting an offering, Chuck said to me, "This is where it happens, Phil. This is where I meet the men I'm discipling."

I was shocked. He hadn't brought me in to show me his business or to talk about leadership or even to discuss the cancer which was ravaging his body. He just wanted to show me the place where he had discipled men. As he neared the end of his life, Chuck wanted to encourage someone else to take up the mantle of discipleship. The manufacturing plant had made a lot of money, and Chuck's managerial wisdom had been appreciated by many, but at the end of his time on earth, all he could talk about were the men he'd discipled. The rest of it didn't matter. You see, Chuck understood that businesses come and go, and trophies just gather dust on a shelf, but changing a life through the love of Jesus Christ is the one thing he'd accomplished which would have an eternal impact. As his time on earth drew to a close, Chuck understood that spiritual reproduction in the lives of others is the only way a man can live on after his death. The men he had prepared and equipped for spiritual leadership were his legacy.

How different Chuck's life is from that of my other friend, Randy. Randy is also dying, a brother with a healthy business but an unhealthy heart. Randy called me and asked if I'd come visit him, but all he could talk about was his frustration. He was no longer being asked to sit on boards any more, nor was his opinion sought on major decisions. Church and business went on without him, and he even complained that his own children no longer sought his advice. A resentment had built toward those who had left him behind. Randy had created a great business and had many organizational relationships with others, but he had never discipled another man. He had spoken to big groups, created jobs, given generously to his church, and served on countless committees, but he had never fostered spiritual growth in others. As he faced his last months of life, Randy realized that no one would weep when he died. Some partners and friends might feel sadness for a few days, but then he'd be forgotten, his life quickly fading like the morning mist on a sunny day.

This book is written for all of us who have a desire to give our lives to the things that last forever. After the will is read, the assets claimed, and the money distributed, the lives of most men and women will be forgotten. For all their success and all their striving, their achievements will turn out to be minor and temporary. But the person who decides to invest in the spiritual lives of others will make an eternal impact. He will leave behind an army—a battle-ready group of spiritual soldiers who are focused on the Lord and who will always remember the wisdom built into their lives by their leader's guidance and example. Randy left behind a will. Chuck left behind a willing army. Randy died frustrated. Chuck died fulfilled. Randy's legacy is like a cloud, fading quickly away. Chuck's legacy is like a crowd, with prepared men marching off to disciple others.

At the end of my life, I want to go out like Chuck. I want to leave a legacy of trained, active spiritual soldiers of the cross, who will stand in the gap for the Lord Jesus Christ, winning and discipling others long after I'm gone. Several years ago I learned how I can have that sort of eternal impact, and this book is my attempt to pass the information along to a new generation. You have probably heard speakers talk about the importance of having a "Paul" in your life who disciples you and to whom you can turn when you need wisdom, advice, and direction. At the same time, you need a "Timothy"—someone in whom you are investing your life. You have been called by God to be light in the darkness and to mentor those who have accepted the light. It's the most exciting assignment in the world to be the spiritual parent for one of God's new babies—to see God use you to reach a man or woman on the path to hell, watch him change before your eyes, and be part of the process of helping him become mature in the Lord, a reproducing Christian who will carry on the Great Commission. It's an important job, and it's been entrusted to you and me.

When Paul first met Timothy, the young man wasn't very impressive. He was a mama's boy, raised by women, with a weak stomach and a retiring personality. But Timothy had a heart for God, and by spending time with the Apostle, his life changed. He was able to see how Paul lived. He observed Paul's teaching, talked with him until late into the night, and had the opportunity to minister to others under his direction. Timothy grew to be a strong, mature man of God. He continued to be different from Paul, more gentle, and perhaps not as quick to confront others, but Timothy became a leader in the early church and a pastor to many. His time with Paul equipped him as a soldier in the army of God, ready to do battle with the enemy.

That same type of relationship is what changed my life. A mature man of God stepped in and became my "Paul," and I became his "Timothy." I watched him work, listened to him talk, and learned from him. Soon we were ministering together, and over time, he prepared me to disciple others. That's when I became a "Paul" and I started working with some "Timothys." And in those relationships I found the key to fulfilling the Great Commission. We've been instructed by our Lord to "Go and make disciples" (Matthew 28:19), but most Christians don't know what a disciple is or how to go about making one. This book is written to help you learn. Chip and I wrote it so that you can learn to be a "Paul."

The events in the following chapters, recording Susy's and my salvation, our mended marriage, and the gift of our family and ministry today, began when God brought into our lives a young single mother who had been a Christian less than a year, who reached out to Susy and began discipling her. It was through that relationship that I was invited to an outreach meeting where I heard the claims of Christ and was later introduced to the man who would become my "Paul."

Men, women, young people – this book is for you. Change the names, the professions, and the genders in the pages ahead to those of your friends, relatives, neighbors, and coworkers, and see yourself as God's instrument to make an eternal impact on the world. Please note that throughout the book, as we talk about discipleship in terms of different relationships with friends, neighbors, and colleagues, we are always assuming that men will be meeting only with men and women will be meeting only with women because of the needs for safeguards as well as the importance of avoiding any appearance of impropriety. In many instances, however, Susy and I have found that God has used us effectively as a couple in the lives of another couple.

I believe you will find the chapters ahead to be interesting and empowering. My goal is to give you a plan for becoming a man or woman willing, able, and equipped with the vision to answer God's call to make disciples.

When I was in Vietnam, I was a soldier on the front lines equipped for battle. I didn't want to wait around in the rear area. The Marines had trained me to fight, and that's what I wanted to do. I feel the same way about my faith. Believers haven't been called to sit in the barracks or to hide behind the lines or to pretend we're not in the army of God. As Christians, we have been called to get equipped and go into the fray. This book will get you ready to fight.

PART ONE

Investing in
the Lives
OF OTHERS

*O*ne night in June 1944, General Dwight D. Eisenhower walked the beaches of England, alone with his thoughts. Occasionally he would stop and stare across the dark waters of the English Channel toward the coast of France, where the Nazi armies had built a military fortress. The next dawn would see hundreds of allied ships and thousands of soldiers storm that coast, and General Eisenhower knew that for many of those soldiers, it would be their last morning.

As he walked along, he came across an American private, standing by himself, also staring across the ocean. The General asked him what he was thinking about. "Home," came the reply. Then the Supreme Commander of Allied Forces suggested they walk together, that perhaps they would draw confidence from each other's company. So the two men walked on—one older, one younger; one experienced in the ways of war, the other inexperienced, but each man drawing strength from the other.

That is exactly what many people need today—others to walk with them, offering wisdom and encouragement, particularly in difficult times. Men in our world are in turmoil. The pressures of our modern age are draining away the joy and leaving people too exhausted to experience the abundant life God has promised. They are physically tired, emotionally drained, overwhelmed by debt, and trying to cope with damaged relationships.

What a person needs is someone to draw close, minister to him, and help him mature. He needs somebody to demonstrate for him another way to live, modeling a godly marriage, biblical parenthood, and the love of Christ. He needs someone who will take the time to parent him in his spiritual walk, helping him find the new life Christ promised. Many women are where Susy was, in a painful relationship, feeling trapped and unsure where to turn. *Many people are exactly like Susy and I were years ago, in need of spiritual parents.*

Dr. Jim Lyon did that for me. Liane Day, a divorced mom, did that for Susy. They spent time with us in the Scriptures each week, inviting us into their home and allowing us to see what a spiritually mature Christian is like. They made their lives transparent so we could see the real Jim and Liane inside, and they showed us the importance of opening our own lives to them as well. They became our spiritual parents, and their investment changed our lives. This part of the book is designed to help you make that same sort of investment in another person's life. It will show you the steps necessary to develop a rewarding discipling relationship and help you make that same sort of impact in the life of someone else.

CHAPTER 1

Success to SIGNIFICANCE

*W*hat is the most important thing that has ever happened in your life? Was it completing your education? Deciding on a career? The birth of your first child? For me, it was realizing that God was recruiting me to play a part in His eternal plan. He has called me to impact the world, even after I'm no longer here. He wants me to help Him fill up His eternal kingdom.

As Susy says about Marilyn, the woman who reached Judi, who was the woman who discipled Liane, who in turn reached us, "I owe everything to that woman. I don't know where I would be today if God hadn't used her to begin this chain of changed lives, that now includes our children, who are now winning and discipling their peers."

God has taken a risk and called us to work with Him. He wants us to take people who are far away from Him and bring them near. He wants us to take people who are near and help bring them into maturity in Christ. The Lord has called you and me to mentor and disciple men, women, and young people so that they begin to reproduce themselves in the lives of others. God is calling us to join ranks with men like the Apostle Paul by faithfully helping other people grow up in Jesus Christ. Rather than merely achieving success at some career while we are on this earth, the Lord wants us to play a significant role in shaping the lives of others. That's the job to which He has called all Christians—including you.

Paul understood this job. When writing to a young protégé, he once said, "You therefore, my son, be strong in the grace that is in Christ Jesus. And the things which you have heard from me in the presence of many witnesses, these entrust to faithful men, who will be able to teach others also" (2 Timothy 2:1-2). In other words, Paul understood his role: he was to pass on God's message to trustworthy people, who in turn would pass it along to others. Paul became the spiritual *father* to Timothy, and as Timothy passed on the message, Paul became a spiritual *grandfather* and *great-grand-father*. There are four generations in that verse—Paul, who trained Timothy, who trained faithful men, who in turn trained others.

Through the centuries, God passed on His message of salvation through ordinary people . . . and one day someone eventually told you. Most of us didn't come to know Christ by watching a television preacher or reading about Him in a tract but through a relationship with a friend or a family member who loved us enough to tell us the truth. They became our spiritual parents, part of a chain that leads back two thousand years, to Jesus Christ and His twelve disciples.

If we are faithful, that chain will lead forward into the future, adding more new links than we can even imagine.

The people who have made up that chain have been ordinary men and women, but they have been given a super-natural power that has allowed them to conquer kingdoms, influence lives, and alter the course of history. And they have done it all one by one, spreading the love of God and taking His message and the new life it promises to every part of the world. Each person who loves Jesus Christ brings a new dynamic to the cause, and a new circle of people who can be changed by His love. Every relationship is unique and carries with it special opportunities, which is the reason friendships are so crucial to God's agenda.

I was a lawyer, focused on my own success, living to please myself, when I met the Lord. It was a woman named Liane Day who took the initial steps that would eventually lead this reprobate lawyer to a saving knowledge of Jesus Christ. Liane was herself a new Christian, still reeling from the blow of her husband's leaving, throwing her into an unwanted divorce and catapulting her into the work force without a college education in order to provide for her two children. However, Liane had a friend named Judi, who loved her through the turmoil, led her to Jesus, and began discipling her. One day Liane found herself at a baby shower sitting on a couch next to my wife, Susy. She didn't know that Susy was a successful lawyer or that she was about to divorce me. She simply sensed that this woman next to her was strug-gling in some way, so Liane reached out and shared her faith in Christ with my wife.

Those two women began working through a popular one-on-one discipleship series called *Operation Timothy*. It was Liane's great sense of God's power and unmatched peace that caused Susy to be attracted to her the first time they met. Through that study and their growing friendship my wife realized that a relationship with Jesus Christ was possible and that it was probably the missing ingredient in facing her biggest problem—living with a tyrannical husband. It was Liane who suggested to Susy they figure out a way for me to attend an outreach luncheon sponsored by CBMC (Christian Business Men's Committee) where another businessman named Paul shared the gospel with me. That event led to my coming to Christ and getting acquainted with Dr. Jim Lyon.

My life was never the same after meeting Jim. He went over God's assurance of my salvation, answered my questions, and helped me cement that decision to give my heart to Jesus Christ. But our relationship didn't end there— it was just beginning. For the next three years, Jim met with me each week. I became his "Timothy" as he shared his life with me and helped me mature in my faith. He didn't merely offer me information or assume going through a workbook would provide me with adequate training. He opened up his life, sharing his joys and struggles, so I could observe how a godly man lived. Mine was supposed to be a new life in Christ, and Dr. Jim made sure I had a chance to see how that new life was operative in another man's life.

Jim wasn't perfect, of course. But without his example I would have had no idea how the Christian life was different from my pagan lifestyle. For you see, Jim wasn't just having a Bible study with me; he was passing on his faith and his life. He was giving me spiritual training so I could become a soldier in the army of God, fully equipped for the spiritual battle. And the whole process started because one divorced young mother decided to start talking with the troubled woman attorney sitting on the couch next to her at a baby shower.

THE CHRISTIAN SOLDIER

I believe every Christian is called to be a soldier for Christ on the front lines; if he stays in the rear, he will see his life detoured, discouraged, and even defeated. I tend to subscribe to the "soldier and donut" principle: a Marine is trained to be a fighting man, not to sit around eating donuts. If he is assigned for long periods of time to the rear, he only gets into fights, gets drunk, contracts venereal disease, and gets busted. This happens because Marines are trained to *stay in the battle.* That's where their equipment works best, where their training is fulfilled, and where their lives are most useful.

The same is true of the Christian soldier. Our lives are best lived in the battle of winning and discipling men and women, whether at the office, in the neighborhood, at church, in a prison, or in our own home. A Marine away from the battlefield constantly has to be reminded to keep his weapon clean, instructed on the chain of command, and counseled about the importance of teamwork and the countless other aspects of soldiering. However, one flash of enemy fire calls the Marine to war. All other problems are suddenly forgotten in a millisecond when he inhales the scent of battle.

A Christian man may argue with his wife on his way out the door to work, but she suddenly becomes a great blessing when he sits across the table with someone whose wife has just filed for divorce. I was having an early morning argument with Susy by telephone just before I met with a friend whose wife had moved in with his best friend. Somehow the pettiness of my bickering instantly melted away, and I realized the gift God has given me in a woman who is faithful. By the same token, I have loved it over the years when Susy came home after spending time with a woman she was discipling and commented, "Next to most women, I simply don't have a problem in the world." If we Christians would stop all the bickering over the color of the pew pads, we could get out into the battle and see what life is really all about. It's time we stop focusing our lives on *success* and begin to focus on *significance.*

Our modern culture is enamored with the concept of success, though most businessmen can't really define it. We all know those who are "successful," and we generally associate this achievement with salary and perks, but if you ask one hundred people to define the word, chances are you'll get one hundred different definitions. To one, "success" means moving up the corporate ladder. To another, "success" is measured in numbers of units sold. *Webster's Dictionary* defines success as "attaining a desired end," and the vagueness of that definition proves my point. We don't know exactly what success is, but we know how it feels. That's the reason I like this definition: "Success is the feeling you get when you reach your goals."[1]

Reflect on that definition for a moment. You might earn a million dollars a year, but if your goal was two million, you don't feel successful. You might be the best salesman in your company's history, but if your goal is to move into management and you aren't offered the job, you don't feel successful. Our culture is in love with success. Our world system feeds on it. The accumulation of wealth and position, the trappings of "success," are the greatest values to our fallen world. But the thing to remember is that, as Christians, we don't share the values of the world. Our values have been changed by the power of God.

Success is based on a feeling, and I've found that feelings come and go. That's why I can feel like a million bucks when I buy a new car, but a few months later I find that my new car no longer gives me the feeling of success and fulfillment it used to. So I need to buy something else to prop up my fragile feelings of success. And not only are the feelings fragile; they are fleeting. During the playoff games in the NFL one season, an announcer referred to a player—a man at the pinnacle of his profession, playing on one of the best teams in the playoffs for the right to go to the Super Bowl—by saying, "He stinks." That announcer didn't mention that the man was playing below his ability or that he was having a difficult day. He simply summed him up by telling the world he was a

---

1. Thanks to Chip MacGregor and Bobb Biehl for this definition.

failure. Success is not just a feeling, but also a short-lived feeling.

One day I was having breakfast with a famous NASCAR racer who had a half dozen airplanes, hundreds of acres of land, a beautiful wife, cute children, and tons of money coming in every month from endorsements. But he had not won a race in ten months. He told me, "Phil, I'm only as good as my last race."

That's the world's perspective on success. You have to achieve, and you have to keep achieving, or you're a loser.

So when you look across your driveway at the family next door that appears so "together" or you gaze across the conference table at the businessman who seemingly has the world by the tail, remember that the message they often hear and will continue to hear throughout their lives, is that they "stink." They had better succeed because the world hates a loser.

It is to this world of losers, however, that Jesus came to say, " I offer you abiding love, unconditional acceptance, and undeserved glory eternally." That's good news, and the Lord has given us the great privilege, as well as challenge, of being His messengers taking that news to the world. (I sometimes accuse the Lord of "negligent entrustment" to consider using the likes of me in reaching a world so desperate for a savior!)

MOVING TO SIGNIFICANCE

Recently a friend of mine was sitting in a small group with a very wealthy Christian man. The man had an expensive suit, a Rolex watch, and a black Mercedes parked outside—the picture of success. But in the group he admitted he felt like a failure because he hadn't met his personal goals. Success is nothing but a feeling, and it has a tendency to be selfish. Unfortunately, the church has largely bought into the world's standard for success. We often consider the pastors with the largest churches to be "successful." The guy who faithfully preaches the Word to a small congregation just isn't a success in our eyes. That sort of thinking is entirely unbiblical. By those standards the prophet Isaiah was a dismal failure. He preached repentance for years in Israel, and nobody listened to him. Dare I say that Jesus Christ was *really* a flop by the world's standards? He never could have made it in the modern church-growth movement because over the course of His ministry, His congregation became smaller rather than larger!

So while our culture values success over almost anything else, the Lord isn't too concerned with success. You see, God doesn't care about our worldly attainments. He is much more interested in the concept of *significance*. If *success* is just a feeling you get when you reach your goals, *significance* is "making a difference in the lives of people over time." Successful men and women have come and gone, but it is the *significant* people who have changed the course of history. They are the ones remembered, because they have left a legacy of lives behind. It is time we left behind the old way of thinking. It's time we abandoned our worldly pursuit of *success* and began engaging in the godly pursuit of *significance*.

Most people *want* to be remembered, to feel that their lives count for something. Paul told Timothy, "I have fought the good fight, I have finished the course, I have kept the faith" (2 Timothy 4:7). I think every Christian wants to "finish well." A popular myth going around the Christian world is that "finishing well" is best defined as "not committing adultery," or "not being exposed a fraud," or "not wallowing in greed." Certainly those qualities are good, but they die at the grave when we go on to our home with God.

Success is the feeling you get when you
reach your goals. . . .

Significance is making a difference in the lives
of people over time.

I believe the definition of "finishing well" is not merely living our lives free of indictment but leaving behind a legacy of men and women set upon a course to reproduce themselves in the lives of other people. After all, however faithful Paul, Timothy, Silas, Priscilla, and Aquilla were, if the Christian movement had ended with their deaths, of what significance would their lives have been? The worth of your life is not simply how you live but how you reproduce your life in others, causing them, in turn, to "Go therefore and make disciples of all the nations." Matthew 28:19). That discipleship process, if multiplied around the world, might truly result in a revival that would shock history. Satan tricks people into thinking they will find meaning for their lives through success, but that's a lie. Meaning in life comes from leaving a legacy of godly people!

To become a person of significance, you have to invest yourself in the life of another. You have to commit yourself to helping someone else mature in the faith. Discipling is nothing more than establishing a relationship with another person, then helping him or her grow up in Jesus Christ. Women have already grasped this fact. While most men are task-oriented, most women are naturally relationship-oriented. That's why at any church gathering, women immediately get together and start to talk, often sharing deep feelings, while men take hours just to build up to a discussion about the local sports teams. For a number of years women have pursued what traditionally have been men's careers, trying to find meaning and fulfillment through *success* the way their husbands and fathers tried. Now we are seeing women leaving the traditional work force in droves, heading home to be with their children, because they have observed the negative impact on the family when both the husband and wife have a career outside the home. Mothers seem to be increasingly understanding that the *significance* they can have in their children's lives far outweighs the *success* of a career.

SIGNIFICANT MEN AND WOMEN

You may be familiar with the mathematical explanation of spiritual multiplication, which demonstrates the power of multiplying your life one by one. If continued over a few short decades, we could actually reach every man, woman, and child in the world. For example, if you were the only Christian on earth and you spent one year sharing the gospel with one other person who became a Christian, and then the two of you both committed to becoming spiritual reproducers, your ranks would double every year. Within ten years your group would have growth from just the two of you to five hundred trained disciplers. After twenty years there would be more than half a million disciplers. In a little more than thirty years, we could reach the world for Jesus Christ!

Undoubtedly, not every person who is reached for Christ goes on to multiply himself, and it usually takes longer than a year for most people to become spiritual reproducers, but the illustration is effective nonetheless. There are many Christians available to reproduce themselves today. If we were all focused on the goal of being spiritual reproducers, of choosing significance over success, what God could do with the resulting army of disciple makers would be enormous.

When Paul wrote from his jail cell in Rome to encourage the Christians at Philippi, he said, "But even if I am being poured out as a drink offering upon the sacrifice and service of your faith, I rejoice and share my joy with you all" (Philippians 2:17). Paul is referring to a Jewish sacrifice, saying his life is like the drink offering that was poured out on the altar of God. When the cup was turned upside down, all the contents were spilled out. There was nothing held back; it all belonged to the Lord.

That's what Paul's life was like—completely sold out to serving God, his life a sacrifice to the Lord. He gave everything to serve God by discipling men and women into maturity. Paul wasn't worried about meeting the world's standard of success. He was committed to making his life significant. He invested in the lives of people over time, and his investment changed our world forever.

Dan Sylvester, who operates a manufacturing company in the Midwest, built a multi-million dollar enterprise from a basement project he started as a teenager. But along with becoming a manufacturer of auto parts, Sylvester devoted a few hours each week to discipling men in his growing company. He started with a delivery boy who went on to become a college graduate and is now pastoring a church. His other Timothys have included the man who later became his director of operations and his top two salesmen. Other business leaders often ask him where he got such a fine Christian staff, and his response is always, "I invested in God's invention—people—and along the way I was investing in my business." Sylvester won't admit to how many men he has impacted, but his friends say it must be thousands when you consider the third and fourth generations of faithfulness passed on from man to man over the years. He's never been much of a traveler, and he shies away from big religious events, but Dan Sylvester has truly impacted the world by influencing many people for Christ.

Dee was a successful single businesswoman, criss-crossing the country lecturing on time management. While she continued to ask God for a godly husband, her specific goal was to colabor in her marriage, discipling others. Along came Bob, a widower with adult children. They joined into an exciting marriage and partnership focused on discipling their neighbors, business colleagues, friends, and his children.

Brother or Sister, *you* are the pivotal factor in someone's eternal destiny. God can use you to bring others to Him, and to help them grow to maturity. Your life-on-life example— sharing your life with that of a spiritual brother or sister—is imperative if you are going to help others grow up in Jesus Christ. Your story, your struggles, and the simple matter of accompanying another on his or her spiritual journey will make all the difference in the world. If you demonstrate a willingness to give something of yourself so others can have a part in the riches of God's kingdom, you can change your world for the cause of Christ. As you get involved in the adventure of helping others discover God's love and grow into maturity, you will find power you never thought possible. You will also be drawn closer to God and experience the wonderful adventure that comes from serving Him.

It may be that you have been active in religion yet are still wondering where you will spend eternity and how you will be judged. I was that way at one time. An elder in my church, serving as a Sunday School teacher, I had acknowledged some religious principles but I had not accepted a relationship with Jesus Christ. Then I attended that CBMC luncheon in which Paul Johnson, a builder from Birmingham, Michigan, explained to me how he had found joy today and peace eternally. He told me that God loved me so much He sent His Son to pay the penalty for my sins. Jesus Christ died as a sacrifice in my place, submitting to death on a cross in order to give me life eternal. He was dead and buried, but on the third day He rose again. We know this is true, for He was seen by more than five hundred people, and their lives were changed because of their newfound relationship with Christ.

Then Paul Johnson read to me Romans 10:9 "If you confess with your mouth Jesus as Lord, and believe in your heart that God raised Him from the dead, you shall be saved." So I believed, and my life was changed. If this is something you haven't done, this would be the perfect time to simply admit that you have sinned and are separated from God, tell the Lord that you choose to repent of your sins, and ask Jesus Christ to be your Lord and Savior. It's my prayer that no one will read past this page without being sure he knows where he will spend eternity.

If you want to become a person of significance, consider the meaning of your life. If you want to squander your life on temporal things, you can join the hordes looking for meaning through success. But if you want to spend your life on eternal things, you can decide to be different by investing in another man or woman. Remember, God doesn't judge us at the end of life, but at the end of time. If you look at the book of Revelation, you will see men are not judged for their lives at the moment of death. Instead, the Lord waits until the very end of time, when this world is destroyed and all mankind is facing eternity. Why? *Because a person is judged not simply for what he does but for whom he influences.*

Adolph Hitler hasn't been fully judged yet because his evil practices are still influencing people today. His ideas are still in print, still poisoning the minds of men. God is waiting until the end of this world to judge Hitler, for it is only then that the full extent of his life's meaning will be evident. By the same token, the ministry of the Apostle John is still impacting the lives of men and women around the world. His words, forceful yet full of love in leading them to a saving faith in Jesus Christ, are still influencing lives. John will be judged at the end of time for the impact his life has had on history. So will you. You can begin right now to leave a legacy. You can choose to lead a life of significance, pouring yourself into the life of another, who will in turn reproduce himself in the life of another, making you a spiritual "grandfather" or "grandmother."

So invest in the life of a new Christian. Forget about making a big splash through *success*. Commit to *significance*. Become a spiritual parent by discipling someone into maturity, and you'll experience the joy of being a part of God's plan to change the world.

QUESTIONS FOR DISCUSSION

1. How do you define success?

2. On a scale of 1 to 10, how successful are you?

3. If you could choose between being successful and being significant, which would you choose?

4. What is the most significant thing you are doing?

5. What is the one thing you would like to accomplish that would make you feel successful and significant?

CHAPTER 2

Christian Growth IN CONTEMPORARY CULTURE

*I*t's tough to be a Christian today. I expect in the future it will be even tougher. Mankind is lost, and man's dead faith causes him to hate God—that's why the crowds killed Jesus Christ, rather than proclaiming Him king. We are starting to see the first steps toward persecution in our nation, with Christians being regarded as second-class citizens. You risk being sued if you pray in school, you risk being criticized if you talk about your faith at work, and taking a stand for righteousness may mark you as intolerant. It reminds me of the times described by the prophet Isaiah, when he said of his own nation,

> "Woe to those who add house to house and join field to field, until there is no more room, so that you have to live alone in the midst of the land! . . .
>
> "Woe to those who rise early in the morning that they may pursue strong drink; who stay up late in the evening that wine may inflame them! And their banquets are accompanied by lyre and harp, by tambourine and flute, and by wine; but they do not pay attention to the deeds of the Lord, nor do they consider the work of His hands. . . .
>
> "Woe to those who drag iniquity with the cords of falsehood, and sin as if with cart ropes; who say, 'Let Him make speed, let Him hasten His work, that we may see it; and let the purpose of the Holy One of Israel draw near and come to pass, that we may know it!'
>
> "Woe to those who call evil good, and good evil; who substitute darkness for light and light for darkness; who substitute bitter for sweet, and sweet for bitter!
>
> "Woe to those who are wise in their own eyes, and clever in their own sight!
>
> "Woe to those who are heroes in drinking wine. . . .
>
> "Who justify the wicked for a bribe, and take away the rights of the ones who are in the right!"
>
> (Isaiah 5:8, 11-12, 18-23)

Those words decry the problems of Isaiah's day. There was *materialism*, with people building bigger and bigger houses and accumulating more and more things. There was *hedonism*, with parties and pleasure being the central focus of people's lives. There was *defiance*, with people openly flaunting their sin and mocking God and His people for taking a righteous stand against their behavior. There was *perversion*, calling the evil things of this world good and the good things evil. And there was *corruption*, as evil personalities gained celebrity status. Those who stood for right were neglected, even persecuted. Those who embraced evil became the heroes.

We could use almost those same words to describe twenty-first century America. The focus of our lives seems to be the acquisition of things and the pursuit of pleasure. Sexual sin and perversion of every sort are not only flaunted but advocated as positive activities. The movie stars and rock stars of the day have become our heroes rather than men and women of character. Worse than that, the good things of God are mocked, His standards criticized, His truth attacked. To embrace biblical standards is to invite ridicule. Take, for example, the issue of abortion. The taking of an unborn life used to be seen by many as evil, while protecting children was a righteous calling. But now killing a baby in its mother's womb is seen as a good thing by many; it is "protecting" that child from an unhappy life—we've even declared it constitutionally guaranteed. Taking a stand against abortion is seen by many as backward and anti-woman. Our society has become perverted in its thinking. In many ways, we've become just like Israel in the time of Isaiah.

A CULTURE GONE MAD

People in America today may look good on the outside, but inside they are plagued with problems. We are a culture gone mad, embracing evil and rejecting good. Unfortunately, that behavior is sure to lead to judgment. In Isaiah's day, the nation of Israel had turned its back on God and, as a result, was coming apart at the seams. The book of Isaiah contains an entire list of nations God punished because of their pride. The problems and symptoms of those nations and their people are strikingly similar to those afflicting America today.

For example, Isaiah 2:6 talks about the nation being filled with evil influences from the east. That same thing is happening in America in the twenty-first century. In many schools today, you can get credit for taking transcendental meditation but you can't take a biblical studies course. Teachers often talk openly about sexual perversion or the occult, but it takes a court order to get the schools to open their doors to Bible clubs. Many of the New Age ideas, which have become prevalent in modern education, arise directly from Hinduism—an "evil influence from the east."

Isaiah 3:5 says that "The youth will storm against the elder." Juvenile violence is apparently not a problem unique to our day. It seems scarcely a day goes by we don't read about a young person attacking a teacher or sometimes even murdering a parent. I actually had a two-day period when I spoke and prayed with three fathers, all godly men—one whose daughter had been arrested for murder, another whose son had been sentenced for killing his mother, and a third whose daughter-in-law was caught by her husband sleeping with another man! That's a wake-up call.

A friend of mine, a famous consultant, confessed he was far more successful answering questions at work than he was talking to his kids at home. His success at work has allowed him to hide out in his career and not face the fact that he doesn't know what to do to spiritually shepherd his family. He loves the Lord and talks openly with clients about his faith but has never discipled his own children. His story is common. We have become a nation of dropout dads, and our kids have responded to neglect with anger. Much of the violence in our culture stems from the disconnection children have felt from their fathers. Young people's inability to draw close to a godly dad causes them to lash out in anger at all forms of authority. Isaiah 3:25 goes on to talk about the men of the land falling "by the sword." Violence was cutting them down, and violence is the number one killer of young men in this country. When men turn their backs on God, they lose their moral authority—and with it their morality.

Similarly, Isaiah 3:12 gives us the detail that "women rule over them." That is, the men found themselves taking a back seat to female leadership, in direct contradiction to God's plan for the family. We are in a situation in America right now where men are often becoming displaced from a leadership role in the family. Mom is usually the glue that holds the family together. Even in Christian families, the mother is often the spiritual leader, making sure the children go to church, hear Bible stories, and get spiritual instruction. Most Christian wives will tell you they long for their husbands to be the spiritual leaders in their home, but many dads have abdicated the responsibility. The result is that women rule over them.

The similarities don't end there. Isaiah 3:16, talking about the daughters of Zion, tells us they "walk with heads held high and seductive eyes." Those words mean that the young women of Israel were involved in sexual sin and were proud of their shamefulness. Sexual sin has become the order of the day with young people in our culture. The old concepts of morality are either mocked or ignored entirely. We have young women today who are not seen as outcasts, the "bad girls who sleep around," but are considered good girls, even though they have a goal of sleeping with the entire school football team to make a statement about their independence and control over men. Rejecting the old-fashioned notion of marriage and commitment, the sexual revolution has helped shape a new generation of people for whom sexual sin is "no big deal." That loss of morality bodes ill for America. The very things that brought Israel down can bring down our own country.

In short, I believe the real problem we face is that the lives of Christians in our land are filled with idols. Some of those idols are money, fame, reputation, business, sports, and sometimes even our kids and our churches. Isaiah states, "Their land has also been filled with idols; They worship the work of their hands, that which their fingers have made" (Isaiah 2:8). In other words, *their busyness kept them away from God.* His people were more interested in what *they* could do than what *God* could do.

THE CHALLENGE OF DISCIPLESHIP

In the midst of that sort of world, what course are we to take? How do we go about changing an entire system gone bad? I think the only answer is that we change people *one life at a time*. Each of us decides to take on one man or woman—older or younger, married or single, similar or dissimilar—and we help them grow into maturity in God. We share ourselves, life on life, so the other person has a model to follow.

That kind of sharing is a hard task, particularly in a culture that places such a premium on success. You see, if we are all worshipping that which our hands have made, that which we can receive glory from, then we won't be involved with discipleship. There is no glory in discipleship. Glory is a *success* concern, and you will get no glory from discipling someone into maturity. After all these years of discipling men, I have finally figured out that this is our biggest challenge. Most of us, having accepted the world's values, are more interested in success than significance, and there isn't much glory in discipling others. We are too busy, too uninterested, and too self-centered to reach out to the people around us. While our day grows darker, most Christian men and women are not reaching out to the unsaved around them, trying to establish relationships with the people with whom they share interests.

Perhaps Christians are staying away for fear of being contaminated by the culture. We've already seen the evil of our society, and it's becoming more so, but Jesus was willing to have dinner with prostitutes and tax collectors so He could love them to God. In the midst of a decaying society, He reached out to win the lost. So when I hear many Christians talk about their fear of spending time with non-Christians, I wonder if the real problem is that these Christians simply lack a heart for God. Having accepted the world's values, they have convinced themselves it is more honoring to God to feign holiness than to cultivate a heart for people.

This describes my life. When I first became a Christian, I didn't have a heart for non-Christians. So I began to pray for God to give me a heart for souls without Christ. Our world is filled with people who are dying apart from the Lord, heading straight to the pit of hell, but it seems many Christians aren't too concerned about this reality. If that describes you, it's time to get on your knees and pray for God to give you a heart for people. Pray you'll begin to see them as God does. Only then can you begin to move toward developing meaningful, redemptive relationships with non-Christians.

Since there is no glory in making disciples, it doesn't get much attention. Discipleship is a relationship, not a program, so most churches don't know what to do with a disciple maker. It doesn't appeal to short-term thinkers or those who need regular recognition as they minister. At its core, discipleship is sharing your life with someone less mature in Christ in a way that causes him to grow in his spiritual walk. You share both your successes and your failures; in the process, you both mature. It is the most significant, long-lasting ministry you can have. But it won't bring you glory today—only glory in eternity forever!

SOFT TIMES AND SOFT PEOPLE

In our culture, to take a stand for Christ means you will become a marked man or woman. It takes toughness to set that kind of example, and I don't know if many people have that sort of grit. We live in a time when a significant number of people have a soft Christianity. We cower at opposition, forgetting that "Greater is He who is in you than he who is in the world" (1 John 4:4). We are too unwilling to do the hard things, let alone serve as models for others to follow.

For example, one of the common challenges people face in developing a discipling relationship is that it simply takes too long. You might spend weeks establishing the friendship, months growing close, and years in fully developing the other person's life. In a society that lives on instant breakfast, fast food lunches, and microwave dinners, that's hard to accept. Christians are consumptive Americans, and we expect immediate fruit for our labors. When things don't go as fast as we would like, or when a couple of people we are discipling quit on us, we get discouraged and want to retreat. We are not seeing the instant fruit to which we are accustomed. But it is God who makes the disciples, and He does it on His timetable.

Compare our attitude to that of Isaiah who, except for a brief moment, preached to a stiff-necked generation that never repented. Or look at Jeremiah, who, except for a short time during Josiah's reign, was a total "failure" as a prophet. Even his own people threw him in a cistern. Yet consider the challenge God gave him. The Bible says in Jeremiah 12:5, "If racing with mere men . . . has wearied you, how will you race against horses, against the king, his court and all his evil priests? If you stumble and fall on open ground, what will you do in Jordan's jungles?" (The Living Bible) Here was a guy with a big challenge from God, but he continued to stay the course. In Jeremiah 45:2-3, the prophet says to his secretary, Baruch, "Thus says the Lord the God of Israel to you, O Baruch: 'You said, "Ah, woe is me! For the Lord has added sorrow to my pain; I am weary with my groaning, and have found no rest."'" And then down in verse 5 he notes, "But you, are you seeking great things for yourself? *Do not seek them. . .* " (emphasis added). In other words, don't worry about your own glory. Even when the days are bleak, God continually challenges us not to seek things for ourselves. He wants us to race with the horses! He wants us to do great things, to be able to race with the kings and stand up in love against the people who oppose God in a condemned culture. He wants to use us and do mighty things through us. As a Christian, you have residing in you the power of the Almighty God, and He seeks to use it to shape the lives of those around you. We need to get involved in what God is doing.

Jeremiah was willing to invest in the truth, and he relates stories of strong people who were willing to take a stand for God. In the middle of all the carnage in Israel he points out one good example of faithfulness: a man by the name of Jonadab. "Indeed the sons of Jonadab the son of Rechab have observed the command of their father which he commanded them, but this people have not listened to Me" (Jeremiah 35:16). In other words, the sons of Jonadab and Rechab showed their faithfulness in the middle of all the unfaithfulness. Because they have been faithful, the Lord goes on to say, they would have generations of people following them who would always be faithful. Verse 19 just jumps out: "Therefore thus says the LORD of hosts, the God of Israel, 'Jonadab the son of Rechab shall not lack a man to stand before Me always.'" In spite of the trouble, Jonadab was willing to stand up for God in a corrupt society. He was willing to set the example for others to follow. Today, just as in Jeremiah's world, we need a few men and women who are like Jonadab and his descendants, standing honorably and faithfully before the Lord.

That is one of the blessings of discipleship, that even after we are gone, there will be faithful men and women reproducing themselves in the lives of other people. There will always be a legacy, someone standing faithfully before the Lord.

GOD CAN USE YOU

Susy and I want our lives to be like that. We want to build deeply into men's and women's lives and walk with them, that we would all walk with God. In the midst of a depraved culture, we want to mentor men and women and help them draw close to the Lord. We want to take a person's hand and put it in the hand of God—to multiply our lives in ways that will change this world through the lives of other people. And we want to do this through our children's lives, as well as through the lives of men, women, and couples with whom we meet.

God wants to use you to shape lives so He can change the world. I want to be part of His plan. For three years I showed up, Sunday after Sunday, to pump out good information to people in a Sunday school class. After a while, I realized there wasn't much happening in some of their lives. Many of those young people, sometimes eighty or one hundred in number, weren't becoming more like Christ. Many were going to the same R-rated movies, listening to the same trashy music, and exhibiting the same rebellious attitudes as the world around them. These were mostly college graduates, in their first jobs, coming from good homes, attending a good church. But they weren't taking a stand for Christ and were just like the rest of the culture—except they went to church on Sundays rather than staying home to read the paper or going to play golf.

So I had the idea to disciple these people. Susy and I decided to start a home Bible study, thinking we could move some of the young people from our Sunday school class into a discipling group to go deep in their lives.

I went to my spiritual grandfather and told him what we were planning. He thought it was a stretch to try and disciple a big group, but we did it anyway. I copied the table of contents from an *Operation Timothy* discipling book and sent it out to everybody in the class, telling them to show up if they were interested. That first night we had eighty people! We didn't have enough books for everyone. Susy and I not only covered the information in the books, but also shared our lives.

Those young people loved seeing a family that worked. They were encouraged to observe a home where Mom, Dad, and the kids really got along and worked together. Everybody became excited about evangelism and decided to have an outreach meeting. We asked whom we should have attend, and everyone was committed to inviting their bosses, people they worked with, parents, neighbors—everybody important in their lives. They asked Susy and me to speak. More than three hundred people came, so many that we had to set up closed circuit TVs in the basement and upstairs just so everyone could hear.

When the Sunday school director, a businessman, came to see where all his people were going, he was met by one of the young women in the group who said, "I'm sorry, but you can't come in unless you have a lost guest with you." The guy just hit the roof. He was storming around the yard, and I had to go out and calm him down before I could share my testimony that night. But the fact is, these kids weren't just sitting in a Sunday school class anymore. Because of discipleship, they had become serious about their faith.

We did three six-month discipleship groups and three outreach meetings. After we moved to Chattanooga, the group was so excited about the fruit of their effort that they continued with periodic outreach meetings. Years later there are members of that group involved in ministry all over the world, either in full-time positions or with the attitude that their jobs provide financial support for their lives of ministry. Many of them first became serious about their faith in those discipleship groups. There is fruit spreading out from that group all over the nation and all over the world. It's not because they were in our group, but *because God used us as part of the process of helping people mature in Christ.*

The fact is, our world needs disciplers. It takes mature people to change the world. Christians need a process for becoming mature, and discipleship is the method Christ used when He was here on earth. But discipleship is a hard road. It requires commitment and discipline, which are in short supply in our culture. There aren't many other things you can do that will help shape the lives of people as significantly as discipling. Sermons can be educational, inspiring, or both, but they are typically not as life-changing as life-on-life discipleship. Christian books and radio programs have great teaching, but they don't offer the context of a relationship. If you really want to impact lives for Christ and help change our world, I encourage you to become a discipler.

QUESTIONS FOR DISCUSSION

1. In your opinion, how are most men or women seeking glory?

2. Where are you seeking glory?

3. What practical impact could discipleship have on a corrupt culture?

4. According to Isaiah 5, what evidence is there of the following problems in Isaiah's culture:
   Materialism?
   Hedonism?
   Defiance?
   Perversion?
   Arrogance?
   Corruption?

5. What evidence of these troubles do you see in our own culture?

CHAPTER 3

The Biblical Basis of DISCIPLESHIP

*S*usy and I once took our oldest child, Abigail, to a conference so she could listen to a famous speaker, a man who has inspired thousands through his many books about the Christian life. Between sessions we had a chance to talk with him about his walk with God, and he asked about my own spiritual pilgrimage. I briefly shared a three-minute outline of how we came to Christ and how our lives were changed through discipling relationships. I told of our marriage being healed, our values being changed, and our entire personalities being transformed by the power of God. He interrupted me to say, "My, I love to hear those stories." Then he said something I found astounding. This famous Christian author and speaker looked at me and said, "I've heard such stories before, of course, but I've never actually seen that sort of changed life happen to anyone before my eyes."

I was stunned. Here was a prominent, faithful Christian, doing an important work for the Lord all over the world, and he was missing out on the most incredibly effective and fulfilling work of reproducing his life in others.

That's why I love 2 Timothy 2:2 "The things which you have heard from me in the presence of many witnesses, these entrust to faithful men, who will be able to teach others also." That verse speaks of the discipling generations we all should produce—four generations. I believe each Christian ought to be committed to being a fourth-generation reproducer.

That verse was written when Paul was an old man, yet he still referred to Timothy as his "son." Timothy was middle-aged and a very competent leader of the church, but he would always be Paul's spiritual son, just as my boys will always be my physical sons. Paul understood the fact that God has made us His children, and it is our responsibility to reproduce our sonship by bringing others into the family of God.

The Lord Jesus gave us the Great Commission, which calls us to "Go therefore and make disciples of all nations, baptizing them in the name of the Father and the Son and the Holy Spirit" Matthew 28:19). We've all heard sermons explaining that the emphasis in this verse is not on the "going," but on "making disciples." Yet even with that knowledge, most Christians I've known never get *close* to making disciples. They're too busy with meetings to ever get around to building deep relationships. They have replaced relationships with busywork—sometimes religious busywork. That's unfortunate, because I believe redemptive relationships are the core of all effective ministry.

JESUS CHRIST: DISCIPLE MAKER

Consider the model of the Lord Jesus. He spent time with the multitudes, but most of His time went toward preparing twelve men for ministry. From the time He called them to join Him until He died on the cross, Jesus was with the twelve. He walked with His disciples, ate with them, camped out and slept in the same area as they did, and offered Himself as a model to follow. The Lord Jesus took twelve guys and poured His life into them, so that when He was finished they would be prepared to take over the work of the ministry.

What else can you do that has the same impact? What role can you fill that will so shape and change another person's life? God knows nothing changes people like relationships. That's why He sent a Son, not a tract. If mankind could get a glimpse of God-as-man, we would be able to see how we are to live.

A short study of the process Christ used for discipling others is helpful. For example, it is important we remember Christ *called* certain men to join Him. Luke 6:12-13 says that "He went off to the mountain to pray, and He spent the whole night in prayer to God. And when day came, He called His disciples to Him; and chose twelve of them, whom He also named as apostles." Jesus didn't put a notice up on the office wall. After praying all night, He *selected* the men whom He thought were right for Him. Then the Lord made sure He didn't just have a class once in a while; He spent all His time with them. He taught the Twelve not only in formal situations but in everyday conversation. He constantly looked for teachable moments, when He could reveal something of the heavenly Father.

Sometimes Christ had a sermon He wanted the disciples to hear. Other times He answered their questions. He made sure they saw Him spend time alone praying, and He used the words of Scripture often, making it a normal part of His life. Christ would occasionally ask questions to get a discussion going, and He spent much of His time ministering to the needs of others. Once, when the disciples were arguing about who was the greatest, He took a towel, wrapped it around His waist, and began washing their feet, performing the most menial of services. The Lord demonstrated putting others first by placing the disciples ahead of Himself. Those twelve men were able to experience the direct ministry of God in their lives. Imagine if someone could spend that sort of time with you!

Throughout my life I have always wanted to be where the action was. In football it was catching passes, in high school it was driving fast cars, and in the Marine Corps it was carrying a machine gun at the front line. When I passed the bar exam, I wanted to become a trial lawyer because that's where the action is in a law firm. So when I came to Christ, I first thought the action was in being up front, making speeches, and becoming an expert theologian. But as I watched the doctor who discipled me serve both his Timothys and his patients, I began to understand the concept that Jesus has called us to serve, not to star. This means, even in our leadership roles, we will be servants of others. He has called us to be servant leaders, putting the needs of other people ahead of ourselves. Servanthood is where the action is in the Christian life.

Month after month, meeting with this godly Christian doctor, I heard about his late night trips to the hospital or working twenty hours a day while serving as an obstetrician in moments of great need. And along the way he would share with me how he had led a couple to Christ. Frankly, I was embarrassed and even ashamed that I was such a lousy servant.

As I came to know Jim better through our meetings, and Jesus better through study and prayer, their love rubbed off on me. I began to love people and develop a sincere desire to serve them. When one of my friends was squashed in a corporate reorganization, I just sat and listened as he poured out his pain, anger, and deep sense of betrayal. After several hours, my friend profusely thanked me for "all that you have done." I thought to myself, "All that I've done? I've done nothing but simply be here and let God minister." And then the light bulb went off inside my head: "You know, Phil, you might really be getting the point. God does the work. . . . He just asks you to come along."

Most of us have grown up being trained to handle problems and give answers. In fact, many successful businessmen are paid for right answers. But discipleship isn't a case of merely offering solutions but of walking with a person through their problems and helping them discover God's answers along the way. As I read the Scriptures, I am amazed at how many questions Jesus didn't answer and how many people Jesus didn't help. Too often I find myself talking before I have even listened. I was shocked recently when a business associate of mine, struggling with a difficult problem, took my advice and wound up in disaster. I had offered him a quick answer instead of walking with him through a process in which God would give him the next steps in His plan. I had taken a shortcut, probably out of my impatience, and it resulted in a greater problem. Discipleship is not giving man's advice but helping people grow closer to God.

SHARING EXPERIENCE

The first few verses of Luke chapter nine tell of Jesus sending out the disciples to do the work of the ministry, delegating responsibilities to particular members. Verse ten notes, "And when the apostles returned, they gave an account to Him of all that they had done. And taking them with Him, He withdrew. . . ." Christ not only had His disciples do the work but also had them talk through their experiences after they had returned so they could share the excitement. Perhaps more important, the Lord was always honest with His disciples about the cost of following Him.

When the crowds began following Jesus, He said, "If anyone comes to Me, and does not hate his own father and mother and wife and children and brothers and sisters, yes, and even his own life, he cannot be My disciple. Whoever does not carry his own cross and come after Me cannot be My disciple" (Luke 14:26-27). Becoming a mature disciple of Jesus Christ isn't easy, and the Lord never pulled any punches in explaining that fact. He wanted the disciples to know from the start the process was going to require major changes. Nothing is the same after God gets hold of your life.

Mark, a new convert, was elated with his newfound peace in Jesus Christ. The first thing he did was go home and unload his newfound faith on his mom and dad. But, in short, they went ballistic. Mark was crushed by what he thought was the final blow in what had been a rocky parental relationship. He even told me, "I knew my mother was serious about writing me off when she told me that she had removed my number from her automatic telephone dialer!" A relationship with Jesus Christ can cause friction and division in a family or a friendship. But the breach is usually caused by our own well-meaning yet overbearing insistence that everyone think as we do. As I sat with Mark, we discussed the principles of lifestyle evangelism, talking about how a man can effectively share the gospel with his family.[2]

As Mark began to follow those principles, loving his mom and dad with no strings attached, he began to see a change in the relationship. He apologized to them for the ways in which he had let them down over the years and started serving his parents physically and emotionally. He didn't force the truth on them but simply began living out his faith before them.

---

2. If you're looking for an effective lifestyle evangelism tool, I highly recommend CBMC's twelve-session video course, *Living Proof 1: Evangelism As a Lifestyle*. It chronicles the struggle of Christians attempting to become effective witnesses in the world and deals with the bottom-line issues honestly and dynamically. *Living Proof 2: Lifestyle Discipleship*, the sequel to LP1, follows the lives of the same people as they move from the evangelism stage to the discipleship stage. This gripping drama will not only answer your questions and fears about discipleship, training you to be effective, but will convince you that you want to be involved in the life-on-life impact of discipleship.

Mark's dad, who had been raised in an orthodox Jewish home, had promised his grandmother—the only family survivor of the Holocaust—that he would never renounce his Jewish faith. For his son Mark to become a "Jesus freak" was almost more than he could stand. But the Christlikeness he saw in his son over the months following his conversion was truly beyond what he could explain. Within a relatively short time, Mark's father accepted Jesus as his Messiah.

Mary Jane found discipleship very much a family affair when her sister, convicted by my message at her church, replaced her sarcasm by sincere interest and her indifference with initiative to spend deep, one-on-one time with her. Matthew 28:19 commissions us to "Go therefore and make disciples" of ALL people . . . even a little sister—or especially a little sister.

One of the most important things we can do with our Timothys is to share our experience. Find someone you believe in; then look for the areas in which he needs to grow. Mark needed to learn how to honor his parents, so that's where we began the mentoring relationship. Many new believers need help in the process of talking about their new life in Christ with relatives and friends. My counsel is usually that they keep quiet and live out the life in Christ. Jesus said His relationship with us will be so intense it sometimes will bring division— even with those we love. However, if we can walk with our Timothys through the inevitable conflicts with people, we can often help them lead many more people to Christ.

Jesus didn't give up on Peter, even though this stubborn fisherman failed Him on several occasions. The Lord worked with Peter, sharing principles and encouragement, and helped him to mature.

Many years ago, Johnny was my Peter, only far more stubborn. Sometimes I would tell my wife that Johnny made me look like a passive guy. Well-educated and obviously brilliant, Johnny had "all the answers" to his company's problems. But Johnny wasn't patient enough for God to put him in a position to meaningfully share those solutions with men who would be willing to listen. I sat with him one morning for two hours, unloading both barrels of the Bible's wisdom about waiting on the Lord and being willing to accept the authority placed over him, to no avail. Johnny was at work less than ten minutes when he marched into his boss's office and unloaded all his wisdom on how the company should be run. This time his boss, the company comptroller, didn't even pretend to consider Johnny's comments. Instead of giving a response, he simply said, "Johnny, I think you'll be happier somewhere else. Pack your office and be out of here by 5 p.m."

I thought to myself, "What a waste! All my counsel, all my months of great Bible teaching is down the tubes—and Johnny just blew a fast-track position in a growing company because he couldn't control his tongue!" So I made up my mind to do the same thing his work had done—dump Johnny. I told him I was sick of his attitude and I didn't think I had any more wisdom that would be of any benefit to him. Instead of looking to the example of Jesus and Peter, I told Johnny off.

Much to my surprise, getting fired was just the impetus he needed to start his own business. He wanted to continue meeting with me because he thought I needed his business acumen in my law practice. I watched Johnny ignore my advice, disregard my precautions, even marry someone I opposed. I felt I was wasting my time. It was like babysitting a temperamental athlete who continually breaks curfew. In my view, the whole relationship was a waste of time.

But that's not the way Johnny saw things. He told other men that he had learned how to develop a deep relationship with Christ just by spending time with me. He talked to my wife about my example and how I had taught him to go to the Lord with his struggles, pain, ambition, and challenges. Today Johnny is a successful financial consultant who works with fast-track NASDAQ companies all over the country, but more important, he runs his business based on the principles of Scripture. I am always embarrassed when he gives me credit for helping him along the way, because I remember all the doubts and frustration I had. I wanted to give up on the guy, but God was willing to be patient. It is obvious Christ was involved in that relationship and used it to His glory in spite of me.

LIFE ON LIFE

Everything Jesus did had two purposes: He wanted to minister, and He wanted to mentor. He shared His ministry with the masses so they would get a glimpse of God, but He shared His life with the disciples so that they could know Him deeply. That's what I call *life-on-life* discipleship, and it's the method our Lord used to train His chosen few.

Almost everything I'm doing in discipleship I have learned from someone else. One of the most effective disciplers I know is a former tennis pro named Dave. It seems like Dave's whole life is discipling one man after another. I've had a chance to sit and talk with him, and I've learned some tremendous truths that have helped me in discipling my family as well as other men. You see, as a tennis instructor, Dave was paid by the hour to give people lessons. During that hour they owned his time. What they chose to do with his instruction later was up to them, but Dave was there to give them the very best advice he could. "That's exactly the way discipleship is," Dave told me. "God owns the process and He owns me, and my goal is simply to be available to Him, to be used in the life of another person for whatever He wants me to do."

My problem is that I often impose my own expectations onto the people I'm discipling instead of entrusting them to the Lord. Sometimes I will put undue pressure on myself to *cause* a certain result in a man's life. But both of those ideas lead to failure. If Dave's tennis student got drunk and broke a leg, failed to practice serving, or continued a bad habit that was detrimental to his game, Dave didn't consider it a defeat. He simply continued to do his best and collect his fee for being the tennis coach. Dave had learned his job was *to be faithful and offer the truth*—it was the tennis player who had to make the decision about how he would play the game.

The same is true of discipling. Jesus gave us an example of how to build a strong church: mentor strong men and women. Help produce strong Christians by discipling them into maturity. We have been "bought with a price" (I Corinthians 6:20). God owns our time, and we are to work toward the fulfillment of the Great Commission. Our job is to be faithful, regardless of the apparent response. My friend Dave devoted great time and effort to studying the game of tennis, giving his students the very best teaching he could. He never tried to play the game for them but was always available to them. In the same way, the biggest need of those we are discipling is often for us to be available, interested, affirming, forgiving, and willing to offer our storehouse of life experiences to help them grow.

DOES IT WORK?

"How much can you really accomplish in an hour a week?" This challenge was thrown at me as I was speaking to a group of men at a large church. My answer was that sometimes effective disciple making takes more than an hour a week. Jesus spent hours each day with His men, so I am willing to do whatever the Lord asks in order to leave a godly legacy behind. But I knew what response that comment would bring from the crowd: "I simply cannot spend any more time, what with my busy schedule at work and at home!"

My reply was simple: "What is God's goal for your life? Do you want to stay busy so you can feel successful, or do you want to disciple the next generation of Christian leaders so your life can be significant?" If all you can do is give one person an hour a week, that is far better than giving nothing at all. After all, an hour a week is more time than most fathers in America devote to their children.

WHAT TO LOOK FOR IN A MENTOR

Is your mentor. . . .

a person of vision?	a person of compassion?
a person of faith?	a person who delegates?
a person of prayer?	a person who sets an example?
a person of humility?	a person who reveals his life to you?
a person of excellence?	a person of integrity?

Discipling works because it offers a person the things he needs most: a model to follow, a person to hold him accountable, and a relationship in which he can learn to open up. Most Christians don't have any models worth emulating, particularly if they came to Christ later in life. They have been living as non-Christians for a long time and may have no idea how their new life is to be worked out. That's why Jesus didn't just give the Twelve a set of directions: He offered *an example to follow.* He showed them how a godly man cares for children, how he treats women with respect, and what his attitude should be toward money. And the Lord *held them accountable,* not allowing Peter to get away with rash statements or actions but bringing him up short when he raced ahead of God's plan. When "doubting Thomas" said he wouldn't believe in Jesus' resurrection until he had put his hand into Christ's side, the Lord confronted his disbelief by saying, "Reach here your finger, and see My hands; and reach here your hand, and put it into My side" (John 20:27). Finally Christ offered the disciples a safe, loving relationship. John, who started out as a "son of thunder," became a sensitive man, unafraid to reveal his love. Matthew, tax collector and outsider who was no doubt calloused by his treatment from other Jews, became a man whose heart longed to lead those same Jews to a saving knowledge of God.

Christ set an example for us to follow. Most Christians have no accountability relationships; few of their relationships get beyond sports results and politics. A discipling relationship offers an opportunity for a man or woman to draw close, reveal his or her heart, and be changed.

One winter I planned a trip to Colorado, where I spoke to a group of men, most of whom did not know Jesus Christ as Lord and Savior. Since this type of meeting was effective in bringing me to Christ, I have been active in speaking to groups of men about what my life was like before I knew Christ and how He has changed my life since meeting Him. Even in the middle of litigating cases in courtrooms around the country, I was able to drive across town or catch an airplane late at night to take advantage of an opportunity to speak to groups about my faith. These are great opportunities to take men with you who are not as far along in the faith as you are. Those are always encouraging times for me, and in doing this I am modeling something I want my Timothys to imitate.

On my trip to Colorado, I had several choices for the best way to accomplish the task. I could fly alone to the meeting, using the time to catch up on my reading. Or I could take someone with me so my activities were accountable to someone and used as an example in another man's life. For that trip, I decided to take two of my sons with me, inviting as well two men who are fifteen years younger than I am to bring their boys for a weekend skiing retreat before the meeting. Over the weekend we three dads shared topics meaningful for both fathers and sons, and of course the boys were absolutely delirious about going off with Dad for a ski trip. "Raising" children is really "discipling" children, and it is a joy to see God use our kids to impact the lives of others. What a privilege to take Josh and Matt on a trip where we could pray, laugh, ski, eat, and have fun together. It was interesting to see Josh, who was ten, and Matt, twelve, impact the younger boys for the Lord. One of the boys even became interested in reading the Bible after hearing about Josh and Matt's quiet time.

In those few days of cooking, studying, sharing a bathroom, and working through the inevitable challenges of three dads and five boys being together, we had an absolutely unforgettable weekend. The other two fathers looked forward to what was ahead, and I hope that my sharing some of my experience with teenagers, parents, and over twenty years of business and ministry was valuable in their lives. More than that, both of the other fathers seemed to have their fingers on the pulse of the younger generation in America, and I used the time together to learn even more from them, I think, than they learned from me. I also was able to get their suggestions on raising sons. My boys were able to be around godly men and build lasting relationships with guys who will probably be here long after I'm gone.

Consider how many generations we had on that one ski trip. I mentored the other fathers, and they in turn discipled their sons and mine. The older boys ended up discipling the younger boys in some ways, and our sons became better prepared to do this same sort of activity with others as they got older. What began as a speaking engagement turned into not only a ski vacation but fourth-generation reproduction.

Jesus Christ invested in discipling relationships because He understood that was the best way to change lives—and thus the best way to shape the future. We neglect this pattern at our peril.

QUESTIONS FOR DISCUSSION

1. What was your life like before you met Jesus Christ?

2. How did you come to know Christ as your Savior?

3. In what ways has your life changed since you became a Christian?

4. Who has been the "Paul" in your life?

5. What would it take to make you a discipler of men or women?

CHAPTER 4

Selecting Your
TIMOTHY

*W*hen the pastor at First Church decided God was calling him to discipleship, the first thing he did was institute a program. Instead of building a relationship, he announced a meeting. Rather than pray about whom God would call him to work with, he put a notice in the church bulletin and waited to see who would show up. After three months, the program died. The only guys who showed up were considerably older than the pastor, and most of them had been Christians since the Truman administration. Concluding that it was just a bad fit, the pastor canceled the whole plan and announced they would be going back to a monthly men's breakfast.

Jesus didn't work the way most churches do. Discipling isn't a program; it's a relationship. It isn't something you can do most effectively with a big group, so it's never going to get the attention of the masses. It requires high commitment to ask a man or woman to share his or her life with another person in informal settings. Rather than breakfast prayer meetings, discipling often takes place in a car, on a fishing trip, or in an office discussing the Christian response to a particular situation. Because it is a relationship, it cannot simply be announced in the bulletin. After all, you don't put an advertisement in the paper that says, "Friend Wanted: Must Be Mature Christian." Instead, discipling is preceded by much prayer, and it is based on common interests.

The Scriptures are clear that Jesus *selected* the people with whom He wanted to work. He enlisted a few men to carry on the ministry after He was gone, and He selected an assortment of men by various means. Andrew and Peter were relatively successful fishermen. James and John were fishermen too, though they were no doubt younger, and their nickname, "Sons of Thunder," suggests they were a bit wild. Matthew, the tax collector, was someone most Jews would stay away from, and Simon was the type of political extremist the Jews admired but feared. Andrew seems to have been a sensitive type who liked helping others, while Thomas was a bit of a pessimist. Peter was a loudmouth, while Philip was not. The key thought is this: *people were the method by which Christ intended to change the world.*

The Lord didn't set up programs; He prepared some people. He didn't focus on the multitudes but honed in on a handful of men. None of them were key leaders, sophisticated socialites, or influential politicos. Instead they were temperamental, prejudiced, and occasionally impulsive. In other words, they were normal people. But they were all willing to learn.

It is crucial to ask God to help you select the people you want to disciple so you will get the man or woman with whom you believe God wants you to work. Jesus made His decisions carefully and Luke tells us that before the Lord selected the twelve apostles, He spent the entire night in prayer. Jesus wasn't hasty or impatient because He knew He had to get the right people. You see, Jesus took the long view with people. His discipling often seemed to have little impact on their lives. By the time of Christ's death, the twelve disciples were still weak and confused. But over time, the significance of Christ's impact in their lives became clear.

You can't transform the world until you transform a person. Christ does the changing, but He has asked us to be channels for His power. Rather than offering a discipleship class with forty people, think carefully about the one or two men or women to whom you could offer life-on-life discipling. I once heard a man say Jesus was unlike most modern Christian leaders because He wasn't concerned with impressing the crowds. Christ understood the importance of shaping a handful of mature believers over a crowd of immature church-goers. In the words of Charles Swindoll, Jesus wasn't drawing a crowd—He was ushering in a kingdom.

So instead of trying to convert your entire city overnight, consider selecting a few people to assist in their walks with God. Then watch God at work through you, and eventually you will see those *few* change the lives of *many*.

GOD CHOOSES YOUR DISCIPLES

Of course the people you disciple have to be selected by the Lord, and He typically speaks through men and women, so the names of your disciples are something He'll often bring to your mind. I try always to be on the lookout for people who could benefit from a discipling relationship—people I like who are teachable and willing to get serious about commitment to Christ. Look for someone in your life who needs to learn from you, has an interest, and is teachable.

Remember, *God chooses your disciples*. He has called us to disciple others—to help others grow into maturity—and He has somebody in mind for you. At this point, you may be ready to put down this book, thinking you're not mature enough to disciple anyone else. But if that's how you feel, consider this: men and women in this world aren't looking for perfection. I've spoken to large groups of men, and as I've described a discipling relationship I have asked the question "How many of you would be interested in a relationship like that?" Always the majority of men raise their hands. But when I ask the next question, "How many of you feel ready to begin discipling another man in that sort of relationship?" very few raise their hands. The problem is one of perspective. We seem to think we need to get to some great spiritual plateau before we can disciple others. I'll tell you right now that if you are waiting for that sort of plateau, you'll never disciple anybody. If you want to wait until you glow in the dark with right-eousness, you'll spend your entire life marking time.

None of us is perfect. If we were, Christ would not have had to come. All of us are sinners saved by grace, and no one is going to achieve a state of spiritual perfection in this world. So give up the notion you are not good enough. Our world is full of men and women in need of a discipler, and you have been called. Your life will contain evidence of God's power, goodness, and love if you have been walking with Him despite your failings. The point is to display His excellence, anyway, not your own.

This feeling of, "I am not ready to disciple anyone" is prevalent in our churches. Maybe we have created the wrong image by perpetrating some mental picture of the Christian Superman, someone who perfectly loves his wife, has children who never misbehave, gives himself fully to both his job and his church, and has overcome any secret sins of pride, selfish ambition, lust, swearing, and materialism. The only trouble is, that person doesn't exist. (If you do come across him, ask him to send me his resume!) Jesus didn't call perfect men (or women!) to be His disciples. He called fallen, flawed people like you and me and He left them in charge of the most important message in history.

If you are a sinner who admits you struggle with temptation, welcome to the club. I'm a charter member. Get rid of any notion that, as you get older and mature in your faith, the Christian life will get easy. I can testify that it doesn't, and anybody who tells you differently is either a liar or a phony. But just because I'm imperfect doesn't mean I can't help someone else grow. All the men I have discipled have been imperfect also, and many of them have been very different from me. But they were more interested in my faithfulness and availability than in my perfection.

I've even seen brand-new Christians, who were themselves being discipled, start discipling. If you get away from the "program" mentality, which seems to require a person to be approaching perfection, you realize every Christian can start building a relationship with someone else, open up his or her life to another, and spur that man or woman on to growth in Jesus Christ.

I will add one important caveat, however: Remember that one of the greatest traps in ministry is believing that you have been called to minister to the opposite sex. It is tempting to think your situation is the "exception"; however, there is a certain magnetism, flattery, opportunity for deception, and self-delusion that accompanies a male/female close relationship. At least one person is headed for trouble or pain that is peculiarly unique to an opposite-sex relationship.

Your job, men, is not to direct your affection, energy, and interest away from the women God gave you—wife, mother, sister, daughter—toward a wounded, needy, and vulnerable female, regardless of your rationalizations. They are the enemy's trap in the area of sexuality. Discipleship, to be real discipleship, must be intimate. The God of the universe, Who created us and Who is all powerful, all-knowing, and all-loving, is able to provide a suitable mature woman to help sort out the thoughts and emotions of the female account executive who is going through a divorce. Sister, that man at work or in the neighborhood who is lonely and hurt or just wants to chat is the hunter's steel trap for a woman's heart or affection, whatever the safeguards you may think you have established.

PEOPLE AFTER GOD'S OWN HEART

Sometimes I begin meeting with someone who is a new Christian and needs grounding in the faith. We talk about assurance of salvation, prayer, Bible reading, and the sort of things a new believer in Jesus ought to hear about. But not all of my discipling relationships have been with baby Christians. I've also met regularly with interested non-believers, hoping to lead them to the Lord eventually and begin the process of helping them mature. There are plenty of people interested in the Bible who have never studied it, and a lot of guys hurting in a marriage or career. A person like this simply needs another to whom he can talk and perhaps get some wisdom from God.

I have discovered, however, that the most common type of person who needs discipling is the one who has been a Christian for some time and yet is not a reproducer. I'll work with that person until he really begins reproducing his life.

Reproducing my faith in others was a breakthrough idea in my life. After I had been a Christian for several years, I realized that the goal of discipling is to make mature spiritual reproducers, not merely converts. It is to help develop those who, like King David, are men or women after God's own heart. Many of the men I've met at church or on the job were Christians who had not been discipled and really didn't have much fruit in their lives. Through meeting with people like these in a discipling relationship, you too can catch a vision for changing the world for Christ. Sometimes these men and women become the most fruitful Timothys you can have—

they long to be mature, to have more of Jesus Christ, and to experience His power. They also are some of those who most quickly begin to bear fruit. They're often not dealing with a lot of baggage, and they're ready to grow.

Sometimes you'll find someone who has an immediate hunger for the Word, and he can make dramatic progress because he is adamant about surrendering his will to God. When you find one of those, get busy working with him because he is the one who will really grow. This person is willing to make the commitment necessary to see rapid changes.

Realistically, however, many people are not like that. Many Christians are what is known in the ministry as "decade men" or "decade women." Typically, these people have come out of a difficult mid-life tragedy that has led them to the Lord, and they have found great peace and abundant life through Christ and the Scriptures. They are hungry for wisdom and have an appetite for Scriptural principles. These are people who will usually take about ten years before they start reproducing their spiritual lives. They have usually had more than one marriage, have children, and perhaps have had problems with alcohol, drugs, sex, or in their jobs— sometimes all of the above. There is not one major issue of conflict in their lives but several, and their lives simply aren't what they should be. Look around your church, your office, and your neighborhood to see who these men or women might be. Try not to create expectations outside of what God might be doing. He has someone in mind, so learn to follow His leading.

I have seen decade men become some of the most fruitful Christians on earth. It takes them a while, but what's the hurry? When we go to the doctor for open-heart surgery or to a lawyer for defending our company's biggest case, don't we usually look for somebody who has been in the profession for ten or twenty years?

Eric was one of those decade men, a guy with two divorces, one attempted suicide, a past problem with alcohol, and the experience of having made and lost a million dollars before he was 30. Eric was a mess—a saved mess, but a mess nonetheless. He would spend time with the Lord, thanking Him for his salvation and feeling overcome with a deep sense of being in the Spirit, and then go out and do the dumbest things you can imagine. Eric was spiritual; he just wasn't spiritually mature. He was going to heaven but making hellacious decisions along the way. The funny thing is the man who discipled him had absolutely no clue what it was like to go through those sorts of difficulties.

Claude and Eric met in bankruptcy court during Eric's business collapse about a year after he came to Christ, and eighteen months after his second divorce. Claude spoke to me and I encouraged him to meet with Eric, but my encouragement was always met with, "Phil, I have no idea where this guy is coming from. His stories make me sick. I feel totally inadequate in dealing with Eric's rawness, brashness, and earthiness. The man is totally ungodly." Of course, we all were ungodly once.

Claude was a third-generation Christian, saved at a church youth camp when he was six or seven years of age, had been married twenty years to a wonderful godly woman, and worked for one of his city's most stable banks. He was accustomed to his bank's loans being defaulted on by people like Eric and, frankly, wanted little to do with the kind of characters that continually hurt his department's profitability. Most of all, I think Claude just felt ill-equipped to deal with a business version of a Hell's Angel!

I gave Claude several suggestions. First, pray that God would give you a heart for Eric. Second, look in the Scriptures to find God's examples and solutions for Eric's problems. Third, pursue Eric and attempt to meet with him once a week for a year—on Eric's terms. Fourth, pray for Eric every day. Fifth, call or write Eric twice a week with a short word or verse of encouragement. Sixth, give the expectations, credit, and outcome for everything that happened with Eric to the Lord.

Pretty soon I started to hear how excited Claude was about meeting with Eric. Claude sensed a new urgency to get up every morning and study the Scriptures, and he found the same old evangelistic sermons at his church on Sunday mornings had new meaning because he was constantly looking for ways to explain the truth of the new life in Christ to his disciple. They began meeting with a small group of other men to talk about discipleship and to pray for their lost friends. Over the course of ten years, Eric sorted through his broken relationships, tattered finances, and habitual acts of destruction and finally became a man whom God began to use. Over that same period of time, Claude became a spiritual reproducer, sought after by his pastor to teach other men in his church the principles of reproduction. Claude's marriage became richer, his ministry more exciting, and his job more meaningful as he began to see his life count for eternity.

The relationship didn't just cover spiritual topics, either, but all areas of life. Claude helped Eric's business evaluate some bad debt situations, and Eric offered some invaluable advice to Claude on the deadbeat thinking of some of the bank's worst customers. When Claude's son was arrested for driving under the influence of alcohol, Eric helped Claude walk through the process with his son. Because of Eric's background, he had great insight on how to talk with the boy and not lecture or berate him. Eric was able to get tough with Claude's son because he had been there and could cut through all the excuses and alibis. Eric was a "decade man," but Claude kept in mind the fact that Christ has called us for life, not for a thirteen-week class. It takes a lifetime to grow an oak tree, and we are aiming to grow a thousand oaks of righteousness (see Isaiah 61:3).

Anabelle was a new lawyer in the firm reporting directly to Lauren, another attorney who had taken a special interest in mentoring her. Anabelle was concerned that joining the new firm Bible study announced by several of the Christian lawyers might intimidate Lauren, so she let the subject naturally come up at work. Lauren said she wasn't sure she would attend the Bible study, but leaped at Anabelle's suggestion that the two of them get together in a one-on-one study to explore the Scriptures.

Who has God put on your heart? Who are the people you believe in and can envision accomplishing great things for God? Which one needs the most help? Spend time in prayer and see whom the Lord puts on your heart. Get on your knees and ask the Lord to point out the one or two men or women He would have you disciple. Start light. Don't dive in and immediately swim to a hundred foot depth. Simply be available and see if there is one person at work or in your neighborhood who might have an interest in meeting with you.

THE TEN BEST THINGS TO SAY TO A PROTÉGÉ:

1. I've been praying for you.

2. You're a winner.

3. What do you need?

4. How can I help?

5. I believe in you.

6. Can you come with me?

7. Did you understand that?

8. What would you like to know?

9. You can do it.

10. You are making a difference.

KEEP THEM IN YOUR HEART

In the disciple selection process, it is important to really pray for the men and women you are considering so they sense the movement of God as much as you do. Often the person's thinking isn't spiritual, and he really needs the Spirit to influence his decision.

After fifteen years as a trial lawyer, I came to the conclusion that picking a Timothy is somewhat like picking a jury. There are a tremendous number of theories, entire organizations you can hire to help you, plus jury psychologists who can analyze the demographics for you. But after all the research and questions, after all the study and prayer, it often comes down to your gut feeling. Do you feel he will become committed to walking with God? That's who you select in building a Timothy relationship. Keep in mind you are setting up a potentially lifelong friendship, however unlikely that may seem at the outset.

If Jesus could spend all night in prayer before selecting His apostles, it's not too great a task for you to spend a half hour seeking the Lord one evening. Simply turn off the television, get down on your knees, and say, "Lord, I want you to use me. Who should I disciple?" Then wait quietly for Him to reveal this to you. It might take a little while, so be patient. I believe Christians too often don't hear the voice of God because they won't be quiet long enough to listen. They'll get down on their knees and talk; then when they're done talking, they get up and go. Prayer is a *dialogue*, not a monologue, so wait and see who God brings to mind. Don't get me wrong—I've never heard the Lord speak to me in an audible voice—but He will often bring someone to mind, and I know that is the man I need to begin spending time with. Don't worry too much about your will getting in the way of the Father's. If you are walking with the Lord, He will shape your will.

Don't fall into the trap of thinking you'll only be called to disciple the "easy" people, the ones who are obvious winners and with whom you have much in common. I once met a man who broke all the norms for me. He came to a prayer meeting where we were supposed to pray for men by name, sat down beside me, and when it came to his turn, said, "I want to ask for prayer for me. I need salvation."

My first thought was, "You are at the wrong meeting! You ought to be at the outreach meeting." But the man had just realized that he didn't know Christ. Terry was raised in a church and had been to a number of prayer meetings, but he had never personally given his life to the Lord. So at the next meeting, he said he wanted to meet with me and go through *Operation Timothy*. I am used to fishing for men, not having them jump in the boat! I prayed about it, and the Lord clearly showed me I should disciple him.

However, Terry and I were very different. As a lawyer, I was trained to keep track of my time and billed my hours in increments of six minutes. Terry kept track of his business by how many sales he made, so the time clock was not as important to him. Every time we met, he would be fifteen or twenty minutes late—and never say that he was sorry. Since it was my hour-and-a-half lunch, it really started to bug me. Often I would begin our meeting so irritated at his tardiness that I had to take the first few minutes just to regain my composure. All I wanted to do was scold the guy for being late.

I think Terry was late for each of our meetings for more than two years. He would get with an interested client and stay with him until the deal was done. If it meant staying until 12:15, Terry would be there, even though we had a noon lunch appointment. I probably could have done well to learn from Terry's attitude of servicing clients, but I was usually too angry to learn anything.

As we began to meet, Terry came to Christ. Being in insurance, he was not someone who held lawyers in high regard. He believed lawyers in his trade usually caused more problems than they solved, and his attitude came through in some of his comments to me. Terry was just someone I didn't naturally click with.

But as we began to work through *Operation Timothy*, sharing our lives with one another, we became the closest of friends. I realized I had much to learn from my new buddy and new convert. During one of our meetings, he had to break the news to me that one of his customers, a client of mine, was about to fire me as his lawyer. "It's not your legal work, Phil; it's your temperament they object to," Terry explained. And then came the bombshell: "They said you sometimes appear to be more concerned with your schedule than with their case."

Pow! Right in the kisser! Not only was I facing a client problem because of my same old "drive too hard toward the task and forget about the people" attitude, but now I was being lectured by one of my spiritual children about the problem. How humiliating! Yet it was that humiliation God was using in my life to get me to mature. Then something remarkable happened. Terry said to me, "Phil, I cannot find one place in Scripture where Jesus rushed because He was under the pressure of time. The Lord was not always jovial, but I can't find a single description of Him losing His temper because somebody was late." It was an incredible truth. I learned from my own disciple—and it could never have happened if I had not prayed about him.

I kept meeting with Terry because the Lord wanted me to, and we both recognized God was teaching us quite a bit. He was one of those guys who really longed to be discipled. After we would finish a meeting, he would go right to his calendar and say, "When's the next time we can meet?" Terry was the faithful man in our meetings. He isn't the guy I would have chosen, but he is the guy God chose for me. And I have found that the people God has brought to me have been a lot better than the ones I have strategically selected for myself.

ASKING YOUR TIMOTHY

When you feel God is telling you to disciple a certain person, a good approach is just to go up to him or her and talk about the concept. I have said to men, "Would you be interested in getting together to talk about growing in the Lord? Would you be interested to see what I do and how I have grown?" Don't ask them to commit to anything yet; just see if they are interested. If they have spent some time with me or have seen God work in my life, they will sometimes say yes, but usually they want to ask questions. I am always low-key in my answers. I'm not trying to "sell" somebody on the idea, I am simply trying to plant the seed so the Spirit can bring growth. Of course, I'm praying for the man all the time so that God will make it clear to him if he ought to enter into this relationship with me.

Another approach is to reach out to a point of need in someone's life. For example, suggest a willingness to sit and talk about his business or family problems. Of course, you want to pray about the process and not be deceptive in your motives, but when you make a decision that you want your life to count forever in the lives of people, God will bring you people in a variety of ways. Sometimes I avoid talking about discipleship, particularly among younger men, because the term can turn some men off. To today's "me generation" the word *discipleship* sometimes carries the negative connotation of discipline, work, and studying under a taskmaster. Sometimes discipleship is misunderstood as being only a glorified Bible study, without a strong focus on life's needs, problems, and challenges. So I'll simply suggest we get together to talk about marriage or job pressures or financial decisions. You see, discipling someone is not just teaching spiritual truth, but sharing your life in such a way that he or she matures in Christ. Often a discussion about money can turn into a wonderful discussion about the decisions we make in this life and how they affect us eternally. That's why it is important to select the right person, and invite him to join you, rather than announcing that you're having a Bible study.

Recently a friend of mine, speaking to a roomful of more than one hundred young men between the ages of twenty-five and thirty-five, asked how many would be interested in having an older mentor. Every single man raised his hand! Mentoring is much more than offering business advice—it is discipleship and seems to convey to younger men and women the idea they will be receiving something from their mentors, not simply committing to an intellectual study. Think about Paul's charge in 1 Corinthians 9:19, 22:

"For though I am free from all men, I have made myself a slave to all, that I might win the more. . . .To the weak I became weak, that I might win the weak; I have become all things to all men, that I may by all means save some."

Invite a person to join you by figuring out what he needs and suggesting you talk about it. Don't overcommit or over-ask at the initial stage. Before you commit to a period of meetings, be sure God is calling you to invest in his or her life and has communicated that desire to the other person.

It is imperative to pray for the individual while he is considering meeting with you, for you want the power of God at work in the other person's life. The next time you see him, ask if he has been praying about the decision. Trust me, ninety-nine out of one-hundred will say "no," but they cannot know the will of God if they haven't talked with God about it. So ask them to meet—and encourage them to pray.

THE IMPORTANCE OF COMMITMENT

As soon as somebody says he'd like to meet, I try to schedule an appointment. At that meeting, I often ask about the man's life to discover what he perceives his needs to be. And I nearly always talk about commitment. The Timothy is committing to becoming Christlike. He is making a commitment in his life to become mature. I don't think most people today understand the word "commitment." The word means "to decide and to make a promise." When somebody commits to discipleship, he is committing to a movement toward Christ. The Bible doesn't just call us to acknowledge Christ as the Son of God, but to give Him our whole lives and let Him develop in us a lifestyle of holiness. It is important for a Timothy to understand this concept from the start.

The message of commitment is received differently by different generations. In my father's generation, men responded to a challenge of commitment with a sense of obligation, responsibility, and perhaps guilt. In my generation of "baby boomers," commitment means success, impressing people, and building a resume. But to the younger generations, a request for commitment is often met with suspicion, indecisiveness, and indifference. That is why many people have labeled the younger generation as people who are uncommitted, and they tend to write off the so-called "Generation-X" as those who will be changed by the world rather than those who will change the world. But the truth is the "baby busters" and Generation X-ers are suspicious of my generation because we busted the sexual revolution with AIDS, the Ozzie and Harriet family model with divorce, the Great American Dream with an enormous national debt, higher education with mediocrity, and an optimistic future with employment rejection notices. Because they feel ripped off, the younger generations want to know what's in it for them before they commit to anything.

This is why we have such a problem in building spiritual reproducers in America today. The older generations are waiting for the younger generations to haunt their doorsteps, seeking advice, counsel, and spiritual disciplines, while the younger people are living out their suspicions with a "Been there, done that, don't want any of your marriage/ business/lifestyles anyway" attitude. In that sort of atmosphere, you can't just expect a man or woman to commit to you. You have to *be the pursuer*.

One of my mentors, Ted DeMoss, spoke all over the country on the topic of "pursuit." He told story after story of people willing to listen to the claims of Christ and actually receive Him as Lord and Savior if only we would pursue them. But pursuing others is inconvenient, unconventional, perhaps even—at least initially—unwanted. That pursuit must be the focus of those of us who want to invest in things that go beyond the grave. We have to decide now that if we want our lives to be significant, *we must pursue people*. We must encourage their commitment to discipleship by committing to them first—seeking them out with the clear intention of staying with them over the long haul, through all their life's ups and downs.

I learned that lesson with Charlie, another man the Lord made clear I needed to disciple. Charlie not only stood me up for luncheons; he once failed to appear at a business celebration he had planned. I am still not sure what happened—he just didn't show. Charlie broke promise after promise to return the briefcase he had borrowed from me for a business trip he took. It occurred to me that he had lost it, but he would never admit to that. In short, Charlie was a mess to deal with. But he was very competent at his job, had been a Christian about ten years, was faithful to his wife, and said he wanted to grow spiritually. Most of all, as I got to know him better, I realized he really didn't have a lot of close friends—a problem with many men these days. It seemed to me Charlie had tremendous potential as a godly leader of his family and community, if he could refine his character and then learn to reproduce his love for Christ in the lives of his generation.

I called Charlie one day to invite him to go with me and spend the weekend with one of the premier experts in his field, but when Charlie answered the phone he immediately started to apologize for the last time he stood me up. I interrupted him to blurt out the invitation to meet with Mr. Big, to which he immediately responded, "Sure, I would love to go." He was the first guy I called, and we both knew there were many others who would have loved to go on this trip. Charlie emphatically assured me he would be at the appointed place at the right hour; he was assuring me he would not fall into his old pattern of broken engagements.

Charlie and I did go together, and we had a great time. He really expanded his connections and business acumen as we had time with the speaker. Most of all, Charlie learned I would give him grace—and I learned once again the importance of pursuing a guy who wanted to be, but was not yet, faithful. Charlie has become one of my trusted confidants, a loyal friend and fellow soldier in reaching this world for Christ.

Sometimes we expect people to be committed and loyal when they have never seen those qualities modeled in their families, professions, or marriages. They don't know what commitment is. How many times did Peter deny Jesus after he claimed to be willing to die for our Lord and Savior? Three times—yet the Lord didn't write off the big fisherman. I have a friend who said he wouldn't meet with anybody who was not a faithful, eager man, willing to prepare every time for his morning meetings. I responded, "I'm glad Jim Lyon, the doctor who discipled me, did not require that from the guys he met with, because I never would have made the cut. Most of the guys I meet with wouldn't either." A Timothy's understanding of commitment needs to be nourished over time.

Keep in mind that crucial commitment needed from you, the discipler. Discipling will cost you. It takes time, which means you will have to give up some other things to invest in the relationship. It takes energy and courage to take the responsibility for another person's spiritual growth. And it takes an emotional toll to stay with him or her through the ups and downs of life. But they won't grow until you start discipling them.

When you disciple someone, you are investing in a relationship. You won't be meeting for six sessions or for nine workbooks or through some series of objectives. You are developing a relational bond centered on Jesus Christ. To think about it any other way is to turn people into objects. Nobody approaches a friend and says, "I'm going to be your buddy for three months, then you'll have to find another friend." Relationships take time—some more than others.

This doesn't mean you have to invest limitless time in that one person, however. There are many men who have impacted me and whom I have impacted, with whom I don't spend more than two or three meetings per year. Discipleship and mentoring can be effectively accomplished through infrequent times in some cases, such as my meetings with Joe and Kevin.

Joe, my spiritual great-grandfather, is an old warhorse. He gets in my face a couple of times a year, and God greatly uses him in my life. It may be on the subject of finances, discipling, my marriage, or any number of other important topics, but I've found Joe just has a way of getting into my life and being greatly used by God. Many times I have had to go away and think about what he said—or more accurately to *recover* from what he said—but in the end I always value my encounters with this man who has walked with God longer than I've been on earth.

Kevin, on the other hand, is 20 years younger than I am. I try to get time with him several times a year so we can sharpen one another. We usually land on issues such as purity, raising children, or walking with God. Though the friendship began with me mentoring Kevin, it has grown into a mutually beneficial relationship.

YOU NEVER KNOW WHAT YOU'LL GET

Entering into discipling relationships also, inevitably, involves some degree of trial and error. I once met with a man who was proceeding through a divorce and offered him everything on marriage I could find. When he finally realized he was not going to convince me his divorce was God's plan for his life, he dropped me like a hot potato. That guy was looking for someone to endorse his position on divorce. I couldn't do that, so the relationship ended. I was hurt for quite a while until I realized that I had chosen to work with him independent of the Lord's leading. I liked him, we had a lot in common, and I was sure the relationship would work out. Instead, it went nowhere.

Another fellow I met with for a long period of time loved my Bible studies, and I think I helped him with his day, but I never moved him much closer to Christlikeness. For all his interest in being spiritually inspired, I was never able to place his hand in the hand of God. I blame it on the fact he was a guy I admired, so I chose to meet with him before approaching the Lord about it. That never works. The Bible says the fruit has to be ripe; trying to disciple someone who isn't ready is akin to a farmer standing in his fields and yelling at the crops to ripen. It won't do any good, and it will only increase the farmer's frustration.

When I first came to know the Lord, friends had me meet with that physician, Jim, who had little regard for lawyers. Over lunch one day, when he asked who I would like to meet with regularly, I reached across the table, stuck my finger in his face, and said, "I want to meet with you." We weren't a natural fit, but God put us together to change us both. Sometimes you never know why the Lord works the way He does. Discipling relationships can be like buying a grab bag— you don't know what you'll get, but you can be sure if God is in control it will be something interesting. Remember, you don't have to be perfect or have calloused knees from spending hours each day in prayer to disciple someone else. But you do have to have a heart for people, be faithful in prayer, be willing to work with the people God gives you, and be committed to helping them grow.

Many years ago a man asked me to take out a 3x5 card and write down the name of every man and woman whom I'd had a part in leading to the Lord. He then asked me to write down the names of people who would say that God had used me to disciple them. I didn't like my answers that day, but the encounter challenged me to do something to change my response. I decided to get involved in the only thing other than the Bible that will last beyond the grave—impacting the lives of people.

Think about what you did of significance last year. What about the last ten years? In what have you invested that will last beyond the grave? Most of what we talk about, think about, worry about, and pat ourselves on the back about is going to burn up. Too many of those close to us will wonder why we never warned them of the carnage coming to those who die apart from Jesus Christ. Perhaps many more who are believers, will wonder why we didn't help them live abundant, mature, spiritually reproductive lives. It's not a question of doing the right thing but of doing the *only* thing that is eternally significant. Why don't you ask the Lord right now to bring to mind the person He wants you to disciple?

QUESTIONS FOR DISCUSSION

1. What reaction do you have when you hear someone say, "You ought to be making disciples"?

2. What does it mean that "God chooses your Timothy"?

3. What people in your life might be your Timothys?

4. Why do you think it's them?

5. What sort of commitment would you need from your Timothys?

CHAPTER 5

Association and ACCOUNTABILITY

A businessman with whom I had worked on several cases burst in my office door and blurted out, "All right, Phil, I *have* to know what you have that I don't! You have the edge on me—we both have kids, we both travel, we both have a lot of pressure from business, and yet you handle it much differently than I do. I need to know your secret. What's your edge?"

Some years ago I would have whipped out the *Steps to Peace with God* tract, confronted him with Jesus, and tried to close the deal. But instead of saying "How about Jesus?" I said, "How about breakfast?" I have learned a man inquiring is not necessarily a man ready to buy. Someone browsing in a store does not like the salesclerk to come up and start pushing a product on him. So I tried to be gentle. We met for more than a year, talking about issues in our lives, with me sharing principles I had learned from Scripture. He came to know Christ at the end of a year, and he has gone on to live his life for the Lord. When you take the time to associate with people, their lives change.

SETTING THE EXAMPLE

One of the things that has become more and more clear to me over time is my *walk* counts more than my *words*. The example I set is more important than the principles I share. Most people know how to have a good marriage: treat your spouse as if he or she is the most important person in the world. But few seem able to live out that truth. *Knowing* the principle is different from *putting it into practice*. Everybody knows the secret to financial freedom: spend less and save more. Yet few are able to live by that dictum. That's why the illustration of your life is so crucial. *People today aren't looking for answers but for examples.* My marriage isn't perfect; neither are my children; and I sometimes make stupid mistakes about my money, my job, and my relationships. But by God's grace, I'm growing into maturity. And I am willing to share both my successes and my failures with others to help them learn. That concept is the essence of discipleship.

For centuries businessmen spoke of "mentoring" others. The word came from a character in Greek mythology. When Odysseus went away to fight in the Trojan War, he left his son, Telemachus, in the hands of a trusted friend. That man, who was to teach and train the boy while the father was away, was named *Mentor*. When a young man wanted to learn, for example, the art of woodcarving, he would spend time with the master woodcarver. He watched the master work, asked questions, and was eventually given responsibility a little bit at a time. With each week the protégé learned more, slowly being shaped into the mold of the master. Christ's work with the disciples was much the same. He mentored them into spiritual maturity.

There has been much debate over the differences between "mentoring" and "discipleship," but I believe most of the arguing is pointless. In many respects the words are almost interchangeable. To mentor someone is to train him and teach him how to live; to disciple someone is to do those same things but with a spiritual focus. When I spend time with a protégé, I try to help him learn both the spiritual and the practical lessons of life. The key to both is association—spending time together in a variety of situations.

Jesus spent time associating with the twelve apostles because *He wanted them to see how He lived*. Peter, John, and the others could watch as the Lord dealt with the sick, the angry, and the hopeless. They observed how He handled material things and maintained a close walk with the heavenly Father. It was their close relationship with Jesus that changed their lives, not just the words He spoke. Remember, thousands of others heard Christ's words, and some of them schemed to put Him to death. It was the *relationship* that set the apostles apart.

When discipling another person, *the relationship comes first*. The other person has to spend time with you, associating with your lifestyle, or the relationship won't work. It will turn into a "fill in the blank" sort of intellectual study. Your Timothy wants to know you are committed to him and his growth, and that your commitment will need to be demonstrated by your actions. Association is what makes any sort of mentoring relationship effective. In business, a young man might spend time with an experienced hand to learn the keys to the trade. He sees the successes and failures and learns more than simple principles. The protégé learns every nuance of the master's way of doing things. In addition to his craft, he learns how to treat customers, how to keep the books, and how to clean up the mess. Discipling a man or woman works much the same way. You aren't merely trying to instill a statement of faith but to help the other person walk with God. Thus, we are called to disciple new believers, long-time believers, and non-believers.

Sometimes an unsaved person is drawn to Christ because of the example of the discipler. As we manifest Christ in our lives, it attracts people. That's what Paul called the "aroma" of the gospel, and it is still the best way to develop a mentoring relationship. Allow another to get close enough so he can see how your life is different. Let him see how you deal with frustration, what's special about the way you treat your wife or husband, and why you spend time in church. Don't worry about the fact that your life is not perfect; show your friend why you have hope for change!

Unfortunately, the most common reason Christians give for not discipling is they don't feel spiritually "ready." They'll say things like, "I have a lot of things in my life I'll have to take care of before I can disciple anyone." My response: "So take care of them." If you're immature, seek out a mature person to disciple you. Then start looking for someone you can disciple. If you have a stubborn sin problem, seek out a friend or a small group to hold you accountable, but don't let that keep you from ministry.

I believe the feeling of not being "ready" is nearly always a deception of Satan. Most people can't define what being "ready" looks like, but they're sure it is something better than their current spiritual walk. The fact is, you are never going to be perfectly "ready." We all have our failures and sins, and the Lord knows I have more than my share. But Christ doesn't expect me to be *faultless*—He expects me to be *faithful*. He is calling you to share your life with another person, and there are very few restrictions on that command.

A LIFETIME OF CHANGE

If you have decided to help change the world, the only way is to change people. The best way to change people is to spend enough time with them so they get to know and trust you, see what difference God has made in your life, and decide to copy your decision to follow Him. That takes time, which is why the Lord allowed Himself three years with the disciples. Those twelve guys came from a variety of circumstances, with a diversity of personalities and needs. There wasn't one *lesson* they needed to hear—there was one *life* they needed to see. Hearing a sermon wasn't going to change them, for change takes place in small increments over long periods of time as a person's beliefs and values are shaped by those around him. Jesus chose to work with people over time, and so should we.

Susy and I are both discipling a variety of people. In each of these relationships it seems we get more in return than we ever give out as we continually learn things from others that we need to know in all aspects of our own lives. These relationships are the most fun, exciting, and meaningful experiences we enjoy outside of our own marriage and family, and we've found working with people to be the most enriching ministry we can have.

Every person we disciple is at a different stage in life, and we have to take into consideration the person's particular needs at each stage. Some are at the very beginning of their spiritual journeys. Others are more mature and looking for someone to help them reach the next level. CBMC uses a chart called "The Critical Process," which traces the spiritual growth of an individual beginning with the cultivation stage and ending with maturity in Christ.

As an individual travels along the path toward Christ, others around him reach out and offer proof of the gospel through their lives. The metaphor in the Bible used for the first phase, the process of evangelism, is *farming*. Just as a farmer cultivates the soil, sows the seed, and gathers the harvest, we are to cultivate relationships with people, sow the seeds of the gospel, and harvest a crop of new souls for the kingdom of God.

But the metaphor changes in the second phase, after the individual has committed his life to Christ. The biblical image for the second phase, the process of discipleship, is *parenting*. As the individual is discipled, he grows in his spiritual maturity. As a spiritual parent, your perspective moves from *sowing to growing*. You recognize your walk with Christ can be multiplied in the life of another, just as your parents helped you to grow and mature. All it takes to disciple someone is to be a few steps farther down the path, coupled with a willingness to share what you know.

The best way to impact another life is to come alongside of a person and become a friend. Share with him the things you've learned through both success and failure. As you cultivate the relationship, sharing things in common and building trust, you'll find yourself given an opportunity to influence his life.

WORKING WITH PEOPLE

Several of the individuals Susy and I disciple are still seekers, willing to spend time with us in search of the truth. Some are believers in the early stages of their walk with Jesus Christ—a tough group because they are often inundated with information at church. They are given "enlightenment" through sermons and Sunday school classes, but often they are not given "en*live*nment"—a living example of someone to imitate in the faith. If a new believer can associate with someone a bit more mature, it will make all the difference in the world in terms of putting his faith into practice.

Susy had met with Kendra for almost a year, helping her to get started in a Bible-reading program, learn some of the life-changing principles of Scripture, and make a few big decisions. Kendra even talked about her relationship with

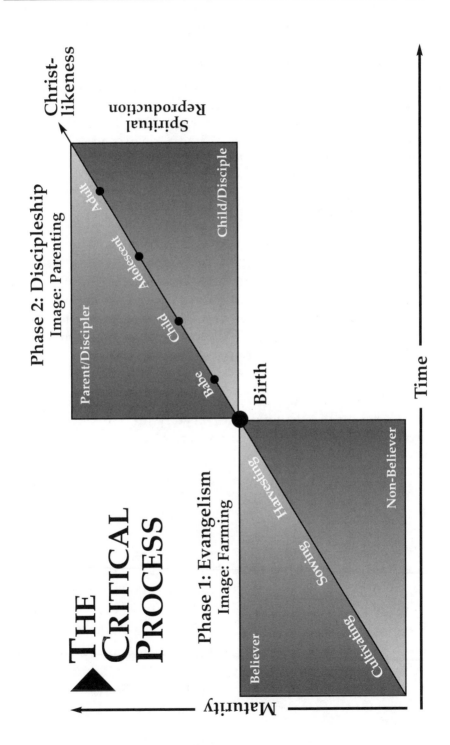

THE CRITICAL PROCESS

Maturity

Time

Phase 1: Evangelism
Image: Farming

Believer

Cultivating

Sowing

Harvesting

Non-Believer

Birth

Phase 2: Discipleship
Image: Parenting

Parent/Discipler

Adult

Adolescent

Child

Babe

Child/Disciple

Spiritual Reproduction

Christ-likeness

Susy as being a "life-changing experience." But when Kendra's father died suddenly, her life started to unravel. She grew depressed and actually began preparing a suicide plan. Even though she felt she was wading into pretty deep waters, Susy confronted Kendra one afternoon over lunch about her unresolved guilt, anger, and bitterness. After several hours of talking and crying together, it became clear to Kendra she had never given control of her life to Christ. That's when Susy took her through the *Steps to Peace with God* booklet, after which Kendra prayed to receive Christ. Her plan for death was replaced with God's eternal plan for everlasting life.

I'm meeting with a variety of men who are in that first stage. They are seeking truth, and I am cultivating relationships with them. They hunger for change, and I'm willing to show them the changes God offers. Those men know I'm not perfect, but they also know God has changed my life—and will continue to change me. All I try to do with each man is to come alongside, listen to questions, and share what I've learned to be true.

A second category of people we're discipling are couples dealing with the struggles of everyday life: career questions, marital difficulties, financial concerns, scheduling, family or parental problems, and physical troubles. These are people seeking a deeper understanding through Scripture. Some are Christians and some are not, but all of them are willing to learn. Susy and I have been greatly enriched by our times with couples, ministering together and walking through their life struggles with them. We decided a long time ago that we wanted to be involved in the battle and not simply assigned to the hospital, so we've attempted to show others how we relate as a couple in a way that moves us both toward maturity in Jesus and into His service to reach others.

A third group with whom I'm working are people I call "Christian leaders"—men who love the Lord but desire a mentor to whom they can be accountable. Some of them are leading godly families, godly companies, or godly ministries;

all of them are looking for the possibility of forming a bold alliance with a Christian brother in order to help move them toward Christlikeness. One of the most overlooked blessings of discipleship is the chance to spend time investing yourself in the strong leaders of our time. Many great leaders today were once weak and ineffective. Unfortunately, some weak leaders are men who used to be strong but were wounded. Too often we wait until somebody is shot before we come alongside and offer help. There is a great need in the Christian community today for someone to come alongside leaders who are lonely, who have fallen into discouragement, and whose lives have been targeted by Satan.

Generally this group of men has tremendous potential because they have their lives pretty well together. They either don't have the huge difficulties others have, or they've grown through their broken relationships and are now impacting the lives of others. Discipling these individuals is one of the greatest privileges I have. They challenge me and encourage me to greater commitment. Sometimes I stay awake at night, challenged by their commitment, vision, and strategies to reach this world for Jesus Christ. But they are also a real threat to my comfort zone. This group is quick to point out my failures, blind spots, and faulty thinking. These are the people I love to get around my kids because they will rivet you with their commitment and their conversation.

A fourth group of people with whom I am working consists of the precious fellow soldiers with whom I co-labor. If the people I'm discipling are my Timothys, then my fellow laborers are my Barnabases. These men are my ministry peers. They depend on me and I on them. These are the men who would be hurt most if the headlines screamed of my failures. They are the ones who go with me when I need help, who drop to their knees when I get bad news, and who trust me enough to forgive me without explanation. The body of Christ is built by interconnecting strengths and weaknesses, and every man in ministry needs to share both so he can be complemented and held accountable. It is awfully tough to fight a battle alone. When you know someone else is there, backing you up, you feel strengthened and encouraged.

Susy and I have trusted a number of people in this group with total entry into our lives for the purpose of accountability. We give these folks the right and opportunity to ask any question regarding our lives. To be perfectly frank, there are times when I really hate the process. At one meeting, a chair was placed in the middle of the room; I was asked to sit down, and my accountability partners questioned me on every aspect of my life. They wanted to know about my thought life, my discretionary spending, and what I was doing to invest in my children. One guy even asked me what sort of television programs I'd been watching. They got in my face and said I was a hypocrite for claiming I wanted to spend time with my wife when I couldn't show them on my calendar a single weekend during the previous year that I had been away alone with Susy without an agenda. That same group will even ask Susy about what I've been doing, to make sure I'm not snowing them. I hate it—but I need it—especially if I am going to be in leadership. Satan despises what we're doing and wants to take effective soldiers out of the battle, so I do what I can to keep myself accountable to my commanding officer, Jesus Christ.

Accountability is an integral part of discipling, and you need it in your life. Without a Barnabas, a friend or two with whom you can disclose yourself, there won't be anybody to check your spiritual temperature. All of the famous Christians who have fallen into sin in recent years have neglected this one area—they had nobody who would confront and force them to be honest with themselves. I've never known a great Christian leader who didn't have this sort of relationship. Over the years I've had the wonderful opportunity to talk personally with men like Howard Hendricks, Bruce Wilkinson, Chuck Swindoll and Joe Stowell, and they all have spoken of the importance of having a faithful brother who would challenge them when they needed it.

A fifth group with whom I'm involved is a senior leadership group, comprised of people fifteen to twenty-five years my senior who have corporations, institutions, and ministries they have founded and led. These are the men who have been through the valley, tasted both victory and sorrow, and survived the compelling sins of their generation. They are now leading multitudes in their most productive years and have already decided they're not going to retreat from the front lines of the battle and become ineffective for Christ. These men are the ones who are finishing well but who are not yet finished. Rather than discipling them, I seek to be discipled *by* them; I need to emulate, imitate, and most of all *to be like them.*

The wonderful thing about this group is they've let Susy and me minister to them as they've ministered to us. We've had the joy of seeing some of their children come to faith or greater commitment through our ministry, for sometimes it takes your spiritual children to reach your natural children. This is the group I turn to for wisdom, and I value their input in my life. Friends, I encourage you to get some people like this in your own life and give them the position of accountability for your finances, vocation, marriage, and ministry. Without these couples, Susy and I would never be where we are today. These are the ones assuming the spiritual parenting roles for us. They're our mentors as we move through the middle years of the Christian life.

WHAT DO PEOPLE NEED?

Now before you get overwhelmed by adding up all the people listed above and conclude you have to quit your job just to meet with all those different folks, let me make one suggestion: go before the Lord and ask Him for the name of *one person* you can mentor. Try to see your way clear to free up one hour a week to disciple a seeker or new believer, or perhaps two evenings a month to meet with other couples. Start looking for someone to whom you can be accountable, perhaps meeting for a weekend so you can go deep in your conversations. Discipling isn't just about giving things to other people, be it advice, principles, or homework assignments. It's about two people together growing up into maturity in the Lord. You may have heard Howard Hendricks say every person needs a Paul, a Barnabas, and a Timothy. In other words, you need a mentor pouring himself into your life, a friend walking beside you, and one into whose life you are pouring your own.

If we keep our focus on Christ and the job to which He has called us, we can live the most exciting, fruitful, and productive lives imaginable. I actually believe we can live the life Paul describes—a life of eternal significance in a temporal world. Even though he was imprisoned in a tough Roman jail, chained to a guard, and hearing about others perverting his work, Paul describes his time as one in which he could rejoice: "Now I want you to know, brethren, that my circumstances have turned out for the greater progress of the gospel, so that my imprisonment in the cause of Christ has become well known throughout the whole praetorian guard and to everyone else" (Philippians 1:12-13).

How many Christians are experiencing this type of spiritual reproduction? How many are willing to reach out to a seeker or a young Christian and share life with that person? The opportunities are everywhere if you simply ask God to bring a person into your life in whom you can invest.

As you take someone along the path toward maturity, you share your life with him. You hold him accountable for his own growth. As you walk the path with him, there are three areas in which you'll want to help him grow: character (who we are), competency (what we can do), and community (with whom we do it as we walk with Christ).

The first priority is to help people know who they are in Christ. Show a person your spiritual life. Let him see how you live your life before God. Reveal your relationship with your wife or husband. You can't disciple without a close relationship because you won't reveal who you really are. Take the time to cultivate the relationship and show your Timothy what a Christian is like.

Once you have shown them who they are as a Christian, you have to help them catch a vision for what they can accomplish. That's why it is a myth that" discipleship" deals only with spiritual development. It really means the *total* development of the *total* person. It must take into account all aspects of an individual's life. If you are just dealing with someone in a Bible study by filling in the blanks in a book, you are not dealing with the whole person. Help them discover their spiritual gifts and begin putting them into practice. Give them opportunities and assignments so they are stretched in their walk with God. People have to develop the confidence that God can use them if they are ever going to be able to reproduce their life.

The final area to emphasize is helping your Timothy recognize he is part of a community. Every Christian is part of the family of God—brothers and sisters in the Lord. We aren't in this world alone; we are part of God's team, placed here to shake the world with righteousness. Because of our competitive culture, it's easy for people to feel isolated and alone. A discipling relationship reminds a person he is never alone; he can always call on you for support.

One Monday morning a young man marched into my office and began criticizing me concerning something to which he had obviously given a great deal of thought. He barked at me for putting "tasks" ahead of "people" and for not offering him the support he needed. I was mentally applying the principle of Hebrews 12:5 not to regard discipline lightly, but as his analytical comments shifted toward ranting and raving, I was about to abandon all of that spiritual stuff and put this guy in his place. That's when the Spirit reminded me this young man was in trouble. If it was so important he was willing to put his job on the line to confront me, I'd better listen.

Wanting to give myself a break and hoping he would cool down, I suggested we get a cup of coffee at a nearby restaurant. What I was facing was the turmoil that had built up in the life of a fellow lawyer who had never felt accepted by his father. Coming in to rant was his way of revealing he had a need to discuss things. After we both cooled down, I had to admit there was some truth in what he was saying about my relational style. In some ways I was doing to him exactly what his father had done, and the problem had grown in his mind from a small matter into World War III. So I suggested we start a discipling relationship, which led us to discuss the abandonment of his father and his own feelings of inadequacy about how he was fathering his own children. It became clear this man didn't know who he was in Christ, had no confidence in his abilities, and didn't feel part of the greater Christian community. As we worked through all of those topics over the next two years, he began to grow and change. This man has now gone on to impact many people with the gospel, having straightened out his relationship with his heavenly Father. And it all happened because a man started talking about his needs. Find out what the people around you need, and then try to meet that need with the sufficiency of Scripture.

YOUR NON-CHRISTIAN NEIGHBOR

I'll occasionally meet with men who say they do not know any non-Christians—and it's usually said by people involved in the ministry. They feel their job has separated them from this lost world. I always suggest they join a follow-up team after an outreach event, to meet with people in their homes or offices and share Christ with them. I'm surprised at the number of

Christians who have never done anything like that. Visiting people puts you face-to-face with those who are interested in spiritual things but have never received the Lord as their personal Savior.

Recently I was speaking at a mayor's prayer breakfast in a medium-sized city, and afterward, different teams of Christians visited more than twenty men who had expressed an interest in knowing more about the Lord. More than half of those visited wanted to get involved in some sort of discipling relationship; five of them prayed to receive Christ right on the spot. In every case, a friend had invited the man to the meeting, he had heard the gospel, was followed up by available men, and committed his life to Christ. Imagine the excitement of those brothers who were on the visitation teams! But we discovered an interesting fact when we did follow-up research. We learned that the men who attended the breakfast were attracted both by the gospel *and by the other men at the meeting*. In other words, the first step in their journeys toward God came from the positive impact of a godly man. The example you set makes a difference.

Too many Christians have developed a "bunker" mentality, hiding out from a hostile world. It is common among Christian workers and pastors to feel a natural gulf between themselves and people in business. After all, they dress differently, work differently, even speak with different jargon. That's why many pastors have stopped going to see businessmen. Now we're seeing this same bunker mentality permeate the marketplace. I've noticed all sorts of believers trying to set up little Christian enclaves so they never have to spend time with anyone who isn't a believer. They work for Christian organizations, send their kids to Christian schools, and only socialize with people from church. Their only interaction with non-believers is during the short dash into the grocery store—and they act like they're on guard the whole time. Living this way, Christians lose their advantage. We're supposed to be lights *in the darkness*. We are to be pointing out the way to those who are lost. Nobody needs a flashlight in a well-lit room. The Bible says we are to be in the world, though not of it. That is, we are to be clearly Christian in a non-Christian world. Learn to enter every relationship asking for God's wisdom on the spiritual "temperature" of the person with whom you are dealing. The Holy Spirit will often show you whether the person knows Christ or not so you will know best how to deal with him.

Before going to one of our children's baseball or softball games (one year we had six children on six different teams!), Susy made a practice of asking the Lord to show her where she should sit during that game. Sometimes it was by someone she already knew, sometimes by someone she had never met. Continuing this practice over many years, Susy built relationships with many moms, some of whom became Timothys, others who brought their children to our Good News Club. This made a great impression on our children who have said that their mom's model has caused them to keep their spiritual antennae alert for opportunities to build a relationship with someone who doesn't know the Lord.

It used to be that the majority of people with whom we came in contact were Christians or at least religious. Now the majority of people in America are completely secularized, with no godly influence in their lives. Yet the typical Christian goes about his day without attempting to distinguish the Christian from the non-Christian. Unless he does that however, he will never know whether he should reach out with the truth of Christ. He often notices the problems in the world but perceives himself as a victim rather than as a conqueror. He goes to work and is confronted with temptation, ridicule, cursing, and integrity compromises. All day long he holds his hands up like a boxer, bobbing and weaving, trying to protect himself from a deadly blow. After fighting this battle all week, he attends church on Sunday, gets bandaged up, then heads out for round two. Instead of focusing on how to reach people who are without Christ, he strategizes on how to stay away from them. Rather than thinking about how to *change* the world, he's trying to figure out how to *survive it*.

On top of these stresses we are now hearing a call for more political involvement by Christians to impact the glaring social issues of our day. While it is clear some Christians are called to political action and each of us needs to be informed and in prayer about the role God would have us take, I believe too many believers occupy the rank of "disgruntled Christian." We need to put aside our complaining about the culture long enough to build relationships of love and introduce others to Christ. He will change people's lives—and thereby change the culture. The man who discipled me disagreed with me on almost every major political and social issue, but instead of trying to win me to the "Christian political point of view," he allowed me to be changed by the Savior. In meeting Jesus Christ, my entire worldview was turned upside down.

FINDING A COMFORT LEVEL

Before trying a case, I always tried to spy out the land and pray through the courtroom. I liked to go to the opposition's office and often thought up excuses to pick up something or do a deposition there, just to get a feel for the team I was opposing. By studying the office I could learn a great deal about the people involved.

Similarly, in discipling a man I want to see his office and home so I can understand what makes him tick. What kind of team is he on? What pressures does he face? I can walk the halls of an office and, as an outsider, feel tensions that may be there, sense his stresses, and develop a better feeling for the kinds of issues with which he is dealing. I can also take the spiritual temperature of his office and see if it's an area where we could comfortably meet. My wife can often determine a woman's needs and comfort level intuitively, but I have to do a bit more investigating.

I once met with a man who continually forgot his Bible. Eventually I realized he hadn't forgotten it; he was simply embarrassed to carry it with him. If people in his field saw him carrying a Bible, it would be like wearing a tank top to the opera. So I bought him a small Bible he could put in his pocket. By being sensitive to his comfort level I was able to develop a deeper relationship with him.

One man I met with would act incredibly nervous during our meetings but really enjoyed our praying together. I finally figured out that although he was a brilliant businessman, he was a very poor reader. So I stopped asking him to read out loud. A few guys I've met insist on praying in public, but most men today are horrified to pray out loud. We do not live in a time where people in churches are standing up, giving public prayers, or doing Old and New Testament readings in their churches, so we need to be sensitive to the environment. Find the comfort level of the person you are discipling.

It is also extremely helpful to get to know the man's or woman's family in some way. Many people have gotten very sensitive about having strangers in their homes. We have gone from an era of hospitality to an era of cave mentality. Our homes used to be open centers for socializing and getting to know someone new, but now the home is a bunker into which we withdraw. It is a haven—a place we go to hide, get away from it all and be ourselves. Often we are sensitive about showing people our homes, especially if we live a busy life where both husband and wife work and the kids are coming and going. The closets will never be straight, the floors will always be sticky, the refrigerator will always be disorganized, and the average wife is not excited about someone coming to her home for an inspection.

The process of meeting the family is made easier by meeting somewhere neutral such as a restaurant, the ball field, or an outing. I think it is interesting that people have no time for church or Christian events, but if you ask people what they are doing on the weekend, they're bound to say, "Well, Friday night we're going to a potluck supper for the school, then Saturday morning we have soccer, Saturday afternoon we have a picnic for the soccer families, and Saturday night we're going to the movies. Then Sunday we're going to that jazz festival unless I go camping with my son, and on Sunday evening we're having a party." You may only be comfortable going to half of those activities, but at least it offers a chance to be involved in the other person's life.

You can begin to invest in a person by simply saying, "Look, do you mind if we just kind of tag along with you to that ball game? It's been a long time since I have gone to a good baseball game—and listen, we'll bring the hot dogs and the drinks! Why don't we just meet you there? My kids would love to see your family!" An important thing to remember is that when you go to the game, be sure you go as invited guests and not as critics. Go as brothers and sisters who love people and are seeking to introduce them to an all-sufficient, all-forgiving, omnipotent Savior. Do not go to try to reform the baseball league!

DISCIPLING YOUNG PEOPLE

Young Christians need a tremendous amount of time and flexibility. Most have no "margin" in their lives. They have growing families, are overcommitted at work, are experiencing strife at home, and are still trying to change their lives in their own energy by overdoing, overeating, overcommitting, and undersleeping. These people have the greatest need for a discipler but the least time and flexibility. In meeting with this sort of person, you have to go as a servant. You see, it seems great to act as a servant for an hour once in a while, but with this type of person, acting as a servant may have to become your SOP (standard operating procedure).

That hour gets repeated over and over again. You have to serve them by moving your schedule, flexing with their travel, finding odd times to get together, and being willing to be stood up when they can't show up because their boss has asked for something at the last minute. It's tough to disciple a young professional person. That is a difficult group, but also a huge joy as you see someone begin to grasp who Christ is.

It is very important to get together socially. Many younger men and women today grew up in homes where the father was gone all the time, so in response they are unwilling to abandon their own families for meetings. When they're not working, their time is family time, so sometimes you have to adjust to their family needs. For example, one man showed up with his two-year-old son the first time we met. As we sat there at the restaurant with Bibles open, trying to talk about Scripture, Joey spilled, chattered, grabbed, and did what all little kids do. It was quite a test for me, because I am a fairly structured person and I hate the thought of getting any goo on my suit or juice on the pages of my Bible. For me it was a tremendous stretch not to become flustered or irritated with this child playing havoc with the breakfast table. But it was also clear, if I didn't accept this man's bringing his boy, he would not spend time with me. I almost died trying to get through our first meeting with that two-year old, but I prayed for patience and we got through the studies that day. The next time I called and reminded my new Timothy of our meeting time, I was thrilled he agreed to come but shocked when he added, "Joey loved our meeting so much I thought I would bring him again"!

A similar thing happened to me when I was a new Christian. I went to a Bible study with Abigail, who was a very rambunctious newborn. As I sat there, Abigail screamed and yelled, until one of the women finally took a pacifier and soaked it in Karo syrup to quiet her for a few minutes while we finished the study. At the next meeting, a very well-meaning individual and a wonderful godly friend, but someone from another generation, said to me, "Phil, I think it was distracting for the leader to have Abigail there. Perhaps it would be better if you didn't bring her next time." That was the last Bible study I ever attended with that group. I am embarrassed to admit it, but my feelings were hurt. I felt I should have received a medal of honor for bringing my child and letting my wife go out of town, taking care of a kid with poopy diapers to respond to my wife's need for a break. These guys were more concerned about interruptions to their Bible study than about ministering to a frazzled father.

So if you want to work with a boomer, a buster, or a Gen-Xer, you will need to learn how to flex. They are not like the older generation. With new converts, it's particularly important to get your families together just to go out and have fun. Avoid always harping on biblical principles or making alcohol and entertainment an issue. Just love them right where they are. That is essential in building relationships.

If you are going to disciple a young person, it is also important to have the spouse on board. Men used to say, "Honey, we're leaving," and the wife would somehow make all the arrangements. Now the wife says, "You can't go. You need to take the kids to school and I have a carpool." Wives have a lot more say over men's lives than they used to. In fact, the average man today has about two hours a week of disposable time he can use without his wife's agreement. Many modern households are run as partnerships, so if the spouse doesn't like you or doesn't understand what you are doing, the discipling relationship is going to be very short.

One of the very first things you need to do with a young man is to ask him about his relationship with his wife. Encourage him to give her time, and explain your meeting will not be in conflict with their time but should actually benefit their marriage as God's Word fills the husband's thinking. One of the things about the younger generation that is shocking is their tremendous drive in the area of relation-ships. I grew up in a time where big boys didn't cry, you didn't show your emotions, you toughed it out and took care of yourself, and you didn't let people inside your life. It has taken a lot to change that, and younger guys can really press me on that issue. If I don't open up, they won't either. So I find I have to talk about the issue of television and how I spend my time in such a way that I avoid sin when I travel. Those are some real challenges, but many young men are serious about developing holiness. I've learned to share my heart and try to help set the example. In truth, we learn from one another. Your vulnerability and willingness not to just teach but be teachable will allow you to have a greater impact on the lives of young couples. If you do not open up your life to build the relationship, you can forget about mentoring a young person. You must courageously share yourself to forge an alliance with a young believer.

STRUGGLING WITH SIN

People today are struggling with sins of every variety. It is important to pierce through the superficial chatter about sin and hit the real issues. For example, I was meeting with a group of men one time who didn't seem to want to deal with any of the tough elements of the Christian walk. Finally, I asked them, "Do any of you guys struggle with masturbation?"

There was not an eye looking at me in response. The room was filled with a sense of embarrassment. How could anyone bring up "the M word" in public? I was somewhat nervous about doing it, but I proceeded to explain that I had struggled with that practice earlier in my life. After I became a Christian, I began to be concerned about it; even as a non-Christian, I hadn't been comfortable with it. So I told the guys I'd read a few books on the topic.

Some of the books I'd read said masturbation was wrong; but one particular book, written by a Christian husband and wife, claimed it was a natural function, appropriate as long as you kept your thoughts pure. So I posed the question to these men, "How easy is it to keep your thoughts pure when masturbating?" They all exploded with laughter. "Impossible!" they replied. Then I revealed I had come to a place where I realized I had to stop that practice for three reasons. First, I could not keep my thoughts pure. Second, it destroyed my self-control. And third, it kept alive a very deep root of lust in my life. As a young Christian, without any counsel from anyone, I sought to end that practice. Years later, other Christian men finally admitted to me they had struggled with masturbating and had also quit upon coming to the same conclusion.

As embarrassing as it may be, men need to talk about gut-level issues like this. They need to be honest about magazines and movies in hotel rooms. I describe for my Timothys how I pray through every hotel room when I first enter, read Colossians 2, and ask God to fill that room with His power so I will not turn on the television. I then spend my time reading the Bible and other good books. I also share with them that I always call my wife when I return to the hotel room each night, no matter how late it is, because that's the time when I am lonely and sometimes very bored.

Susy tries to talk with the women she is discipling about such sensitive issues as submission and its role in sex in marriage. It is a tough topic, one people don't want to deal with openly, but that is the very reason the discipler has to bring it up. Many women never talked with their moms or dads about the topic, so any information they learned came from movies, women's magazines, romance novels, or perhaps an outspoken friend. There is no guarantee they received good information from any of those sources, so a godly woman in a discipling relationship can have a significant impact on their thinking. We must steer our Timothy's thinking toward God's thinking.

In talking about these delicate subjects, I have found lectures only drive people away. But if I honestly share my own struggles, pointing the finger at myself, it allows me also to be able to talk about biblical principles. It is always difficult to cover such sensitive topics, but I have had dozens of men come back to me later and say how much they appreciated an open discussion about them. If we can talk openly about our struggles with sin, we can help the Timothys in our lives follow our example to maturity.

DEVELOPING ACCOUNTABILITY

I want to set an example with my life, then share that example with others. Sometimes I succeed; sometimes I fail. But I always try to see where men need help and offer it to them. If I can spend time at a man's house and at his work, then have him visit my house and my work, we'll both have a better understanding of each other.

Let me emphasize again that as God is refining me as a Christian, I find I need someone with whom I can be accountable. A friend of mine in ministry put together twenty questions he wanted his staff to ask him each week. The questions concerned his quiet time, the sun going down on his anger, diet and exercise, and the use of his money. Soon each staff member was creating his or her own sheet of accountability questions so they could check up on one another. You see, we all have idols in our lives. We have lusts for money, power, or position. I find it sometimes easier to talk about a man's struggles with his sexual purity than his drive to accumulate monetary reward. Those are often the darkest secrets of a man's heart. But as such, I have to ask the hard questions.

For example, I often question a man about the amount of time he puts in at the office. We'll talk about his schedule, his family, and his time in the Scriptures. Questions about why and how long he works can lead to a lot of areas that reflect his focus on something other than Christ. A man who works all the time may be trying to accumulate assets. He might be in love with possessions, not Christ.

TWENTY QUESTIONS

1. How often did you have a quiet time last week?

2. What did you study in your devotional life this past week?

3. On a scale of 1 to 100, where would you rate your spiritual life?

4. Besides Scripture, what constructive material are you reading/studying?

5. How did you build up your wife this past week?

6. Were there any times last week when the sun went down on your anger?

7. On a scale of 1 to 100, where would you rate your marriage?

8. What significant investment of time did you make with each child?

9. What one thing have you done recently that your family will remember five years from now?

10. When did you last struggle with your thought life, and how did you respond?

11. What did you do for exercise this past week?

12. What did you do for relaxation?

13. Is your weight up or down? How much?

14. Did your total indebtedness grow or shrink? Why?

15. What percent of your income did you give away outside your family?

16. Whom did you encourage?

17. With whom did you share your faith?

18. What were your emotional highs and lows?

19. What decisions or problems are weighing on you right now?

20. What are you praying for God to do?

From Dr. Chip MacGregor's *Organization Resource Handbook*

My struggle used to be that I had to own something before I could enjoy it. If I was on vacation, visiting a nice location, I would start to think "How could I buy a building lot? How can I own part of it so I can enjoy it?" I had a hard time going to shops and looking at pretty things because I always wanted to own them. I tell my Timothys that falling in love with Jesus Christ moved me away from falling in love with things.

There are a thousand reasons men become workaholics, but if you are discipling someone who can never leave his office, you have to make him face facts. Perhaps he works long hours because he hates to be home. Maybe his wife nags him about the things he won't change and should change, or he or she has allowed the spark to go out in their marriage. A discussion with him about a few things he could do to better serve his wife can be both helpful and revealing. A man might work all the time because of a fear of losing everything, so a discussion about the security of the Lord and the security of the believer is in order. We have no security in temporal things, only in eternity with God. Another man may work constantly because he had a lousy father who never allowed him to feel he measured up. I have a friend who is a very successful businessman, with a gorgeous wife, a beautiful home, and a magnificent career in industry. He is on numerous boards, supports ministries all over the world, and is a leader of leaders. But as I was talking about his father and his lack of approval, this man, who is past sixty, burst into tears. He told me how wonderful it would have been if his father had even once said to him, "Son, I love you and I appreciate what a good job you are doing." He had been driving himself most of his adult life to satisfy an earthly father who had been dead and buried for more than thirty years. By talking through our relationships with our fathers and doing a Bible study on our relationship to our heavenly Father, this man was able to make the attitude changes necessary for his spiritual growth.

If you want to disciple others, you are going to have to be ready to discuss these types of issues. Don't just talk with people, *associate with them*. Let them see how a godly person lives his life. And don't just allow your time with them to be a "holy huddle"—an opportunity for Christians to hang out together in order to commiserate on the state of the world. *Keep them accountable*. Ask the hard questions. Talk about the important issues in their lives. God will use you as an impetus for growth in the lives of others.

QUESTIONS FOR DISCUSSION

1. What people have influenced your life the most?

2. Whom do you go to when you have a question or concern in your life? Who is the Barnabas in your life?

3. Men, what have been your best male relationships? Women, what have been your best female relationships? Why do you suppose so many men struggle with relationships?

4. How are the needs of new believers different from those of Christian leaders?

5. What activities are you involved in that you could invite non-Christians or new believers to?

CHAPTER 6

The Cycle
OF LIFE

*D*iscipleship is like going camping with the family. You sign on for all of the unexpected crises, weather problems, intrusions, snake bites, sleepless nights, forgotten sleeping bags, and burned dinners, but you do it because it is good for everybody—and in the long run, you find it fun. Snake bites and all. When you disciple someone, you agree to take on their difficulties and immaturities and recognize you will also have to face a few of your own. Receiving people in grace is the starting point of discipleship. Be thankful for the opportunities God gives you to walk with someone else through the process of spiritual growth—it will change you every time.

Over and over again those I have mentored have impacted me as much as I have them. I once met with a young businessman who said he appreciated how much he was learning from me about walking with Christ, but when our discussions turned to business troubles or a problem I was having with a person on my legal team, that young man gave me the perfect solution for my problem. God used me to shape him spiritually; then the Lord turned around and used that man to shape *me*.

We sometimes approach discipleship with the attitude that we expect our Timothys to be open to our input and schedule yet fail to reciprocate. I have been guilty of this. I remember the time Jon showed up to help Susy plant a garden in the backyard—in the middle of a day I had set aside to work on "my projects." My maleness, unable to allow another man to help Susy without my expert assistance, sent me across the yard looking for another shovel to join them with the plunge, lift, and turnover of the soil project they had underway. In about fifteen minutes, I remembered why so many farmers had sold their shovels and moved to the cities! Jon kept instructing me to plunge the shovel a full twelve inches into the ground, then turn over one foot of soil to reach the necessary depth required. After about the third suggestion that my shovel was negligently shallow, I began to realize he was serious about teaching me farming, which only added a headache to my backache. At the time it did not seem nearly as funny to me as it did to Susy. But I did learn a lot about farming!

I used to think disciple making was easy. You met with another individual, talked about the Bible, spent some time praying, and discussed your life. If the other person wasn't committed, you dropped him and moved on to the next one. My life was full and my schedule busy, so I didn't have time for those who seemed to lack commitment. I hate to admit it, but I became pretty bent out of shape when I was stood up for a discipling appointment. I figured the other guy just wasn't "serious" about his relationship to the Lord. I came from a marketplace mindset, which told me to "move with the movers—or move on." I wanted things to go my way, and the other person had better meet my expectations.

In retrospect, I was acting like a spoiled child. This world is filled with many hurting people who can't get with the program for a number of reasons. Their marriages are bad, their kids running amok, they have job and financial pressures, they are pulled in thirty different directions, or their schedules are out of control. In the midst of this, I'm asking them to put God first by making our meeting the number one priority in life. It sounds good, but it's unrealistic. Contemporary culture won't allow that to happen very easily.

I once wrote off a guy because he would not meet with my program—forgetting my program was not necessarily God's plan for his life. Instead of sticking with him and checking from time to time to see how he was doing, I bolted from the relationship. In my mind, that guy was either uninterested or unwilling to keep his commitments, so I told myself he wasn't worth my investment of time. It was a terrible mistake, for that man desperately needed a helpful friend. The biggest error I made early in my discipling relationships was having a "program" that I followed. No deviations were allowed. That sort of thinking put *my* desires ahead of the other man's needs. It put *me* in charge rather than God. You see, the Lord isn't as concerned with my program as He is with my relationship to others. The Timothy in your life is not a task to be accomplished but a relationship to be developed. When we look at people as tasks, we are not only ineffective disciple makers but run the risk of injuring others' spiritual lives.

The good news is that I got help. My spiritual parents reminded me that I wasn't perfect when I began and everybody grows at different rates. As a Christian, I'm called to be like Jesus to other people—and Christ came to spend time with the sick. He didn't turn Peter away just because he made some mistakes. Christ worked through the various stages of growth with Peter, and the end result was a man who became the rock of the early church.

Jesus isn't the only disciple maker found in the pages of Scripture. Elijah took pains to prepare Elisha for ministry. Daniel did something right with his three friends Shadrach, Meshach, and Abednego. And Moses certainly made sure Joshua was ready for his role as leader of Israel. I have always appreciated how the Bible gives us the details about how Joshua, when he was ready to take the Promised Land, sent *two* spies to view the land. Those were the two men who went secretly and arranged for a signal with the harlot Rahab. The reason Joshua sent two trusted men, and sent them in secret, is because he saw the mistake Moses had made forty years earlier in sending a big group of twelve. Ten of those guys came back and reported in fear to the masses, inciting a cowardly response. Joshua sent only two, using faithful men, and had them report directly back to him. Joshua learned from the mistakes of his mentor.

BECOME AN IMITATOR

In one sense, when you decide to disciple another person, you have decided to become an imitator. In Ephesians 5:1 Paul tells us to "be imitators of God." In speaking to the believers at Corinth, Paul told them to "imitate me" (1 Corinthians 4:16). The word he used in Greek actually says, "mimic me." In other words, he wanted the Corinthians to observe him carefully, see how he lived, then live that same way. Those two verses offer a wonderful thumbnail sketch of the discipling process. I am to spend time with God through His Word. I'm called to worship Him, to get to know Him so I can imitate Him in this world. As a believer, I am to live like Jesus Christ. Then I am to invite another to watch what I do and imitate it so he, too, can grow into maturity in the Lord.

Christians have a tendency to think about discipleship as being the same process as evangelism, but it is not. Too often the church has attempted to help new believers by offering bits of advice instead of a caring, trusting relationship. Things like "Hey, new Christian! You need to go to church!" or "Read this book, you need it," or "Hey, you'd better stop that! Oh, and can you help with the youth group?" seem to replace people's coming alongside and showing them how to live the Christian life. Somehow we expect there to be growth, but we often get frustration and rebellion because we have not developed a relationship that allows a context for life change.

As mentioned earlier, the metaphor in Scripture for discipleship is parenting, which usually means a long-term commitment to help a new babe in Christ grow into maturity. Spiritual growth is not found in imparting intellectual information but in sharing your life. Paul said to the people in Thessalonica, "For you recall, brethren, our labor and hardship, how working night and day so as not to be a burden to any of you, we proclaimed to you the gospel of God" (1 Thessalonians 2:9). In other words, Paul modeled godly character to the believers so they would know how to live. He proclaimed the gospel, worked hard, and spent night and day with them so they would know how a godly man lives his life. The people in Thessalonica, even though they lived in a crooked and perverse time, were known for three things: "We give thanks to God always for all of you . . . constantly bearing in mind your work of faith and labor of love and steadfastness of hope in the Lord Jesus Christ" (1 Thessalonians 1:2-3). The Thessalonian Christians were living faithfully for Jesus Christ in a pagan culture.

It is interesting that Paul notes, "You also became imitators of us and of the Lord" (verse 6), for they must have been following Paul's example. "In every place your faith toward God has gone forth, so that we have no need to say anything" (verse 8). Paul didn't have to brag about the Thessalonians. Everybody already knew about them.

Everywhere Paul went he heard about the way the people of Thessalonica had changed. Out of lives of paganism they developed into men of God. They matured in Christ by imitating Paul's example.

That's why Paul wrote to the church at Corinth, urging them, "Be imitators of me, just as I also am of Christ" (1 Corinthians 11:1). The New International Version translates this, "Follow my example, as I follow the example of Christ." It was not that Paul was arrogant or had reached some sort of perfection. He was simply further down the path than the other believers and wanted to help them mature. So he revealed his life to them by spending time with Christians, and then he encouraged them to follow his example. He did the same thing with the church at Philippi, telling them, "The things you have learned and received and heard and seen in me, practice these things" (Philippians 4:9).

The result of all this imitation was that the believers grew, and Paul rejoiced in their growth. That is the example the apostles have set for us. "I have no greater joy than this, to hear of my children walking in the truth," John said in 3 John 4. But that's what many Christians are missing today. Too often we are bound up in who won the game, how much our new car cost, the taxes we owe, or the squabbling in the church. We miss the pure joy of celebrating the work of God in the lives of people. We spend our time on other issues instead of getting this tremendous, profound, eternal blessing of having spiritual children and knowing they walk with God.

That's a shame when you consider the impact you could have by revealing your life. The Lord told the prophet Isaiah, "The least of you will become a thousand, the smallest a mighty nation" (Isaiah 60:22, NIV). In other words, God can take the smallest thing and multiply it. He can take your walk with Jesus Christ, even though it isn't perfect and you have a few rough spots that need smoothing, and use it to help others grow. Remember, one can become a thousand through the work of the Lord in your life. So if you want to have a profound impact on your world, invest deeply in one person.

STAGES OF CHRISTIAN GROWTH

Christian maturity is not a static thing. Just as there are new babies and senior citizens, there are infant believers and spiritual elders, babes in Christ and mature saints. Helping someone grow from spiritual infancy to spiritual maturity is the process of spiritual parenting, and there is an incredible need for it in the church today.

One of the biggest problems the church faces is the mass of immature believers. Mature Christians stand for what is right; immature Christians fall for the compromises of Satan. Mature believers speak the truth; immature believers want to make sure everyone is happy. Mature men and women of God know the truth and do it; immature people know about the truth and do the parts they like. Mature reproducers change their environment; immature Christians are still being taken in by the deceit of this world. An immature Christian's temperature is changed by the world like a thermometer reveals the heat of a room, but a mature Christian controls the temperature of his environment, acting as a thermostat. Learning to grow up in the Lord, and helping others do the same, is the hurdle we must clear if we are to help those immature believers become effective members of the family of God.

There are four distinct stages to Christian growth, each with specific needs. John, writing to a first-century church, described the growth process this way:

"I write to you, dear children,
because your sins have been forgiven on account of
    his name.
I write to you, fathers,
because you have known him who is from the beginning.

I write to you, young men,
because you have overcome the evil one.
I write to you, dear children,
because you have known the Father.
I write to you, fathers,
because you have known him who is from the beginning.
I write to you, young men,
because you are strong,
and the word of God lives in you,
and you have overcome the evil one."

(1 John 2:12-14, NIV)

Just as each of us goes through the process of being a physical baby, then a child, next an adolescent, and finally an adult, every believer moves through this same spiritual process. Each stage has its own struggles and joys. John describes as babies those who have met the Father. As spiritual children, they are immature but know their sins have been forgiven. Spiritual adolescents are struggling with sin, trying to overcome the temptations of Satan. And spiritual adults, the "fathers" John speaks to, have learned to simply enjoy the presence of God in their lives. When we think of this spiritual process, it helps us better understand how people grow and change.

THE NEWBORN

Baby Christians need to experience the benefits of salvation and demonstrate its fruit. Like a physical baby, their primary cry is, "Feed me!" They need information about this new life, and they need help to survive it. One of the best things you can do for a baby Christian is simply reveal your life to him. Let him see how you survive as a believer.

One of the men I used to meet with, Evan, was a brand-new Christian. He had struggled in his job, but as near as I could tell he truly received Jesus Christ as Lord and Savior and was being transformed by Him. Along with that change, as we know from Scripture, Evan received power over sin—but he still had a will the size of a tank. One Wednesday morning, he skipped the meeting with me. We had planned to discuss 1 Corinthians 10:13: "No temptation has seized you except what is common to man. And God is faithful; he will not let you be tempted beyond what you can bear. But when you are tempted, he will also provide a way out so that you can stand up under it." (NIV) Instead of meeting with me to talk about scriptural principles for business, Evan continued his pursuit of "get rich quick" schemes. He met with a man who wanted to do business with Evan's firm so much he offered Evan special favors in return. Unfortunately, the payoff plan was quickly disclosed. Evan was dismissed and learned a hard lesson. Had he told me about his plan, I could have shown him from Scripture why it was a bad idea.

Surely new babies learn hard lessons with the bumps and tumbles that inevitably come, but they don't have to learn to stay out of the street by getting run over by a truck. They can simply listen to their parents' warning, understand the risk, and use special caution to avoid the consequences of taking one too many steps off the curb.

Paul nailed the bottom line when he said to the believers in Thessalonica, "But we proved to be gentle among you, as a nursing mother tenderly cares for her own children. Having thus a fond affection for you, we were well-pleased to impart to you not only the gospel of God but also our own lives, because you had become very dear to us" (1 Thessalonians 2:7-8). Paul cared for his spiritual children, cherishing them and nourishing each one, fostering growth and making them feel loved and accepted.

The newborn spiritual babe needs a family, a caring community of brothers and sisters who can help him grow. He requires intimacy and caring by those around him so he can mature in a safe, healthy, spiritual environment.

THE CHILD

When my son, Paul, was young you didn't offer him water or soda. Paul loved milk. The rattle of the refrigerator door was often the signal he was getting another glass of milk, which he drank all morning, afternoon, and evening to satisfy his thirst. Concerned about fat, he switched to skim milk but still drank it all day long. At fourteen years of age, he had grown into a size-14 shoe and had outgrown his father's jeans.

Some new Christians—about one in five—are just like my son Paul. They simply drink the milk of the Word every chance they get; all they need is guidance. The other 80 percent need to be spoon-fed the Word of God; without a daily dose of the Bible, these spiritual children will grow up malnourished.

Not only do children need good food; they need an example to follow. We don't teach our kids table manners by having them eat every meal at the school cafeteria; we make sure they spend time eating with mature adults who can show them proper table etiquette. That's why I appreciate what the Apostle Paul went on to say:

> "You are witnesses, and so is God, how devoutly and uprightly and blamelessly we behaved toward you believers; just as you know how we were exhorting and encouraging and imploring each one of you as a father would his own children, so that you may walk in a manner worthy of the God who calls you into His own kingdom and glory."
>
> (1 Thessalonians 2:10-12)

More than anything else, children need an example to follow. They are crying out, "Teach me!" And your example will drown out your words. In your home, if you want your children to be polite to others, you must set an example of politeness. If you want them to keep a clean room, you must keep your own room tidy. And if you want new believers to assume the habit of daily Bible reading and prayer, you must model it for them. Explain to your spiritual children the Christian life; invite them into your life so that they can see firsthand how a mature believer lives.

The relationship that grows out of your interaction will change your life. Something special happens that enriches both of you when you disciple another person into maturity. That's why Paul closes his passage to the Thessalonian believers by telling them, "For you are our glory and joy" (verse 20). If you've ever had children, you know the joy that comes in knowing you've given someone life. Ask someone who has raised up spiritual children and they'll tell of the joy that comes from helping someone mature. The spiritual parent holds a special place in the heart of every Timothy.

It's wonderfully fruitful to meet with someone and study God's Word, but that experience is greatly enriched by all the other moments of social and relational interaction that may appear on the surface not to involve the Scriptures; instead, they involve a life lived out in Christ. Patty and Christine make a habit of including another young woman or two who are not Christians in the children's get-togethers in the park or at a picnic. So there you have mothers with their natural babies reaching out to their spiritual babies!

Many years ago I began to realize that going skiing with friends who didn't know Christ could be every bit as productive as a formal study of God's Word. In fact, in some cases it is even more productive because of the shared life experiences. If you're a hunter, take men hunting. If you like to garden, invite someone to join you in a special landscape project. If you're a couple who enjoys travel, think of a neighborhood couple who would like to go with you overnight to a neighboring city. Susy's mom and dad own a house in Colorado that they share with the world; couples and families use the home week after week to get away from it all. Many weekends are used by people bringing friends who do not know Christ or are brand-new believers. Often spiritual discussions are not even attempted until the drive home, after firm relationships have been built and life experiences shared. The simple act of revealing your life to a spiritual child can start that individual on the path toward maturity.

THE ADOLESCENT

If the goal of parenting a child is to help him develop a heart for God, the goal for parenting adolescents is to help them live lives worthy of God. As John put it, the spiritual young man is learning to overcome evil and discover victory in the spiritual battle. The adolescent believer needs to assume responsibility for his own life. He has become responsible for his own behavior so he needs a little more room to try things—and to fail at some of them. The adolescent needs experience, and his cry is, "Show me!"

The best thing you can do to help a spiritually adolescent person is encourage and exhort him. Call him to action, and help him succeed. Testify through your life and words the effects of your faith upon your life. Help him know what path to take and how to develop the discipline needed to make the hard choices. That will help him become strong and teach him how he can "overcome the evil one."

Take your adolescent Christian with you as my spiritual father did with me. I'll never forget the first time Jim walked me into a man's office who had shown interest in knowing more about Jesus Christ after a CBMC meeting. As I sat there praying, Jim gently moved the conversation toward the Lord. I saw firsthand how to lead a man to Christ! Instead of merely focusing on myself, I began to learn that the mature life of obedience reaches out to others in need.

Tim Philpot, lawyer, businessman, state senator from Kentucky, and now judge, invited our son Paul at fourteen years of age on a ministry trip to Tanzania, Uganda, Kenya, and Ethiopia. Tim could have gone alone. After all, he was the one invited to speak at the outreach meetings. He was the one with all the experience needed to teach young Christians and businessmen all over east Africa how to give away their faith to their colleagues, neighbors, relatives, and friends. But Tim has a vision of building into the lives of other people, so he invited Paul to go with him for a life-changing experience. Tim's three-week investment in Paul has reaped great heavenly rewards as Paul's heart for ministry has deepened over the years.

Defeating sin and developing a life of obedience are the core issues for spiritual adolescents. They are ready to become significantly involved in ministry, equipped to begin helping others in the faith.

THE ADULT

The fourth stage of the Christian life is that of the adult, in which the former spiritual child becomes a brother or sister and fellow soldier in the work of God. At this point we aren't nurturing as much as we are endeavoring to get him involved in a mature Christian walk and ministry. The adult Christian is saying, "Follow me," working *with* you for the growth of the gospel.

The apostle Paul treated mature Christians as his peers. He had formed an alliance, standing shoulder-to-shoulder with them, working for the purposes of Christ. He never forgot them or stopped praying for them but insisted they go on and develop their own ministries. Timothy would always be his spiritual son, but Paul made sure Timothy was also a fellow leader in the church.

Early in the life of a new believer, the initiative of the spiritual parent is much greater. The discipler takes care of the spiritual child like a nurse cares for a baby. But as the new Christian grows, the role changes to that of father, offering advice and direction, and eventually the role evolves into that of peer.

This all takes time, of course. An acorn doesn't grow into an oak tree overnight, and we can't expect to develop "oaks of righteousness" in a few short weeks. Immature Christians shouldn't be put into positions of responsibility they cannot maintain (1 Timothy 3:6). They may have had their lives radically changed by the power of God but new believers cannot be mature. Maturity comes with time. True spirituality is learned. If we do not fuel our faith with an understanding of Christ, it will weaken rather than mature. Immature people are vulnerable to Satan's temptation and false teaching. But mature Christians who have grown over the course of time develop Christlike character, perseverance, and the power of God in their lives.

Baby Christians: "Feed me!"
Primary Needs: information about the new life in Christ and loving care to help them survive it.

Child Christians: "Teach me!"
Primary Needs: the basic truths of the Bible and someone to explain them.

Adolescent Christians: "Show me!"
Primary Needs: to find victory over sin and to develop a life of obedience to Christ.

Adult Christians: "Follow me!"
Primary Needs: to use gifts in ministry and begin training others.

CATCHING THE VISION

Proverbs 29:18 tells us, "Where there is no vision, the people perish" (King James Version). It is really important that any time we are meeting with someone, we share with him the vision God has for him. The Lord intends for believers to become mature and begin impacting their world for His purposes. Just as having a baby is more than just going through a pregnancy. The real work begins after the baby is born. In the same way we shouldn't be satisfied with someone's simply saying the words of the sinner's prayer. We are after *disciples*, not *decisions*. We need to catch the vision for moving an unbeliever all the way through the process of evangelism by sowing, cultivating, and harvesting, and then become a spiritual parent to help him move through the process of being a newborn, child, adolescent, and adult. I have found it very effective to sit down with someone and ask where he sees himself on the Critical Process chart in Chapter 5. It will help you evaluate people and will help the other person see where the Lord wants to take him as he matures.

We need to remember that Jesus called Peter a "rock" long before he *was* a rock. In fact it was after being called a rock that Peter denied Christ three times. Jesus had a vision for Peter based on his future maturity. Paul later had the vision to begin sharing the gospel with Caesar's household—even the guards he was chained to. He was so effective that in his letter to the Philippian Christians, he passes along warm greetings from the members of Caesar's home. Paul's vision allowed him to win to Christ the very men sworn to restrain him.

I share this thought because we live in an age of burnout. Workers feel burned out in their careers, wives feel burned out with their marriages, and parents feel burned out with their children. A generation of people has risen that lacks the staying power to accomplish what they set out to do. But there is no mystery to the cause of burnout: lack of vision. Vision is the ability to see—and people with spiritual vision will see farther and more clearly than others. They *envision* what most people cannot see. They glimpse the future possibilities.

Most people can't see beyond the next pay period. For many, having "vision" in a family means keeping everybody from complaining for an entire weekend. But real visionaries are driven toward a picture of the future. They know where they are going and why. Their vision sustains them through the bumps in the road they are sure to come across. A visionary spiritual parent always has the potential of the disciple in view. Paul faced the prospect of ministering by letter to numerous churches from a jail cell, but he still made time to minister to his young friend Timothy. His vision extended beyond his cell, beyond the churches, to the next generation of Christian leaders.

Two thousand years later, nothing has changed. Modern Pauls are willing to spiritually father their own Timothys because they have vision. They have the commitment to make time in their busy schedules for regular appointments with a new Christian. Rather than being tyrannized by the urgent, they make time for the ultimately important. Time spent with their Timothys is an investment with which one more business meeting or errand cannot compare. God's agenda is served by spending time with another as a spiritual parent.

I am constantly amazed when I stop to evaluate the casualness with which I take small steps and how those small steps have led to momentous decisions. Can you doubt for a minute that your commitment to a new believer is any less critical? Catch a vision of the importance of discipling another person. You can become another link in the long chain of believers stretching back to Jesus Christ. Once you have a vision, you can begin sharing your life.

LIFE ON LIFE

When the Lord was on earth, He spent a lot of time asking questions:

"Do you want to be healed?"

"Where is your husband?"

"Whose head do you see on the coin?"

When discipling another person, you'll find yourself asking a number of questions to gauge the current status of his spiritual life. At the same time, you'll be answering questions in a transparent manner, sharing with the new believer your own struggles, pain, and pleasure. Your Timothy will be relieved to find you are flesh and blood rather than some sort of spiritual superhero. This is what I mean by sharing "life on life," and it will keep the two of you close.

You'll also find yourself making a long-term commitment to the individual. Christ spent three years discipling twelve men, and He stayed with them until death. Paul's ministry was similar. It takes a sacrifice of time and energy to become a spiritual parent, so Jesus didn't assign a semester for each person. He made an absolute commitment to be with the twelve disciples, preparing them until they were ready for ministry. He took into account changing roles and situations, dealing differently with Peter from how He did with John. If you have children of different ages, you parent them accordingly. A good parent accounts for various stages of life, displaying patience and adjusting expectations as each child grows.

"Like newborn babes, long for the pure milk of the Word," we read in 1 Peter 2:2, "that by it you may grow in respect to salvation." Growing in spiritual maturity has many peaks and valleys. Growth often occurs in the trials of life. The Spirit dwells in the life of the new Christian, setting up an internal civil war that requires the wisdom and experience of a mature believer to guide him to victory. But spiritual change occurs as the believer spends time with God, His Word, and His people. As a spiritual parent, you can help shape the growth process of your Timothy by sharing with him, encouraging him, and arranging for ministry opportunities.

WHOM GOD USES

The church used to focus its energies on changing behavior: "Don't drink, don't swear, and stop those wicked thoughts!" But that sort of ministry often didn't produce real changes in people. The process of transformation ought to first affect the worldview and values of the individual, and those will eventually translate into new behaviors. You can't clean up the outside before you deal with the inside. Paul had this same struggle, which is why he complains in Romans chapter seven about his opposing desires to do good—and to sin. But the goal of growing in Christ was always the ultimate goal of Paul's life (Colossians 1:28). That's why he could say, "He who began a good work in you will perfect it" (Philippians 1:6).

Relationships are what change people, not prescriptions. For example, my friend Martin was a lawyer who handled product liabilities cases and consulted with me in regard to expert witnesses. Over the course of about five years, Martin and I often had lunch to talk about his cases; along the way, I took those opportunities to share my faith in Christ. One time I told Martin about my failure to act like Christ, describing for him how I had to swallow my pride and make apologies around the office.

He listened with very little comment. However, he started attending meetings where businessmen shared their faith in the Lord. Once, when I spoke at a luncheon and Martin attended, he indicated an interest in talking to someone further about Christ. The next day I went to his office and we discussed the events of the previous evening. Just as my spiritual father had trained me, I took Martin through the small tract called *Steps to Peace with God*, which describes the way to eternal life. At the end of the booklet he prayed to receive Christ, and his life was dramatically changed. For a number of weeks he would call and describe how he was finding greater peace in his life and growing as he read the Bible.

However, there was the issue of Lori, his live-in girlfriend. I knew that topic was no-man's land for my comments. I had mentioned several Bible verses dealing with sexual sin without so much as a twitch from Martin. Somehow I knew I had to let the Lord deal with Martin's conduct and not hound him with my convictions. Over the course of about eighteen months, his affair with his girlfriend continued and he would eagerly talk to me about all aspects of his life—*except* Lori.

Then the day came I had been praying for. "Phil," he said one morning over coffee, "I feel uncomfortable about Lori—I mean, what we're doing. The fact that we are living together, in the same bed. . . ." Then he reddened and said, "But I haven't touched her! I mean, we haven't. . .I told God I just couldn't." He was quiet for a minute, then he went on to tell me how his relationship with Lori was perfectly normal, and he had not had any sexual relations with her for months, although they slept in the same king-sized bed.

To that I exclaimed, "What do you mean normal? That's not normal!"

Martin went on to admit he had tremendous guilt and shame over his relationship with Lori, and was deeply wanting to "make her an honest woman," so he was going to propose marriage. As I saw it, he was going to try to solve his problem of their living together by jumping into another problem of being unequally yoked with an unbeliever. I counseled that he needed to apologize, ask her to forgive his selfishness, and move her out. Further, I was concerned he was taking such a step of marriage out of guilt, so I strongly urged him to end the affair and see if Lori truly evidenced a lifestyle that honored God. He did, and the Lord graciously led him into a wholesome relationship with a different, very godly woman.

You see, the Spirit will grow us into maturity; the spiritual parent's role is to guide, counsel, and care for the new believer. God uses faithful men and women willing to pay any price to fulfill His will in their lives, servants who love God and are able to teach others, who have a heart for people, and are willing to commit to another person for the long haul. They don't have to be perfect, but they do have to be faithful.

The parent can't deprive himself of spiritual food while feeding others, or his own life will dry up. Just as a river that feeds a tributary must receive fresh water from a greater body, so the mature believer must remain grounded in God's Word and prayer, staying in fellowship with other growing Christians if he expects to teach another.

As I've said before, some people are reluctant to disciple others because they fear they lack the ability, knowledge, or maturity required. But being a discipler is ultimately not a matter of ability but of obedience. We often don't feel qualified to be biological parents when our children are born, but we take up the task anyway. God is much more concerned with your *availability* than with your *ability*. He won't call you to something you are unable to do. The question is, are you willing to be obedient when He does call? If you have some competence in the Scriptures, a heart that seeks after God, and are part of a healthy culture of believers so that you don't have to go it alone, you are needed as a spiritual parent.

My wife Susy was surprised to learn that Liane Day was at first very hesitant to consider discipling her. When her spiritual mother suggested it, Liane's first reaction was, "I can't disciple Susy; I've only had one year of college and am in my first job as a secretary—she's a *lawyer*! What if she asks me a question I can't answer? I've been a Christian for less than a year, and I'm still struggling with my husband's leaving the children and me. Susy is so self-confident and together. The only problem she has is Phil!"

That may be the way it appeared on the surface but the reality was that Susy had all the knowledge a person could stand, but it was God's wisdom she needed, and His peace. Liane ultimately decided to disciple Susy not based on Liane's confidence in herself but because of her confidence in the One who had changed her life.

As I've traveled around the world in ministry, I've seen many gifted and godly people, well-positioned to influence many lives, who shrink from the responsibility. They feel inadequate to the task. The point is, they *are* inadequate—but God is sufficient to work through them and accomplish His purposes. After all, He is the One who has called us to go into all the world and make disciples, and He said, "Lo, I will be with you always" (Matthew 28:20). That means even when discipling some brash young neighbor whose life is falling apart, or a business colleague who seems like his life is all together but who is headed on a course of destruction, God is with you. Through all the cycles of life, the Almighty God is on your side.

DISCUSSION QUESTIONS

1. In your spiritual walk, who have you imitated most?

2. At what stage in the spiritual life cycle are you?

3. At what stage would you like to be?

4. What steps do you need to take to get there?

5. What are the areas in which you need to grow?

CHAPTER 7

Spiritual
PARENTING

$\mathcal{M}$any of the New Testament writers described their ministries in terms of parenting. Paul called the Galatians "my dear children," told the believers at Thessalonica he cared for them "like a mother caring for her children," and called Timothy his "son." John repeatedly addressed those to whom he wrote as "my children." Peter encouraged his readers to long for the milk of the Word of God so they would grow. Even the writer to the Hebrews talked about spiritual infancy and the importance of moving toward maturity in Christ.

If you are going to disciple a fellow believer, you need to take the approach of a parent. Even if the person is your peer, you will need to decide in your mind you are offering spiritual guidance the way a father tries to guide and assist his son. With a baby Christian, you'll need to be attentive, giving a lot of individual attention, explaining things and protecting the new believer from harm. Babies don't know much—more importantly, *they don't know that they don't know.* So the greatest thing you can do for a new Christian is to create a strong personal bond so he knows he can rely upon you. Young unmarried women and men can effectively learn God's principles of parenting through parenting their peers in one-on-one discipleship.

The church has had a tendency to create discipleship programs as a substitute for personal care, putting people through a particular curriculum in hopes of helping them mature. That's a recipe for failure because the new believer doesn't need information as much as a meaningful relationship with a spiritual parent. It will be through that trusting relationship that he can receive information.

Keep in mind, the believer needs Scripture to grow; but without a relational context, it is easy to get the mistaken notion that spiritual maturity is simply a matter of having the right answers. It is possible to go through a Bible study, have all the right answers, and still not grow spiritually. However, by developing a relationship with a spiritual mother or father, the new Christian has a model to follow, a guide to lead him, and the strong support of a mature person to help him through the hard times.

My spiritual parents helped me learn responsibility, discover how to pray, study God's Word, and develop a love for people. The love, support, and accountability they offered was invaluable. I also saw their willingness to stick by me, even when I failed. Think of it as a comparison between a self-taught golfer and one who has had professional instruction. The self-taught golfer might have developed a few good strokes, but the job would have been much better and the learning much faster with tips from an experienced teacher.

It takes patience and love to be a spiritual parent, but if you try it you'll experience the joy of seeing new believers begin to move down the path of maturity. Some things will change quickly, others will change slowly. God knows the needs of each person and is working in each life to help establish growth. We want instant maturity in our culture, but the spiritual life is a marathon, not a sprint. There is a clear-cut start, a definite ending, and a long, arduous race in between. But if a Christian is identified as a follower of Christ, then he should live as Jesus would live—and learning to do that takes time.

When you met Christ, you became a new creature. Unfortunately, your new creature is trapped in an old body. God has to work in your life to slowly transform you so your new creature can take control of that old body. The war waged between those two factions is the spiritual battle between sin and holiness. Although ultimately defeated, the flesh has seniority; like an athlete in training for the Olympic games, the new creature must *train* to take control. Remember, nobody just shows up for the marathon; the runner has to train and prepare himself for the race. So the Christian life is all about preparation. What we do flows out of who we are, and Christ is in the business of changing who we are. A spiritual parent can be a mighty tool in the hand of God for shaping the life of a new believer in training.

CHANGING FROM THE INSIDE OUT

New Christians need education, but more than that they need relationships. They need to experience what it's like to walk with Jesus, and a parent can offer them that unique experience. The personal attention a spiritual parent offers is much greater than what the new Christian could get from a classroom. We don't send our babies to class to teach them how to be "good babies," do we? Why would we send spiritual babies?

The church is the family of God, which allows us to rely on one another as an extended family. It used to be that people growing up in this country were shaped not only by parents but also by aunts and uncles and grandparents. We've lost much of that because of the mobility of our modern age, but the good news is that the church still offers an extended family experience. As brothers and sisters in Christ, you can disciple someone as part of a team. No one individual has everything it takes to bring another to maturity, but every healthy Christian community does. Together we can teach the skills of spiritual survival and nurture the character of those new to the family.

The Spirit of God is at work in our lives, helping us to become like Christ. We'd all like to see continual upward growth, but in reality most of us experience a "three steps forward, two steps back" pattern. Some people seem to get stuck in perpetual babyhood, which can be disastrous. A church made up of immature believers soon begins mistaking immaturity for maturity. They substitute carnality for holiness, losing their ability to impact the world for God's purposes. But someone who has been discipled has *seen* a righteous man, and has grown up into maturity. That's why the writer to the Hebrews says, "solid food is for the mature, who *because of practice* have their senses trained to discern good and evil" (Hebrews 5:14, emphasis added).

In my own life, it seems the more I know about God, the less comfortable I am with myself. I keep wanting to improve the old me, but that can't happen. God isn't interested in "polishing" or improving the old me because it has died (Romans 6:6-11). Rather, He has made me into a brand new me (2 Corinthians 5:17) and wants me to walk worthy of that new calling. The Lord wants to change me completely.

I fear being co-opted by our culture, becoming more comfortable with the things of this world than the things of God. For you see, if God is at the center of how I view the world, my life is bound to change. I'll begin to see things His way. I'll find myself surrendering some things I thought I couldn't live without. My values will eventually become His values. When this happens, my behavior will start to change. What I do will begin to line up with who I am.

Christians have had a tendency to think the most important thing we can do to reveal our maturity is change our behavior, but God wants to change us from the inside out. He's not satisfied with simply watching us try to change ourselves. The Bible says we can't change ourselves (see Galatians 3:3). But the Spirit can change us as we walk close to Him, as we spend time in the Word and in prayer, and as we learn to imitate Christ. If He can help us see the world from His perspective, our worldview and values will change, having a significant effect on our behavior.

The role of the parent is to keep new Christians close to the Spirit. Let them see how God has changed your life. Reveal your God-given perspective and values to them, so they begin to think a whole new way. Remember, our goal is not to change all of the world at once, but to help change one life at a time. As God works through us as spiritual parents, we'll see Him change people from the inside out.

RESPECT AND COMMUNICATION

The discipleship process mirrors the growth process. We have to understand that our Timothys are going to be moving from baby to adolescent to adult, so we must adjust the focus of our relationships accordingly. As a baby, the new Timothy requires daily feeding, attention, and some diaper changes. The diaper changes are not always when the baby asks for it, but rather when he needs it. If he has made a mess of his life, as a spiritual parent you are there to help clean it up. You'll sometimes have to ask the hard questions, holding him accountable for his actions.

As this child becomes an adolescent, we have to be sure we don't demand they clean up their room before they have the conviction that their room is a mess. In other words, the relationship becomes much more two-way and consensual, rather than a strict father/son relationship. Your Timothy will have doubts and ask questions about the faith, and it's your role to try and answer them.

Often with adolescent Timothys, you will find a real need for them to try things on their own and to make mistakes. It is advisable at this stage to get them involved in evangelism and discipleship in their own right, so they can share the excitement of bringing someone else to maturity. Often early attempts to share their faith or disciple someone else are marked by a few disasters, but along the way they'll discover that God wants to use them in the lives of other people. This type of training can sometimes be done in a group setting, where you and your Timothy, together with your spouses, if you are married, can meet with a third or fourth couple to share your faith. Your Timothy may lead, may simply provide the home, or perhaps just give prayer assistance. The idea is you don't want the person you are discipling to think he will always be a spiritual baby, dependent upon your instruction. Begin to move him into some type of activity where he can stretch his spiritual muscles by getting involved in evangelism and discipleship.

Two-way communication is essential for the adolescent stage of discipleship. Rather than always considering yourself the "leader," there needs to be mutual respect and approval between the two of you. If you are discipling someone you never listen to and you expect him to take your advice, you will end up with rebellion.

I met with a brand-new Christian, a man sixteen years younger than I am, to help him with the challenges of his family, his job, and his walk with the Lord. Along the way he asked how he could pray for me, and I just briefly mentioned a problem I had at work with a young man named Del. He started asking questions, which really irritated me because I was ready to go. I had to admit, underneath my irritation was a sense he couldn't have much wisdom on my situation because he was a brand-new believer. After about the tenth question he said to me, "Phil, if you were to do it over again, would you have hired Del?" After I told him no, he said, "Well, then you need to admit your mistake and let him go."

I was struck by his abrupt conclusion and began to explain it would be unfair to simply cut Del loose. But this man went on to point out the biblical principles that God has a wonderful plan for our lives (I could hear myself telling him those same words several weeks ago), and how Del was God's child and by my keeping him in the wrong position I was perhaps depriving Del of God's best in his life. At that point I had to admit my blind spot. I took his advice, and it was absolutely the perfect result for both Del and the team.

Had I ignored him, not only would I have lost his wisdom, I probably would have lost his respect. No one wants to be ignored. No one likes feeling unappreciated. This was a successful businessman, and my treating him like a child would have killed any mutual respect we had. Respect and communication are two of the most important elements of the discipling relationship. They reveal trust, appreciation, honesty, and your belief that the other person is growing in the Lord Jesus.

After I'd been in Vietnam for just a few short months, I found myself in charge of a team of new Marines patrolling a territory infested with booby traps. The little explosive devices were nearly impossible to see on the jungle trails, but when they were stepped on, they would detonate an artillery shell that would turn a man into a mass of raw flesh. It was one of the hidden enemies that haunted your every step in Vietnam.

While we were on patrol, Frenchy and Frank tripped such a booby trap and we had to medevac them out before taking up positions for our night ambush. With the scent of the explosion in our nostrils, their screams of pain in our ears, and the horrible sight of loading our riddled comrades on the chopper still imaged in our minds, we moved down the trail several hundred meters with great caution. Our team was to set up on a small knoll that looked like a perfect position but was also likely to be a booby-trapped area. My temptation was to send one of the new Marines to scout out the area and set the machine gun position, but I knew my responsibility was to look out for these men's lives. Because I had the greater experience in dealing with booby traps, I knew I should be the one to clear the area.

On my hands and knees, I crawled along the trail to the clearing and searched out every inch in preparation for setting up the machine guns. As I squirmed along the ground, I could picture what would happen to my head if there were an explosion (not a hypothetical thought, as one of the men with me actually was decapitated a few months later by a booby trap). These men had only been with me for a few hours and knew nothing about my leadership or my concern for them, but after I took the risk to sight out the trail and clear the area for the machine gun position, they gave me a loyalty and respect beyond belief. We Marines forged an alliance that carried us through fierce battles, and God is calling you to a bold alliance with your Timothy to reach this world for Him.

Sometimes you will have to risk your neck for someone you are discipling. On one occasion, one of my Timothys called to ask me a question about an organization I knew well. The problem was that if I told him what I knew, he would not become involved with them, and I bore the risk of being ostracized from relationships in that organization that were important to me. I wasn't violating confidences but rather taking into confidence a Timothy at the risk of a relationship I needed to maintain. Yet discipleship means laying your life on the line for another, so that's what I did.

The results, as predicted, were difficult. It cost me a business relationship, but I felt called to protect this man whom God had entrusted to me. His growth and protection came ahead of my own personal interests.

One of the most exciting things about discipleship is when your Timothys become not just brothers or sisters in the faith but mature spiritual warriors you can count on. Sometimes they'll even grow into spiritual big brothers and sisters. Many of the men I've discipled have gone on to master aspects of the faith far beyond my expertise. One of my Timothys is the finest lawyer I know. Now, when one of your Timothys becomes the best lawyer in the state, and you become his client and he helps you sort through a bad business decision, it is truly humbling. At the same time, it is wonderful since you had a hand in helping him grow up. It is fulfilling to see how a man's obedience to Scripture can lead to tremendous growth in both spiritual things and professional pursuits.

THE PITFALLS OF PARENTING

We need to be careful to approach our spiritual children in love, particularly those of us who have had terrible parental models in our lives. A spiritual parent should never become an autocrat or authoritarian figure of fear. When we treat Timothys that way, they exit the relationship quickly. If the parent is demanding or impossible to please, he will never develop the long-term relationship necessary to the process. But if we sacrificially and unconditionally love the individuals God has entrusted to our care, discipleship will become the most fulfilling ministry imaginable.

One of the most common pitfalls of parenting is *performance-based relationships*. We often make the same mistake parenting our disciples as we make in our families: making children, both spiritual and natural, feel they are loved and accepted if they perform properly. Fail to perform, and the other person fails to love you. This can lead to legalism or it can flow out of our own legalism; it is always destructive in a discipling relationship. The disciple isn't living to please *me*; he is living to please *God*. If I insist on some particular behaviors from him, he'll quickly sense that my love and my commitment are conditional and he will look for a better relationship elsewhere.

We need to allow space for God to work in our disciples, understanding He is in ultimate control and maintains absolute authority over those with whom we are working. We each need to be able to listen to a problem, encourage a right response, and then have the freedom to forgive when a Timothy decides to take a wrong turn and suffers the consequences.

A second common pitfall that some parents have is the problem of being *overcontrolling*. Remember, we don't own these disciples; they belong to God. Often they need to be involved in other activities beyond our experience and our giftedness. For example, the man who discipled me never sought out speaking opportunities at outreach meetings in large settings. I, on the other hand, enjoy speaking and every time I shared my testimony to a crowd it seemed to drive more deeply into my life the need to focus on Christ and the changes He wanted in my life. Before I went out each time, I would evaluate my life and realize I'd slipped into some old patterns. So sharing my testimony became a very important part of my spiritual life as an early disciple. My spiritual father helped and encouraged me to do this, though he never chose to become much of an outreach speaker himself. As parents, we need to realize our children are different from us, then encourage them to be unique while raising them in the fear and admonition of the Lord.

Reproducers are typically a combination of the inputs from many different ministries and people, not just their spiritual parents. My tendency early in my Christian walk was to try and protect my Timothys, to shelter them from other influencers beyond myself and a handful of other like-minded men. My narrow-mindedness ignored the workings of the body of Christ and God's desire that *He* be in charge of the growth of His children. After all, these are His disciples, not mine.

In my early discipling time with one man, I had covered all the bases pretty well except for financial stewardship. Susy and I were always big givers; the problem was that we were also big spenders. We looked at our finances as being ten percent God's and ninety percent our own. Because of my immaturity, I never helped that man in the financial area, and he suffered from my narrowness and unwillingness to share input from others. I learned something from that relationship: I am not an expert at many things so I'd better learn to listen to those who are. That thought has saved me from being overly controlling with different men on various occasions.

A third pitfall is that we *assume everyone is like us.* The position and location of your disciple is different from your own. His background is different. His position may be one of a vocal support of Christ in the workplace if he is a co-founder or owner of a business, but if your Timothy is the youngest member on a team of lawyers working on a case, his strategic position may dictate keeping his mouth shut and having a ministry of prayer until God gives him an obvious opportunity to speak.

Your Timothys will be different from you. Don't expect that just because you like classical music, the men you disciple will share your taste. We need to help others grow in accordance with their bent. If you're discipling someone who is a technician and you're a generalist, you may need to seek the assistance of someone else who has an accounting background, or perhaps a math or engineering background, someone who can relate to the man in his own context. You can still have a strong relationship, but you'll find yourself more effectively reaching and understanding your Timothy if you arrange to get someone to help you speak his language.

Overprotection is another pitfall that parents fall into. Typically, we want our children to be perfect or totally competent before taking on new challenges. Just as it is important for our own children to stretch and take on areas in their lives in which they may fail, it's important to let your Timothys do the same. For example, new Christians are often asked to serve on boards in dead churches. This may be the church at which the person is a member at the time of his conversion, so his natural inclination is to try to change the church. While you may want to counsel your Timothy as to the difficulty and challenges with respect to that process, once he has in his mind that he wants to do it, you must be careful not to break the relationship just because he hasn't followed your advice. Support him in his endeavor, offer your wisdom and encouragement, and let him learn the hard lessons if he needs to.

Parents also want to protect their children from sin, but often if you give your child a list of "do's and don'ts," you'll just drive his behavior underground. Set up some sort of regular accountability session with your Timothy where both of you are checking on each other, and learn to openly share both your joys and your struggles. You can't protect your Timothys from temptation, nor can you take responsibility when they fail, but you can arrange for open communication so there is somebody they can talk to about what they are facing.

GROWING AS A FAMILY

Some of the best friends I have on earth are the men and couples with whom Susy and I have been involved in discipleship. We've been through some severe challenges over the years, and it's often been not just our spiritual parents but our spiritual *children* as well who have come to our aid, with support and counsel at crucial moments in our lives. We have grown as a family, brothers and sisters in Christ, and have developed the love and commitment families have toward one another.

Moving into full-time ministry from a legal career was a wonderful yet bumpy experience for us, during which the Lord worked a lot of needed humility into our lives. The law firm from which I came broke up, which significantly changed our financial position, and the home we had bought several years before leaving full-time law practice did not sell for four-and-a-half years! We put the house on the market just before the Gulf War, and the economic downturn in the housing market in Atlanta continued for a number of years. We had a lot of people praying for us, and it became a growth experience not just for us and our children but also for our spiritual children. They were praying with us, supporting us, and helping us through the toughest times.

One of my Timothys helped us immensely. He gave us the best counsel we received from anyone with respect to how to sell the house and reduce the price at the appropriate time, stood with us shoulder-to-shoulder over some of the financial obligations we faced, and ministered to our family while I was occupied with my new job. In other words, the spiritual father became the son, and the sons became the spiritual leaders in many aspects of my life. That is, of course, a natural process we go through. As your parents get old and infirm, you become the leader of the family. The roles get reversed. This is what God allowed to happen in my spiritual life, and it made me humble and caused me to grow. It turned some of my spiritual children into spiritual leaders. As a family, we can all see God working to make us like His Son.

If you will invest in the lives of others, and choose to make a significant difference in their lives rather than settling for worldly success, you can be part of God's plan to change the world. If you ask the Lord for the name of one person you can disciple and with whom you can form an alliance—spending time, holding him accountable, and developing a relationship that will thrive as you both mature through the spiritual life cycle—you will find you have friends who are closer than family. You will find fulfillment that can never come from making money or acquiring material possessions. Instead, you will have the satisfaction of knowing you are one of the links in the chain that stretches back to the Lord Jesus Christ. The eternal impact of your life will be weighed by God at the end of time, by your spiritual children and grandchildren.

You have the chance to be part of the greatest ministry ever. It all starts when you make the decision to come alongside a friend, helping him to grow.

QUESTIONS FOR DISCUSSION

1. Whom do you most admire? Why?

2. What person has had the greatest influence on your life? In what ways did he influence you?

3. What is the difference between hearing information from someone and watching him put that information into practice?

4. How would you describe your father?

5. In what ways are you influencing your children?

PART TWO

Living with
POWER

"And one of the scribes came and heard them arguing, and recognizing that He had answered them well, asked Him, 'What commandment is the foremost of all?'

"Jesus answered, 'The foremost is, "Hear O Israel! The Lord our God is one Lord; And you shall love the Lord your God with all your heart, and with all your soul, and with all your mind, and with all your strength." The second is this, "You shall love your neighbor as yourself." There is no other commandment greater than these.'

"And the scribe said to Him, 'Right, Teacher, you have truly stated that He is One; and there is no one else besides Him; and to love Him with all the heart and with all the understanding and with all the strength, and to love one's neighbor as himself, is much more than all burnt offerings and sacrifices.'

"And when Jesus saw that he had answered intelligently, He said to him, 'You are not far from the kingdom of God. . . .'"

(Mark 12:28-34)

God has given us a command to love Him and love others. This fundamental truth exercises a direct influence on our lives, and it helps us know how we are to shape the lives of those we disciple. If we can help foster a love for God and for others, we'll be moving them toward maturity in Christ.

With that in mind, six principles are essential for a new believer to grow in the grace and knowledge of God:

First, he needs to commit to Christ. Often this will mean discovering what commitment really is.

Second, the new Christian must learn obedience, not out of rote activity, but out of love for God.

Third, we need to help him become consistent in his daily devotions. Without the direct influence of God's Word through prayer and Bible study, the babe in Christ can receive no nourishment.

Fourth, the spiritual parent must help shape the character of his Timothys so they become strong soldiers for the cause of Christ.

Fifth, we must help those we are discipling learn how to handle adversity. God often puts hard things in our paths because He knows we grow most when we go through tough times. Great things are seldom accomplished apart from a hard path.

Sixth, we must help our Timothys discern God's will. The Lord has gifted each person and He wants us all to be serving Him, working with others to fulfill the Great Commission.

These six things will help the believer live with power.

CHAPTER 8

Fostering COMMITMENT

The first time I met with Ryan, he came late. He didn't bring his Bible. He forgot about the booklet I'd given him. He told me he'd have to leave early—to make it to another appointment he'd just set up. I smiled.

Years ago I wouldn't have smiled; I would have scowled. I'd have shown disapproval. I would have begun to lecture Ryan on the importance of our times together. But I've learned some things over many years of building into men. My number one goal early in the discipling process is to build a relationship centered on Christ, not to keep the other man on schedule. So instead of lecturing Ryan, I started to talk.

"Ryan, I'm excited about our times together. A few years ago, I too made the decision that it was time I became serious in my walk with God. But I didn't know how to do it. So one man, Dr. Jim Lyon, made a commitment to me. He promised me he'd walk with me in my relationship with Christ. He would always be there for me. We would meet every week to talk about spiritual things, but he would always be available when I needed to talk about other things. He made it clear to me he would be there, week in and week out, to help me grow. He also promised always to be honest with me and share what he had learned from his successes and failures. We talked about marriages and money, things personal and professional, and social as well as spiritual issues. Jim committed to share his life with me, then followed up on his commitment. He did everything he could to help me because he believed in me, loved me, and wanted to help me. If I've achieved any measure of success in my spiritual walk, it's because of Jim's commitment to me."

Then I leaned over the table, looked Ryan right in the eye, and said, "Ryan, that's the same commitment I'm going to make to you. Anything you need, if I can do it, you'll have it. I believe in you, and I'm willing to commit to helping you any way I can."

Ryan just sat there for a minute, staring. Then he looked away, blinked, and said, "Gee. You'd do that for me?" From then on, his commitment wasn't in question. Ryan was waiting to see if I was serious about all this "come alongside" stuff. If *I* was willing to be serious, then *he* was willing to be serious.

Commitment is not easily established. It must be modeled by us, prayed for, and most of all, waited for upon the Lord. Jennifer is someone Susy had invited to many events and outreaches who basically said, "I don't know what relevance those stories have to my life." She seemed pretty uncommitted to Susy, and actually she was not ready to make a commitment to the Lord, but that is no reason to abandon someone. As Susy continued to pray and include Jennifer in family events, God brought to her a need, which she then felt safe to discuss with Susy. Through the course of discussion, Jennifer jumped at the chance to meet with Susy one-on-one and "look at some things in the Bible." Wait on the Lord and don't give up on people. He never gave up on us.

Let me make one thing clear right from the start: your Timothy must know what it means to be committed to Christ. That means you both must be willing to commit to a discipling relationship. One of your first jobs as a discipler is to tell your Timothy of your commitment—to Christ and to him—then help him make that same commitment. Offer love and encouragement, and be patient, but make sure he commits. Without commitment, the discipling relationship won't really get into important issues. It will always be a social hour and a "feel good" time.

Some people get involved in discipling just to make a friend or because they want to please someone else or simply because of the emotion of the moment. I've seen men enter into discipling relationships because they thought it would look good for their businesses! But those few quickly drop out when they find the goal is really to form a bold alliance to spur one another on toward maturity in Christ. A commitment to Christ says God will be in control of your whole life. Nothing will be held back. He'll come in and change everything, and it will be worth it. A commitment to the discipling relationship says there will be a growing and open friendship between two people.

Both of the parties, really, are committing. The Timothy is committing to growing in Christ, and the spiritual parent is committing to help the Timothy grow. If either of you doubt that you can make that commitment, you'd better think carefully before getting involved in discipleship. Some people struggle with commitments, but I believe a discipling relationship cannot be built on a short-term or "drop-in" basis. I'll usually arrange a convenient time for us to get together each week and make that part of my permanent schedule.

Whether it's early morning, over a breakfast or lunch, or one evening per week, I want him to know I'll be there. Of course, I also try to make sure we spend some social time together, but a regularly scheduled meeting when we know we're going to talk about spiritual things is essential for building a trusting relationship. As I've said before, when you're discipling someone, you are not taking him through a program but becoming his friend. And friendships require commitment.

Every new Christian needs to know what he is committing to. He needs to have commitment to the Lord and to the relationship with you. Of course, there are different types of people, and schedules and pressures will eventually challenge that commitment. There have been many relationships I've had where the man's schedule and mine were well-suited. Our practices were fairly routine, and we could count on meeting on a weekly basis at the same time, on the same day, in the same place. However, there have been other times when either the Timothy or I have totally failed to meet the commitments we made. Remember the warning of James 5:12: "Above all, my brethren, do not swear, either by heaven or by earth or with any other oath; but let your yes be yes and your no, no; so that you may not fall under judgment."

THE UNCOMMITTED

I've met with Timothys who were uncommitted for a variety of reasons. One reason might be they are simply unfaithful men, only trying to please people and impress peers. That kind of person will soon burn out on his commitment. Entering into a Timothy relationship is like committing to run a marathon, but that sort of person is not willing to train for it. When I've run up against this type, I have simply had to cut him loose and move on. However, I've also found him to be in the minority.

Don't be too quick to drop someone who struggles with his commitment, however. His problem may simply be that nobody has ever put expectations on him. Churches have failed to challenge people over the years, expecting little and receiving exactly that. Sometimes a big challenge is exactly what a person desires. All it takes is someone willing to challenge him to make a more serious commitment to Christ.

If a person has difficulties with the commitment, it might be because some sort of secret trouble is sapping him emotionally and physically. An explosive home situation, troubles with a teenager, or struggles over an unethical practice at work can weigh on someone's mind and make him appear uncommitted. If your Timothy is struggling with his commitment to be discipled, there may very well be a significant reason. As you talk, God will eventually bring to the forefront the reasons for the lack of commitment and enable you to reach deeply into his life so you can help him. Nothing can assist someone more than becoming accountable to a brother or sister, face-to-face.

Busyness, fear, immorality, materialism, laziness, and spiritual coldness can also keep someone from making a commitment. An overcommitted person just can't find time to meet with you regularly, and one who lacks self-discipline won't get up when his alarm rings. But you can help a person develop self-discipline by walking him through the commitment phase. There are times I've called a man at five or six o'clock every morning, just to make sure he was up and reading his Bible. On many occasions I have gone through a friend's calendar with him, asking some hard questions about where he invests his time. Of course, if a man or woman is secretly harboring sexual or financial sin in his life, he will struggle with making a commitment. He fears having to face his own sin, though he recognizes he will never grow close to God until he does. A person who uses excuses all the time to miss meetings is a person afraid of growing close.

If you find yourself making commitments you can't keep, take some time to reflect on your life goals. What drives you? Where do you find fulfillment? Why do you find it necessary to fill up your time with activities to give your life meaning? One of the biggest secrets in the church is that we have men who, though outwardly successful, feel like failures because they could never please their fathers. A man may build a successful business empire, but if his daddy didn't tell him he was a success, he'll always feel there is something left undone. Years ago Johnny Carson asked movie star Burt Reynolds when a man knows he has become a man. Reynolds thought a moment, smiled, and said, "A man knows he's a man . . . when his daddy *tells him* he's a man." Though we may not want to admit it, Mr. Reynolds was right.

It's tough to get a commitment from someone who feels like a failure because his father never acknowledged his success. But commitment is part of the path of maturity. To commit to being discipled is to commit to grow. Perhaps that's why so many men in discipling relationships ask each other, "Do you think I'm a success?" They want to finally get the approval their fathers never offered. As a discipler, be ready to give that message. Make sure those you are working with know that the reason you are committing to them is because you see them as winners.

MOVING TOO FAST

Sometimes a lack of commitment results from going too fast with your Timothy. We have discipleship programs, like *Operation Timothy*, that used to have twelve chapters, six per book. Often we would think we could go through these chapters with lock-step proficiency, one chapter per week, and "finish the course" within twelve weeks. The goal seemed to be to fill in all the blanks, rather than to sharpen each other as we see in Proverbs 27:17. We were studying truth, but the truth was coming too fast. It was like trying to get a drink from a fire hose, when all the Timothy needed was a sip from a fountain. It takes time and our God to turn new information into experiential knowledge.

Be wary of getting way ahead of your Timothy. You have agreed to come alongside of him, so don't get out on the track and race well ahead. Once people get information overload, legalism sets in, and discouragement is sure to follow. You see, if a person expects to develop a relationship but sees you focus entirely on "working through all the questions in the book," he'll soon start to think being a Christian consists only of knowing a bunch of rules. As soon as he knows all the rules, therefore, he'll be mature. That's the same mistake the Pharisees made. And it will suck all the life out of a person's faith, for no one can ever obey all the rules. Legalism always leads to discouragement.

Keep reminding yourself the discipleship process is not a teaching course but a lifelong relationship through which God wants to build character, obedience, and a servant for Himself. It is God's timetable we need to be concerned about, not our personal schedules or a recommended timetable in some book. If you enter into a discipling relationship and say you're going to spend one year at it, you will probably do everyone a disservice. First of all, it's a lifetime process, so you can't limit it to a year. Your spiritual children never cease to be your disciples, just as your sons and daughters never cease to be your physical children. The intense time of regular meetings may extend from six months to three years or more, depending on the growth experienced and the needs of the individual. Later, periodic meetings and encouragement for accountability may be all that's necessary. Your schedule may change, but the relationship remains. You don't put a time limit on a friendship.

One of the men I was working with had a problem with his wife, but I was insensitive to it. He had married a woman who did not know Christ, so his home life was strained by their different values, goals, and perspectives. It took me months to figure out why this man struggled with our meetings and wrestled with his commitment to study and memorize Scripture—he had a demanding job and a needy wife who did not appreciate his times of study and Bible memory; she saw those times as competing for her love and affection. He found himself getting up in the middle of the night to do his discipleship assignments, then sleeping through our meetings. It took me a while to figure out we had to work on his marriage first and worry about book chapters later.

Initial commitments in the discipleship process vary. Some will ask their Timothy to "finish the course," whether it's a twelve-chapter study or a free-flowing discussion. I find more and more people today are hesitant to make long-term commitments, so I always ask the potential Timothy to pray about meeting me regularly. I'll explain the relationship, then ask the man to take a look at the materials we may use and get back to me on whether he'd like to talk about the first couple of chapters. Sometimes, if I know a man is in crisis, I'll skip any discussion of study materials and just ask if he'd like to get together and talk about principles for helping his marriage, or business, or whatever the person is facing. Then we'll sit down over lunch or breakfast and start talking.

THE BIG COMMITMENTS OF LIFE

There are six key commitments every Christian makes. First, and most important, is his *commitment to the Lord*. It is important to instill in every new believer the concept of total commitment. God doesn't just want our money or our time or our families or our energies or our possessions. He wants it all. He wants our hearts, so we must focus on nothing else. Anyone who tries to commit to Christ and something else is going to be double-minded, as James put it, "unstable in all his ways." In the Sermon on the Mount, the Lord Jesus said you cannot serve two masters. Either you love God, or you love something else. You can't love both.

I have seen men abandon their faith when they finally faced this truth. They had been in love with their own pleasure, or their own success, or their own image. When they realized what becoming a Christian was really all about, they weren't willing to give up the other focus of their lives. It's sad to see someone abandon the eternal faith to pursue a temporal gain, but I've watched it happen. I believe a person who isn't willing to focus his life on Christ at the start of the spiritual growth process will continually struggle. But the one who recognizes the huge cost of discipleship, and is willing to surrender his life to be found in Jesus, will find himself starting to grow in the Lord. As Jim Elliot put it, "He is no fool who gives up what he cannot keep, to gain what he cannot lose."

The second commitment a married Christian must make is the *commitment to his or her marriage*. A man has to commit to his wife, whether she loves him in return or not. A woman must commit to her husband, whether he loves her in return or not. I've yet to find many strong, fulfilled Christian leaders who have unhappy marriages. Marital strife just seems to sap a Christian of energy and vigor. God intended marriage to be permanent and fulfilling; anything less will make a person feel like a loser. Paul said a man ought to love his wife "just as Christ also loved the church and gave Himself up for her . . . so husbands ought also to love their own wives as their own bodies. He who loves his own wife loves himself . . . and let the wife see to it that she respect her husband" (Ephesians 5:25, 28, 33).

How did the Lord love the church? He loved it sacrificially, giving up His own life to make it pure and holy and beautiful. Brothers and sisters, we have been called to love our wives and husbands in that same way. We must put their needs ahead of our own, serving them sacrificially, doing all we can to make them pure and holy. It's hard work because we are naturally selfish. But by the power of the Holy Spirit at work in our lives, we can become *super*naturally serving. Help your Timothy to see that as he spends time with God, his attitude toward his wife or husband will change and his marriage will improve.

A new Christian, particularly if he is having marital problems, ought to commit to stay with his wife (or husband), regardless of the troubles they are having. He will have to commit to marital faithfulness and to working out their troubles. It won't be easy, and he may not feel like loving his wife, but the first step of moving toward maturity in Christ that he needs to take may be committing to his wife. Every man should make a commitment to love his spouse because that's God's plan for a couple. Our culture has substituted happiness and sexual fulfillment as the bases for a marital relationship, but the true basis for a marriage is commitment founded on the truth that God loves us and wants what is best for us. The reason He has instructed men to love their wives sacrificially is because that's how marriage works best and how they will be blessed in His love.

I've worked with men on the brink of divorce who, when they drew close to the Lord, swallowed their pride, and made the conscious decision to serve their wives in love, experienced a miracle. Their troubles did not disappear overnight, but they found new strength to work through them. The wife finally felt she counted because her husband was willing to listen to her and put her needs first. When a wife sees her husband truly committed to her, many of the other problems seem to fade into insignificance. Even a man who doesn't *feel* love any more can find his feelings renewed as he makes a commitment to love his wife the way Christ loved the church.

Teach your Timothy to trust God and commit to his marriage. Open up your home so you and your spouse can model a good marriage—not a perfect marriage with no problems but a good marriage, where you communicate with each other and care for one another. Many men and women have never seen a good marriage, even those who grew up in church. They don't know how a couple disagrees or how the man is to put his wife's needs ahead of his own. By spending time with you and your spouse, seeing a couple committed to each other, your Timothy will begin to see what a marriage is supposed to be like. Don't fall into the trap of thinking you have to have some sort of model marriage to do this, where you never fight and everybody always smiles. There aren't any marriages like that. A good marriage takes work. But if you have committed yourself to your wife or husband, and your spouse recognizes your commitment, you should display that commitment to those you are discipling.

A third commitment a Christian makes is his *commitment to his family*. Psalm 127:3 says, "Children are a gift of the Lord," so to neglect them is to neglect God's gift. A person who is more committed to his career than to his kids is asking for trouble. God has placed your children into your care, and He expects you to lead them. I've seen too many men make the decision to provide for their kids but leave the leadership to their wives. That's a mistake, for it is an abdication of the responsibilities God has placed on the father and puts the mother in a role she was not intended to have. The number one complaint Christian women have is that their husbands will not take spiritual leadership in the home.

If you're a dad, you can't leave the spiritual leadership in your home to your wife, your church, or your youth pastor. God has placed those other people around to support what you do, but the responsibility for spiritual leadership is placed directly on your shoulders. That means you have to make a commitment to be pro-active when it comes to the spiritual temperature in your home. Be the leader in getting up on Sunday mornings with a good attitude and getting everybody to church. Pray with your family—and not just around the dinner table. Read the Bible to your children and let them see you reading the Bible on your own. Talk with them about spiritual principles and how you apply them. Pray with your wife, and pray for the members of your family each day. At some point you are going to want to disciple your children just as you disciple other men, so let them see the role God plays in your life.

EVALUATING YOUR LIFE

On a scale of 1 to 10, where would you rate . . .

Your commitment to the Lord?   ____

Your commitment to your wife or husband?   ____

Your commitment to your family?   ____

Your commitment to your job?   ____

Your commitment to your church?   ____

Your commitment to ministry?   ____

Your commitment to others?   ____

The main reason there are so many juvenile delinquents today is because there are so many deadbeat, disassociated dads. Impress upon the men you are discipling the importance of committing to their children and of spending time talking with them about the important issues of life. I suppose every father can expect some bumps in the road when his children hit their teen years, but nothing will help to smooth out those bumps like healthy communication built upon the trust of the father's commitment to his kids. I have sat beside dying men and not once have I heard one complain he didn't have enough time to complete another business deal. At the end of life, a man always talks about family and friendships—people he has loved and those who have loved him back. Get your Timothys to commit to spending time with their children, training them and investing in their hobbies and interests. Then he'll be able to turn his home into a ministry center that strengthens his faith rather than a turmoil-filled activity center that saps his faith.

The fourth commitment a man needs to make is to *his career*. This is no problem for most men—they already spend all their time at work. Of course, a man must commit to his work in order to take care of his family. The Bible says, "If anyone will not work, neither let him eat," (2 Thessalonians 3:10). But for most American men, the struggle isn't over making a commitment to work, but committing to put work in its proper place. The important thing is to realize where this commitment falls: *after* one's wife and family.

Occasionally I'll begin meeting with a man who really doesn't have this commitment. He is either perpetually out of work or his family is struggling with having enough money to survive. Usually a man like this lacks confidence, self-discipline, and a vision for what he can accomplish. We'll start talking about all these things in our discipling meetings, to get this man to make a commitment to his work.

The fifth commitment a Christian must make is a *commitment to his church.* It is critical for every Christian to attend and be accountable to a local church and body of believers. The writer of Hebrews instructs, "Obey your leaders, and submit to them; for they keep watch over your souls, as those who will give an account. Let them do this with joy and not with grief, for this would be unprofitable for you" (Hebrews 13:17). Many struggle with the idea of being under the headship of a church. They want individual freedom, with nobody telling them what to do. But one of the cardinal rules of life is that you will never accomplish much of anything great without leadership and a Christian will flourish in a church body with proper leadership. When you are discipling a new Christian, help him recognize the importance of the body of Christ. It is in the context of a body of believers that we love one another, care for one another, and bear one another's burdens. The body of Christ is a person's new family, and he needs to be committed to it.

In addition to being involved in the ongoing ministry of our local church, the sixth area of commitment is *to minister where God has placed us strategically in our neighborhood, school, business, hospital, community, and world.* This ministry may be very direct such as the proclamation of the gospel, a Christian school board, or discipling someone one-on-one. It may be indirect such as building the community welfare by feeding the hungry, coaching a baseball team, or serving in a political position. Wherever we minister, however, the gospel should be demonstrated through our lives by our countenance, competency and character. The direct connection with Christ may be only incidental to the activity but one purpose should always be to build relationships through which we can share our love for Christ.

God doesn't want a part of a person. He wants the whole person. He wants the total commitment. And He will settle for nothing less.

THE COST OF COMMITMENT

Over the years I have found that some people are just afraid of commitment. They are what we call in the legal profession "forum shoppers," always seeking the latest idea or new fad, which they quickly abandon when it comes to making a commitment. A.W. Tozer said to commit oneself to God is to decide that one's mind, will, and emotions are going to belong to Him. It takes a person of character to commit to anything, so we shouldn't expect this first step in the discipling process to be easy.

As we look at characters in the Bible who made commitments, we see there is a steep cost. Matthew gave up a lucrative career as a tax collector to be martyred for his faith. Peter gave up what the Bible suggests was a successful fishing business to become the first great preacher in the Christian church. It cost Noah his reputation, Moses his peaceful life, and Elijah his security to obey and serve God. Abraham was called to give up his only child for whom he had waited years. Hebrews 11:35-38 says, "Others were tortured and refused to be released. . . . Some faced jeers and flogging, while still others were chained and put in prison. They were stoned; they were sawed in two; they were put to death by the sword. They went about in sheepskins and goatskins, destitute, persecuted and mistreated—the world was not worthy of them. They wandered in deserts and mountains, and in caves and holes in the ground" (NIV).

Being a Christian has never been easy in this world. We have a tendency to read about the sacrifices of first-century Christians in a hurry, as though God would never call a modern person to make that sort of commitment. But the fact is, God is still in the business of calling men and women to make a serious commitment, and commitment can come with a high cost. Some people make a commitment and it costs them money. I've known men who have had to significantly alter their business practices to satisfy the Lord, at a cost of hundreds of thousands of dollars in profits. With others, the commitment is one of time. Many men I've discipled have felt compelled by God to stop spending so much time with business or recreational activities to invest themselves more fully in ministry toward others. Every time you commit to discipling another person, it costs you something. Sometimes the cost is energy, health, or an emotional toll on your mind and body. Making a commitment to God can cost you a promotion, a reputation, even a job. It takes courage to be committed, but that's what Christ had in mind. There are no "hangers on" with the Lord Jesus. You are either committed to Him or you are opposed to Him.

"If anyone wishes to come after Me, let him deny himself, and take up his cross daily, and follow Me," the Lord says in Luke 9:23. The price you pay to become a Christian is your very life. You are not in control any more. Your life is in God's hands. You have voluntarily surrendered it to Him. Some people will find that price too high. The rich young ruler didn't want to pay the price, so he couldn't make the commitment (Mark 10:17-31).

In Susy's early years with Delta, we both became Christians; as Susy matured in Christ and was discipled, she began to speak out for the Lord at opportune moments. One day a well-meaning friend took her aside and cautioned that her discussions of religion might be dangerous for her job, warning her to "cool it." She thanked her fellow attorney for his advice but responded she felt God had given her that position to be His ambassador. In light of what the Lord had done to save her and our marriage, she wanted to share Christ and her newfound peace and joy with as many people as possible. Susy even had the opportunity to share her testimony with the top officers of the company.

The next week Susy was promoted to Assistant Corporate Secretary of Delta, which made her not only the youngest officer but, at the time, the only woman officer of the company. She enjoyed a phenomenal career with Delta Air Lines for another six years until she felt impressed by the Lord to resign to raise our children full-time. Her testimony didn't detract from her ability to do her job. Of course, Susy's positive results are not always what happens to Christians when they stand up for Christ in the marketplace. One of our dearest friends, the man among the most responsible for bringing huge success to his city, was singled out and unfairly fired from his top leadership position primarily because he was active in sharing Christ personally and inviting his colleagues to meetings where they could hear the claims of Christ. The Bible says the world hates Christ, and if you represent Him you can expect to face similar hatred at times.

You can expect that your commitment to Christ will cost you something. Both Susy and our friend did what God called them to do. Neither has any regrets. One was promoted, the other fired, but in both instances there are people who will go live with God through eternity because of their testimonies. In a similar vein, John chapter six tells of crowds following Jesus when He was healing and feeding the multitudes. But when Jesus started saying some hard things, the crowds departed. Jesus told the people He was the bread of life, the only way to God, and declared everyone would have to be completely committed to Him if they were going to enjoy eternity with Him. "On hearing it, many of his disciples said, 'This is a hard teaching. Who can accept it? . . . From this time many of his disciples turned back and no longer followed Him" (John 6:60, 66, NIV). The cost was too great for some. But for those who can make the commitment, Christ offers a new life.

KEEPING A COMMITMENT

We walk a fine line when people do not keep the commitment they've made to us. But remember, you have no doubt failed a few times yourself when it came to commitments, so you need to be willing to confess and ask forgiveness for your own failures. It is important the Timothy who fails you not feel condemned. However, discipleship is an accountability relationship, so for his own good you need to gently point out his lack of commitment.

In my *Operation Timothy* meetings over the years, I've had to deal with some pretty sensitive areas. I've found that a lot of business etiquette, common sense practices, and corporate culture can be taught to others. For example, I have gently approached and discussed wishy-washy commitments, limp-fish handshakes, and even the need for deodorant and breath mints. I've faced men I was discipling and told them they needed to give up their favorite sins and find strength in God. Often in a discipling relationship you have a unique opportunity to tell your Timothy the things no one else would tell him, or things that would not be well-received if they did.

A man with poor commitment is often a man entangled with integrity issues over expense reports, shady deals, or manipulation at work to make himself look good. As you delve into these commitment issues, you often find the root cause is a lack of faith in Christ for the outcome of events. Manipulation is used to reach the desired goal. Dealing with those types of nitty-gritty issues is one of the most important aspects of a discipling relationship. In dealing with a person's commitments, your goal is not to impart information or your own opinions but to demonstrate the truth of the Scripture in everyday life. Continually pointing to the Scriptures is essential.

I was talking with a man struggling with thoughts of unfaithfulness and asked him to read about Joseph. Tears came to his eyes as he saw in Scripture the way God can use a faithful man. I've talked with complaining men about the children of Israel destroying leadership through murmuring; with deceitful men about David's cowardly attempt to cover up his sin; and with those experiencing tough times about the example of Stephen's trust in God, evident even while he was being brutally put to death. As a spiritual parent, you have a lot of opportunity to deal with the issues rarely mentioned in church or shared in prayer meeting. The people you disciple have made a commitment to Christ, so part of your role is to help them understand and keep it.

BEING FLEXIBLE

Along with commitment, it is essential to learn to be flexible. We can disciple in our own strength and end up with frustrated Timothys who never do anything as a result of our discipling. Or, compelled by the love of Christ and empowered by His Spirit, we can seek to impact the world by establishing, equipping, and mobilizing men and couples to become spiritual reproducers. The goal is to let God use the relationship to move both you and your Timothy to a place of maturity for the good of the kingdom.

In chapter two of the *Operation Timothy* materials, there's a question that asks, "In your own view, to what extent is God involved in your everyday life and problems?" Answering that question, a man might say, "My dad, who is a real S.O.B., used to pound into our heads that God is in control of everything." Having heard this kind of remark, you may be reluctant to dig into such a painful area and simply turn the page to go on to the next question. But God brought out that area of pain in the man's life for a reason. Simple follow-up questions like, "Tell me what that was like" or "What happened?" can bring real insight and get you started on the path toward deeper communication.

I once was talking with a man who started telling me about what a jerk his father was. When I asked, "Are you bitter over that?" he just stopped and stared at me. After a long pause he admitted, "I guess so. I pretty well hate my father for what he did, and feel like I can never measure up to his standard." Those words allowed me to talk about my own father and reveal my personal struggles in that area.

If your Timothy is willing to open up on a sensitive topic, you could spend a couple of meetings just discussing the ramifications of his view of his father and how that compares to his view of God. Perhaps he would be open to a study of Joseph, whose brothers hated him so much they sold him into slavery. You will be amazed at the pain people have, and the ministry the Scriptures have in dealing with that pain. I'll never forget discipling Bernard, a Jewish man who had been rejected by his entire family. He had a great deal of pain in his life, but incredible changes came over him when he realized God had mightily used Joseph to help the very family that had rejected him. This study seemed to encourage Bernard and fill him with a passionate conviction that God was eventually going to use him as a tool for reaching others in his own family.

Sometimes there will be areas in a person's life too painful to discuss and you will just get glimpses of them. If your Timothy is not willing to open himself up, you will need to take those areas to prayer because the Lord wants to deal with the hurts of a person's heart. Always remember you can gain great insight into others if you listen. Keep in mind what I call "the lesson of Johnny Carson," who made his fame interviewing guests on nighttime TV simply by being willing to listen to the answers of others and following where the answer led.

THE PROBLEM OF OVERCOMMITMENT

One of my closest friends, a man whom I had led to the Lord, moved to a different city. I committed to keep him accountable by tape. As a new Christian he was growing very rapidly and would send me these very long tapes—I could barely get through one before I would receive another! I soon became bogged down with a busy schedule, was unable to keep up the tape communication, and completely failed in my role as a spiritual parent. Checking in with him once or twice a year was not sufficient. I had to apologize to my friend, for I had failed to keep my commitment.

Overcommitting is a real challenge for many men. Perhaps they are trying to please everyone or achieve some internal standard they have set, or maybe they just have too many options. We see so many needs and want to fill them and help others, but if we take on too many commitments, we soon can't do any of them well. Like having too many people reporting to you in a business, you soon feel inundated with requests. You get "need overload." You won't be able to do anything right if you don't monitor your expectations.

I have found I can disciple several people at once, plus a few groups of people. That may be too much for many, *but simply taking on one person to disciple is better than not investing in the lives of any.* Ask one individual to commit to a spiritual relationship with you and see what happens. If you're already spending some time together and he has seen what your life is like, he'll be interested.

WHAT DO I SAY?

"Fred," I said to the man with whom I was having breakfast, "it's been fun to get more time with you this morning, and thank you for sharing with me your struggles at work. I've had a lot of similar struggles and I will pray for you about the decisions you have coming up. By the way, one thing I have found very helpful in my growth as a Christian was meeting with a man one-an-one and going through a little study called *Operation Timothy*."

"Operation what?" Fred asked. "You want to do a study of the book of Timothy?"

"No," I replied, "it's a Bible study called *Operation Timothy*, and it's fashioned after the relationship of Paul and Timothy in the Scriptures. The content of the study is really exciting, useful material, but it's the relationships that both people build that's really helpful to them."

"Really? Well, what would be involved?"

"Well, here's Book One," I told him, holding out a copy. "Why don't you take a look at the chapters and pray about it. Ask God to show you if this is something you might be interested in."

"Okay," said Fred. "Then what?"

"Well, if you feel it would be good, we could start to go through it together. I want to impress you with the fact that God tends to put two people together. We never really are sure at first who those people will be. We can pick a lot of teams but it turns out God really has His say about who will get together. Maybe it wouldn't work for you and me to meet. It might be a difficulty with schedules. Maybe because you're an engineer and I'm a lawyer, we may just talk on a different plane. But if God would put this together, what we'd typically do is meet on a weekly basis. . . ."

Fred interrupted me with the question, "When will we meet?"

"Well, that would be up to you. I find meeting in the morning is good."

"Nope. I carpool my kids in the morning."

"Oh, well, maybe we can meet for lunch."

"I don't go out for lunch," Fred said, shaking his head. "My team pretty well works through lunch. Lunch is served at the office each day, and because of the deadline I have on this project, going out for lunch would probably be out of the question."

"Well, again, if God has this in store for us, He'll raise up time to do it. Why don't you pray about when we might meet if this would be something you would want to do?"

There was a pause. "Well," he finally admitted, "there is one thing I could do, Phil. How about Saturday morning? I usually go out and play golf with some of my buddies, but maybe we could meet before we tee off at seven."

"Hey, that's a possibility. Why don't we pray about it. Take a look at the material and. . . ."

Before I could finish, Fred interrupted me again. "What's the meeting like?"

We usually talk about the topics involved in each chapter, then talk about our lives. . . ."

"So you teach me this material?"

"No, Fred, we really kind of go through the material together. I've found I have learned as much from going through this material as the men I've gone through it with. Again, the primary aspect is two people getting together, committing to grow in Christ and grow closer to one another."

"What about Gloria, could she join us?"

"Well, she could if we wanted to do this as couples. But 6:00 a.m. on Saturday morning . . . we'd probably better stick to the two of us. Maybe we could meet as couples or Susy and Gloria could meet together."

"O.K., Phil. That sounds great. Let me pray about it, and I'll let you know next week."

There are a number of reasons that people may not continue with the meetings. A number of men have only met with me a couple of times because of scheduling conflicts, other interests, or having decided the cost of commitment was too high. Frequently, however, they will come back at a later date and get together with me either one-on-one or with a group. Group discipleship has become more popular and effective as the men's movement motivates them to become more honest with one another. However, I believe one-an-one discipleship probably will give you the best opportunity to dig deeply into another person's life. Often a man is at odds with his wife, and the wife will not open up in a meeting. In fact, the two of them meeting together could put a chill on the process of healing the relationship. So typically, I would ask them to commit to separate discipling relationships.

In the book *Built to Last*, authors James Collins and Jerry Porras point out that it's a myth to believe everyone in a visionary company will have an impact. Actually, only those who are willing to embrace the core values of the company will succeed as a part of that company. While I don't embrace the view of God and science Collins and Porras espouse in their book, they do make some very good points. Some people simply are not willing or ready to be involved in a high-commitment relationship such as discipleship. But everyone who is serious about discipleship needs to commit. Without commitment, there will be no growth. And without growth, the Christian remains a baby the rest of his life.

QUESTIONS FOR DISCUSSION

1. What pressures do you have on your schedule?

2. Is it realistic to think that a person can balance commitments to the Lord, spouse, family, and career? What principles have helped you the most in maintaining a balance?

3. Have you ever failed after making a big commitment? What happened?

4. Would you say you are overcommitted? What could you do to gain better control over your schedule?

5. What is God doing in your life to help you grow spiritually?

CHAPTER 9

Encouraging OBEDIENCE

*W*hat is the first thing taught in boot camp? If you never had the pleasure (ahem), you might be surprised. Many might guess it's how to shoot a rifle or how to throw a grenade or perhaps how to fight. Others would say it's how to read a map, or how to administer first-aid. Some might think the first thing you learn is battle strategy or war plans. Actually, the first thing they teach you in boot camp is *how to march*. My Marine platoon spent hours on the parade deck marching and learning how to follow commands. Through marching, we learned how to work together as a team. There's nothing more ugly than a disheveled bunch of recruits stumbling along in a supposed formation, each one doing his own thing. But after a few weeks of Marine boot camp, it was amazing to see such a well-disciplined platoon of Marines marching by with the heel of each boot pounding the pavement at the same millisecond as the person in front of him, arms, shoulders, and heads also moving in complete unison as the men followed the commands of their drill instructor.

That discipline is essential for combat. Putting a rifle in the hands of someone without discipline endangers his life and the lives of everyone around him. Soldiers have to learn to obey before they can be trusted with anything more significant than marching around. That's the first thing we learned—marching. The next things were equally important: how to make our beds and eat. It seems as though the military understands a basic principle of life: you can't teach someone the complicated matters of life until they've proven they can obey in the simple matters.

The same holds true in discipling relationships. You will never produce a mature disciple without developing obedience, and obedience is learned developmentally over time. The root word of disciple is *discipline*. Without discipline, it is hard to achieve godliness. Take the example of Abraham, a great man of God who faced some daunting challenges in his life. God called him to leave his ancestral home, travel across the country, and settle in a new land. Gradually, a bit at a time, Abraham learned to trust God. But the real test of his obedience came when he was asked to sacrifice his son. Here was a man who had waited for years to have a child, even making the mistake of fathering a baby with someone else as a way to hurry God along. Abraham and Sarah finally received a son, long after anyone thought it was possible, and the Lord later directed Abraham to kill the boy.

I'm always amazed, as I read that story, that Abraham obeyed the Lord. He could have said no. He could have rationalized his refusal by saying, "It must be a mistake. Surely God would never ask something so evil. Besides, I'm supposed to grow my family into a nation. That will never happen if my son dies. It can't be right. I must have been mistaken." I see myself in those words. God asks for something difficult, and immediately I start thinking up excuses. But not Abraham. When he was told to go sacrifice his boy, he grabbed his knife and headed up Mount Moriah. That test revealed the true condition of his heart. Abraham, as a disciple of the Lord, was willing to obey no matter what the cost.

THE ESSENCE OF OBEDIENCE

The Bible is clear on God's perspective of obedience: "And by this we know that we have come to know Him, if we keep His commandments. The one who says, 'I have come to know Him,' and does not keep His commandments, is a liar, and the truth is not in him; but whoever keeps His word, in him the love of God has truly been perfected. By this we know that we are in Him: the one who says he abides in Him ought himself to walk in the same manner as He walked" (1 John 2:3-6). Obedience is the prompt, personal practice of God's will. You can tell the mature Christian—he's the one who obeys God. Once an individual has committed himself to Christ, the next step involves becoming obedient to the Lord.

Obedience is *prompt*, so there is no waiting to see how things will turn out. Either you obey God or you do not. There isn't any "wiggle room" with the Lord; He knows if you are obeying. Obedience is also *personal*—something you choose to do or not do. Paul tells us in Romans 14:12 that one day each of us will be called to give an accounting of our lives to God. The personal choices we make, to obey or disobey the Lord, will have eternal consequences. Obedience is a *practice*. It is an action. We don't stand around and talk about obedience. We do it. Noah didn't just discuss the coming rain; he built the ark. Paul told the Philippians to "put into practice" the things they had heard and seen in him.

If you want to increase your maturity, improve your obedience. If you want to help your Timothys grow in Christ Jesus, help them work on their obedience. God is calling us to become more and more obedient to His voice in our lives. "By this we know that we love the children of God, when we love God and observe His commandments. For this is the love of God, that we keep His commandments; and His commandments are not burdensome" (1 John 5:2-3). In other words, our obedience reveals our relationship with God. An obedient man or woman obviously loves God. Conversely, a disobedient man or woman is spiritually immature and loves his own pleasures.

You see, love is the essence of obedience. When you love God, you obey Him. Jesus even said, "If you love Me, you will keep My commandments" (John 14:15). Helping a new believer learn to love God by sharing with him the beauty of Christ in your life is imperative. Let your Timothy know how much you love God. Talk about Him in the everyday course of things. Share your blessings. Let others see the role the Lord plays in your life. Jesus loved us so much He was willing to die on the cross for us, so we owe Him our very lives. We can return His love by obeying Him: "He who has My commandments and keeps them, he it is who loves Me; and he who loves Me shall be loved by My Father, and I will love him, and will disclose Myself to him. . . . If anyone loves Me, he will keep My word; and My Father will love him, and We will come to him, and make Our abode with him. He who does not love Me does not keep My words" (John 14:21, 23-24). Love is the essence of obedience.

A man in my city runs a very successful company that his father founded and now his two sons operate with him. One of his boys is the company president, and the other is in charge of personnel. These two young men are a couple of the finest men I've ever known—godly in conduct, faithful to their families, ministry-minded, with a real community conscience. They are truly the kind of men I want my sons to emulate. One day I sat down with Chuck and his wife to ask what they did with those boys that resulted in their extraordinary maturity. Their answer was simple: "We taught them to love God. Once you love Him, the rest will pretty much take care of itself."

Later I talked with the sons. One of them told me, "I loved and respected my mom and dad so much, I simply could not sin in high school the way the others did." In other words, his love for his folks kept him obedient, and that obedience had grown into a mature and godly character. My interview with those young men renewed my passion to foster in my own children a deep love for God, regardless of the cost.

About three years after telling my kids of that interview, my son Matthew, who was then ten, was returning in a van with his baseball team when they stopped along the side of a road to venture into one of the many caves in this area left over from the days of coal mining. All the boys, the coaches, and the coaches' wives went into the cave, stepping over the rubble that had fallen from the ceiling and throwing rocks in the cool water lake deep in the cave. They were cackling, horsing around, and having a lot of fun with this great adventure.

Matthew, however, stood at the mouth of the cave. Being an unusually people-focused boy and one who often acts first and thinks second, his fleshly desire was to join the boys inside the cave. But his feet wouldn't move inside. "Come on in," screamed the other kids, and one of the adult coaches actually came out and asked him why he was not coming inside the cave with the others. Matthew, resisting the peer pressure and even his coach's encouragement, simply said, "Coach, I just couldn't go home and tell my dad I went into a cave without his permission."

Matthew loved me, and his love caused him to obey me. Even though I wasn't in his presence, and he could have gone inside without my ever knowing it, his love compelled him to obey. This same principle holds true in your relationship with God. If you want to increase your maturity, improve your obedience; if you want to improve your obedience, learn to love God. As your heart fills with love, you will find yourself desiring to obey rather than fight Him.

What are the caves of your life right now that you have not talked over with your heavenly Father? Who are the people you are following without the consultation of the One who loves you? What are the questions you have not asked your eternal Accountability Partner because you are afraid He won't give you the answer you want? We live in a world where obedience is a matter of life and death, and the key to obedience is loving God more than ourselves, our friends, our feelings, and our fun.

WHY AM I HERE?

What is the purpose of your life?

How would you describe your gifts and abilities?

What are your life goals?

What is the one verse of Scripture that best characterizes your life?

The Lord Jesus, in delivering a message to the church at Ephesus in Revelation 2:4-5, warned, "You have forsaken your first love. Remember the height from which you have fallen! Repent and do the things you did at first" (NIV). The Christians at Ephesus had allowed their exciting faith to degenerate into a cold orthodoxy. They had forgotten Who it was they loved. So Jesus encouraged them to remember back to the days when they were new believers, excited about working for the Lord. Sometimes in a marriage, a man needs to be reminded of the days he courted his wife, when he couldn't wait to see her. In remembering that love, his romance is rekindled. By the same token, sometimes Christians need to be reminded of those days when they couldn't wait to serve God. By focusing on loving God, their hearts are renewed— and obedience to His Word will surely follow.

DEVELOPING A LOVE FOR GOD

You can help your Timothy develop a love for God by teaching him God's Word and helping him see how to obey it. Talk specifically about putting the Bible into practice. The Scriptures aren't just a general account of good ideas, *but an owner's manual for Christians*. We are to obey it, not just give verbal assent to its value (see 1 John 2:4-5). A believer's life will change when he develops a love for God. The individual who delights in the Lord will discover a new, obedient life. He is transformed by the power of God.

I've never met a committed Timothy yet who didn't want to be transformed. Paul told the believers at Corinth that anyone who is in Christ is "a new creation; the old things passed away; behold, new things have come" (2 Corinthians 5:17). This new life is manifested in obedience to God's commands. It is built by learning how to obey, one step at a time, even during difficult circumstances.

One painfully apparent aspect of discipleship is that we're dealing with life-and-death situations every day. Truly in our culture the guard rails have come off. When I was growing up, police who found us teenagers drunk behind the wheel allowed us to sober up in police stations and then sent us home. Today drunk drivers are jailed. Being promis-cuous in high school used to result in a bad reputation not a deadly disease. It used to be you could work too hard and neglect your spouse, but she would stay around; not any more. Now you find yourself in divorce court. We routinely deal with situations in which discipline is literally a life or death decision. The stakes have escalated. Drunken driving is the number one killer of teenagers. AIDS is going to end the lives of millions of people who decided to engage in sex outside of marriages. Divorce has become a first resort for people unhappy with their marriage. Without the discipline of obedience, you can find yourself in serious trouble amazingly fast.

I used to wonder what people who were "sloppy" in high school did when they got into the service. After I joined the Marine Corps, I found out—they grow up and become sloppy Marines. "John Wayne" Sammons was a guy who frequently did things wrong. He wasn't a bad guy, just lazy, and his lack of obedience in small matters sometimes caused serious problems in large matters. In Vietnam, we used to pull what were called "drop-off patrols," taking a large column of Marines deep into enemy territory and secretly dropping off a squad somewhere. Nine Marines would break into three groups, hide in the bushes until nightfall, then set up an ambush for the enemy. One time I was manning a machine gun position with John Wayne and another man in the center of an L-shaped ambush. Being thousands of meters away from our company position, we had a high level of risk and short life expectancy if we encountered enemy forces. The idea was that we would spring an ambush, then race for our home positions, calling in artillery to cover our path.

These ambushes were very effective but also very dangerous. They took place under cover of darkness, with one man keeping watch while the other two slept at each of the positions. This particular night, I woke up and found John Wayne, who was supposed to be keeping watch, fast asleep. The one supposedly manning the heavy weaponry in event of an ambush—the M-60 machine gun—was out like a light, putting my life and that of all the others at the mercy of his self-indulgence. I thought I should do him the favor of waking him up, so I thrust the butt of my rifle just above his shoulder, as a reminder that our lives were counting on him. Hitting a man in that position prevents him from making any noise, so at least he was quiet when he awakened. Though he groaned with pain, he did stay awake after that.

Here was a man without the discipline to stay awake, even with men's lives at stake miles behind enemy lines. His lack of obedience could have gotten us all killed. Sometimes you may find it necessary to "wake up" your disciples by confronting them with their sin. Help them identify where they have gotten off track, and encourage them to get back on track. Part of your role as discipler is to help foster personal discipline in the lives of your Timothys.

Occasionally you will discover that someone you are discipling has made a serious mistake. There are few things so painful as having your Timothy fall into sin. I feel like a parent to the men I'm discipling, so I tend to blame myself, second guess what I did and said, and be angry. One good friend, a Christian leader whom I'd been discipling for a year, started growing distant during our meetings together. Then I received a phone call from someone telling me Leonard had been having an affair with a woman in his church. After I confronted him with the facts, Leonard confessed he had been unfaithful to his wife. I felt hurt, ashamed, angry, disbelieving, and responsible—all in the same moment. I knew a lot of people were going to be deeply wounded, a ministry was over, and the name of Christ was going to be dragged through the mud. All I could do was cry, "Lord! Help me to do a better job! I pray Susy and I will never let down all those who have invested in our lives by defaulting in being qualified for ministry."

Chuck Swindoll says, "In ministry, you get *one* chance." I know there have been a few men who have humbled themselves, rebuilt their marriages, and reentered ministry, but they are among the very, very few. Most Christians who fall into sexual sin disqualify themselves for effective ministry. Their sin draws them away from God and ruins their reputation in the eyes of men. It's a painful truth, but no more painful than watching someone you've helped nurture have to repent and start all over in his spiritual journey.

Of course, I can't control another man's actions but I still hurt over the ones who have fallen. I've learned the best response is not anger or guilt when a friend falls into sin, but love and grace in humility. For you see, we are all sinners saved by grace. It could have been me who fell, for I certainly haven't reached some plane where I'm above temptation. I work and pray every day to stay away from sexual sin by making sure I don't compromise in my love for and awe of God. That seems to be the key for the men I know who have fallen into sin. They stopped fearing God. Something interrupted their love for the Lord. They typically got out of the Word, became isolated from other Christians, and started being untruthful to their accountability partners.

Accountability is vital in Christian lives if you are determined to walk with Him. It's part of God's plan for obedience. I firmly believe one of the reasons David had so many problems in his kingdom is because he got into a situation where he had no accountability. He not only sinned but also involved his friend Joab in his sin, causing problems that plagued him the rest of his life. But Moses and Joshua before him maintained their integrity by keeping godly men around themselves to hold them accountable.

On the day I'm writing this, there is a news story of a famous football player who has again been accused of a crime. This incredibly gifted superstar's career is once more in great danger because of drug charges—just before a big game when all his team and fans were counting on him. "How could this happen?" my ten-year-old son Joshua exclaimed. "How could this be true when he's already been through a drug arrest once, been punished, and now just before the big game, everyone's counting on him!"

My response was no team, no contract, no amount of money, no promise of fame or fortune, no national or cultural pride, and no admiration of 10-year-old boys will keep a man from sin. Only a love for and fear of the Lord Almighty will be sufficient to keep a man from sin. We must first be His if the power of sin is to be broken in our lives, and we must daily renew His power in our lives by maintaining a deferential awe of God so that we can walk with Him and finish well. As soon as we take our eyes off the Lord and look at anything or anyone else, we fall into a path that ends in destruction.

I love the words of David in Psalm 18:20-24:

"The Lord has rewarded me according to my right-eousness; according to the cleanness of my hands He has recompensed me. For I have kept the ways of the Lord, and have not wickedly departed from my God. For all His ordinances were before me, and I did not put away His statutes from me. I was also blameless with Him, and I kept myself from my iniquity. Therefore the Lord has recompensed me according to my righteousness, according to the cleanness of my hands in His eyes."

In other words, David drew close to God through His word, and it helped establish both love and discipline in his life. The essence of obedience is love; the end result is a life changed by the hand of God.

GOD'S PURPOSE AND PRIORITY

The Lord is calling His people to be obedient. He desires His followers to live holy lives, fulfilled in Him and impacting the world with His love. It's a high calling and means turning away from self toward Christ. His purpose is to make us holy.

Joseph understood the importance of holiness. He suffered being attacked by his own brothers, sold as a slave, unjustly imprisoned, and forgotten by those whom he had helped. But in the end, his holy life saved not only his own family but an entire nation.

The Lord is looking for obedient followers in this lost world, those who can face the truth and follow His plan. It takes all of our strength, our prayers, and the grace of God to hold together our families, our spiritual walk, our businesses, and our ministries. We need others around us to help with the challenge of maintaining obedience.

One of the most painful experiences I've had in discipling was working with a man who was lazy about his work. He had moved from job to job, always requiring his wife to work. She resented having to take a job and had no interest in getting back into the marketplace because her children were very young. But to support the family, she found a job, while the husband spent most of his time at home taking care of the children. The problem I saw was that his sweet wife received all of the praise, encouragement, and recognition at work she should have been getting at home. I warned Grant that women of today do not stay in troubled marriages the way they used to. As predicted, within a year his wife was traveling on the road with her boss and having an affair with him, which resulted in her leaving both her husband and her family to move in with her boss. I really believe the entire situation could have been avoided had Grant developed the discipline to work hard.

I used to think my generation was just weak, that the younger generation had a sexual enlightenment and self-control that we didn't. For example, several of the men I've worked with talked about going home with their dates and sleeping on the couch. "Nothing bad happened," they'd tell me. I'd hear young men tell of going off to cabins as couples, spending the weekend together enjoying boating, Bible study, and bacon and eggs. I was horrified by this conduct, believing it was impossible for men and women to do so without sin. But when I'd raise objections, my concerns were rebutted with what sounded to be well-reasoned explanations on how, for adult men, sexual temptation was not a problem. However, this was a short-lived myth. One of the men confessed he and his "casual friend"—who happened to be female—fell into sin at just such an outing, and now there were troubles ahead. If you're working with young men or women, warn them about allowing the culture to press them into its mold. Just because couples act that way on popular television shows doesn't mean we can live that way in real life. We must not compare ourselves to the world and gain a feeling of confidence and accomplishment; we are to compare ourselves to Jesus and see ourselves for the depraved and sinful people we are, taking courage that through the Holy Spirit's power we have been made new and have the resources to fight temptation.

God has given us the Bible for our own good. His purpose is to make us holy. His priority for us is to learn to obey Him. God wants us to be joyful and fulfilled; we can never be that until we develop a lifestyle of obedience.

DISCIPLING INTO OBEDIENCE

Scripture is always unchanging and true. We ourselves need to abstain from even the appearance of evil and flee from temptation if we are going to help our Timothys develop a pattern of obedience. We have a commitment to operate in truth, love, and purity. I've had several instances when, because of the weakness of my own flesh, I had to stop men in mid-sentence who were about to describe in very sordid, sensual detail the events of their sin. I simply am not strong enough to listen to every detail without impure thoughts racing through my mind. I've also had to get up and leave in the middle of the testimony of a woman who had been saved out of her life as a prostitute. Her stories were so graphic and vivid it took me months to get them out of my mind. Frankly, I left about ten minutes too late in the testimony.

You see, I believe that, as a spiritual parent, I have a responsibility to set an example, not just talk about one. Anything you can do to let your Timothy see your obedience at work will help him to grow. When I was a new Christian, a mature older man approached me and asked, "Phil, do you know what you get when you take a stupid person and make him a Christian?" I admitted I didn't. He looked at me and said, "You get a stupid Christian." In other words, I wasn't immediately mature. When we're saved we receive the *Spirit* of Christ, but we don't instantaneously receive the *mind* of Christ. It takes discipline and hard work to develop an obedient lifestyle. In my life, it's been hand-to-hand combat every day.

Once I had to fly into one of those east coast Navy towns to prepare for a big case. After getting set up in the hotel, I went to dinner with another man before beginning a long night of preparation for the case. The other man started to talk about the incredible "sex for sale" area in the town, and I'll have to admit my curiosity was somewhat aroused. After about the third comment, I felt if I gave him the slightest encouragement we would have been headed toward that part of town! So I finally said, "Tom, men and marriages all over the country are failing because of men's temptation to 'go take a look,' and frankly, the more you mention this, the more I'm likely to go take a drive-by glance. Yet as Christians we know we should flee from evil. So please don't bring that up again. Let's be very sure to stay far away from that section of town as we travel back and forth between the local attorney's office and the courtroom. Agreed?" With another man to keep him accountable, he agreed with a sigh of relief. Sometimes all our Timothys need is a brother to walk beside them and set the example.

A HEART OF OBEDIENCE

Regardless of where a person is in his spiritual walk, it is always important to begin at the beginning. Whether you are dealing with a growing Christian, a pre-Christian, or a Christian in sin, it is vital to take each of them back to the foot of the cross and be sure they have a biblical view of their position in Christ, how that position is attained, and what the guarantees of that position are. Understanding who Jesus is, the purpose of His coming and how He accepts us through forgiveness, and understanding the assurance of eternal life are good places to begin in discipleship. That's why I always begin by talking about commitment, so my Timothy understands who the Lord is. That's also why the second thing I try to cover is obedience, because nobody develops obedience to God without first having a heart of love for Him.

Rick Honeycutt, a hometown hero of Chattanooga, Tennessee, was a major-league pitcher with the St. Louis Cardinals. He defied the aging process by remaining a valued pitcher on his team well into his forties. Rick missed serious injury and in an interview was justifying why he continued to play the sport at a comparatively low salary. The interviewer made at least three references to the fact that Rick's salary was low and asked why he would continue to play baseball for such a relative pittance. Rick simply answered, "I love the game." What a great attitude! When a non-Christian asks you why you would consider giving up your career, your reputation, your money, and your very life to serve a God you cannot see, your answer should be the same: "Because I love Him."

The goal of coaching children's baseball is not simply for the player to learn how to catch ground balls, throw straight, and swing a bat. It is to teach him to love the game. Our goal as spiritual reproducers isn't only to help people learn how to pray and study their Bibles; it is also to help them learn to love the Lord Jesus Christ. Obedience will follow. Some of your work may require going through the basics of ground balls bouncing off foreheads, getting brushed back off the plate by an inside pitch, and watching a line-drive ricochet off the kneecap. But by working with them over time, you'll soon start to see them hitting home runs. As they develop discipline and a love for God, and as they walk with you and observe how you live your faith daily, they will begin to build a lifestyle of obedience.

DISCUSSION QUESTIONS

1. How does God define obedience?

2. Why is *love* the essence of obedience?

3. In practical terms, how can a Christian fight temptation?

4. As you examine your life, when are you most susceptible to sexual temptation? What do you do to help keep yourself pure?

5. Why is refraining from the "appearance" of evil important?

CHAPTER 10

Establishing DEVOTIONS

I was speaking at a conference on spiritual growth not long ago when a man approached me in the hallway to ask, "Phil, do you really think it's necessary to do my quiet time in the morning?"

I looked at him and said, "No. Absolutely not. I do not think it's necessary for you to do your quiet time in the morning. Plenty of men don't. But I will tell you this: of all the men I know who have consistently walked with the Lord over a long period of time, *every one of them* has had a meaningful time of face-to-face communication and worship with God early each morning. So if you're satisfied with where you are spiritually, you don't have to do a thing. But if you want to be like Christ, then, yes, I think a morning quiet time is necessary."

Becoming consistent in your daily devotions is simply a prerequisite for growing in Christ. There are no shortcuts and no other methods. *You will not become mature until you spend time alone with God each day.* It is important for your disciples to understand this clearly. If you aren't having a quiet time in the morning, I suggest you start. If you have tried and failed, then find yourself an accountability partner to help you get started again, because it is nearly impossible to disciple another person long term without spending time with the Lord each morning. It is an obvious truth, but for some reason it is one of the hardest to put into practice. Starting off each day with the Word of God in your life simply puts you on the right track. Satan must really hate a person's quiet time, for he will do just about anything to keep him from spending time with the Lord.

If you are really committed to your spiritual growth and helping others find the Lord and grow into maturity, make a daily quiet time part of your life. Then let others see how you spend time in the Word. Invite them to join you for an early morning time of prayer. Go away for a weekend together so they can observe you reading Scripture, meditating on His Word, and praying about the things most important. Remember, this is foreign to a new believer, so he needs to observe someone else doing it before he can be expected to do it himself. In the discipleship process, the material often becomes the gateway that leads someone to a lifetime of devotion to the Scriptures. Frequently the Timothys with whom I am working will use the *Operation Timothy* material as their quiet time—a good starter course for almost anyone. If I can get a man into the habit of rising each day to spend time in prayer and Bible reading, I know we have laid a solid foundation for spiritual growth.

Jesus, our ultimate model, rose early in the morning, before the break of day, and prayed to His Father. Even the Son of God required time alone, when He could pray and meditate (see Mark 1:35). It kept Him close to His Father and helped Him get focused for each day. If our Lord had to do that, how much more do we need that as His followers?

STARTING A QUIET TIME

How to begin establishing a quiet time is always a challenge. As with starting anything else, you need to have a goal, a comfortable place, an accessible time, and a reasonable plan. Without anyone of these elements, success becomes increasingly difficult.

Some years ago, I was thirty pounds overweight. I could not run a mile or do twenty pushups. One day I looked in the mirror and realized I didn't like what I was seeing. My testimony of self-discipline seemed phony, and I didn't have the physical stamina my job required. So I took out a pencil and paper and put together a plan. My goal was to shed thirty pounds and experience a noticeable increase in energy. I decided on a method for losing weight, a time that would work, and a location for working out. In addition, I tried to make my goals reasonable and incremental—rather than going on a crash diet to drop some weight, I wanted to develop a more healthy lifestyle.

It took a year to get the weight off and another year to develop the discipline of daily running, pushups, and sit-ups. The key to my success the first year was my goal of simply not eating a few desserts, spending twenty minutes outdoors each day moving at whatever speed I could, and at least *trying* to do some pushups. As time has passed, this has developed into a pretty extensive exercise program that has increased day by day. The torturous discipline necessary to achieve this program daily has been replaced by a delightful respite in my day where I commune with the Lord through prayer and Scripture memory and review at the same time I happen to be running three miles a day. This is not a replacement for my quiet time, when I actually study the Scripture, memorize, and meditate, but it has become a time with both spiritual and physical focus. By having a clear plan, reasonable goals, and a time and place set aside for exercising, I have actually developed a healthier lifestyle.

This is exactly the pattern I used to get my quiet time going. My schedule was incredibly hectic, so I decided to carve out time early each morning, because I knew if I left it until later in the day it would never happen. I decided on a place for reading my Bible and praying without interruption. My long-term goal was clear: I wanted to spend significant time praying, reading my Bible, meditating, studying, and memorizing the Scriptures seven days a week. But my plan was incremental. At first I was satisfied spending just a few minutes, but eventually my time with the Lord grew. At first it was work; over time it became the highlight of my day.

In book three of *Operation Timothy*, there is a section entitled, "Pursuing Intimacy with God." In that section, J. I. Packer is quoted as saying, "You come to realize as you listen that God is actually opening His heart to you, making friends with you, and listing you as a colleague—a covenant partner. It's a staggering thing, but it's true. The relationship in which sinful human beings know God is one in which God, so to speak, takes them onto His staff, to be henceforth His fellow-workers and personal friends." Our time alone with the Lord is in pursuit of that intimacy with Him.

WHERE DO I BEGIN?

The first challenge someone faces in his quiet time is knowing how to begin. Early in my spiritual walk I tried the "one strategy." That's the "one minute, one inch, one point, one prayer, one insight" method, which worked reasonably well. Even if I was going out the door late for court, I could at least stop, open up my Bible, read *one inch* of Scripture, try to find *one point* in the passage I could apply, and say *one prayer* for the day. God would inevitably honor my decision to be one minute later. I would find that one inch offered me a meat-and-potatoes answer for some problem I'd be facing that day. And of course, as I did this, it encouraged me the next day to spend a bit more time.

Next I tried the seven-minute strategy, spending *seven minutes* reading one chapter from the Bible and praying through a short prayer list. That's also when I decided to do two more important things. First, I began writing down my prayer requests and prayer answers so I could keep track of them. Second, I began reading through a book of Scripture rather than reading passages randomly. Both of these activities gave me encouragement and motivation to deepen my walk with God. The little booklet *Seven Minutes with God* describes how you can start your Timothy on the right path to a healthy quiet time. Remember, it is better to gain a small victory than suffer a large failure. Help your disciples do something small and achievable at first so they establish a pattern in their lives and grow from there.

Start with a daily goal of reading a portion of Scripture, asking God to intervene in one or two aspects of your life, and then listening for Him as you review a Scripture verse from your reading. This can be expanded into daily reading of, say, three chapters a day (and four on Sunday), which would result in reading through the Bible in a year. More extensive study can be done through chapter analysis or outlining. If you enjoy word studies or commentaries, you can open up a whole new world of study materials for your Timothy to explore.

There are many other methods of devotional time that have worked for various disciplers. Several men I know use the late Richard Halvorsen's "Words of Wisdom" idea. On the first day of the month, they read Proverbs 1 and the first five Psalms. The next day they read Proverbs 2 and the next five Psalms. At the end of the month they have gone through both books in-depth, prayed over the wisdom literature of Scripture, and had a chance to consider some extremely important life issues. The next month they repeat the same process. Within a few months they have become quite familiar with the wisdom of God as evidenced in Scripture. That begins to influence their business decisions and makes an impact on their personal lifestyle choices. "Words of Wisdom" is a great intermediate plan for those desiring to begin getting more in-depth with their Bibles.

Many people enjoy using Bible-study guides, like the materials available from Walk Thru the Bible or Precept Ministries; others enjoy the short, profound thoughts of devotional writers like Oswald Chambers or A. W. Tozer. Whatever you use, the idea is to have a track to run on every day so your devotions become a part of your daily routine. Better than flipping through your Bible at random, these sorts of tools offer an incremental plan for learning the truths of Scripture.

Another tool I like is the *One Year Bible*. It has reading selections of the Old and New Testaments and the Psalms each day. By following its reading program you will read through the entire Bible in a year. It is available in various translations, and it is an easy way to get through a big chunk of Scripture in a short amount of time. However, the tool I like best is *The International Inductive Study Bible*, a tremendous tool produced by my friends Kay and Jack Arthur at Precept Ministries. Following their inductive study methods and using the wide margins for my own notations and outlines, I have been able to create my own personal "study Bible," complete with topical and exegetical study notes I've created myself. Nothing has helped me more in getting deeper into the Scriptures on a daily basis.

Another wonderful thing about discipleship is that the student often outgrows the teacher. When our oldest daughter, Abigail, was sixteen, she had the incredible privilege of attending Precept's *Summer Teen Boot Camp*, where young people from all over the nation come together to pray, praise the Lord, and learn how to feed themselves through inductive Bible study. After boot camp, Abigail came away tremendously encouraged not only to study her Bible but to memorize large portions of Scripture. One of my greatest challenges has been to join her in a father-daughter accountability relationship for Bible memorization. God has greatly used her life to challenge and encourage me to hide God's Word in my heart.

The goal here is to model, encourage, and through instruction help the person you are meeting with begin to believe that time with the Lord is not just valuable but essential to his life. The ultimate goal is for time with the Lord to turn into a love relationship, not just dutifully performed but a natural part of a person's life—just as taking a shower, brushing your teeth, and getting dressed for work are part of your life. Maybe a better comparison is my weekly date with Susy, a joyful and fun time for two people devoted to one another.

TIME TALKING WITH GOD

There have probably been more books written on prayer than on any other topic in history. They explore the theology of prayer, the impact of prayer, and even various outlines for prayer. But sooner or later they all share the same truth: prayer is nothing less than a conversation with the Almighty Creator God. If you don't believe you can benefit from talking with Him, you might as well take this book back to the store!

I believe we need to help our Timothys understand that prayer is a *dialogue*, not a monologue. Prayer is not simply telling God everything you want; it is a time when you can pour out your heart to God, then sit in silence while He pours His out to you (see Proverbs 1:23). This concept of dialogue, of sitting in silence before the Lord, has become almost a lost art in our culture. With our hurry-up lifestyles, we've had a tendency to relegate prayer to nothing but quick thanks at meal times or a wish list thrown up as we're sitting in church. My point is if prayer is meant as a dialogue with God, we rarely allow Him to speak. If the Christian life were a play, most Christians would have cast God as a bit player—the script talks about Him a lot, but He rarely shows up on stage.

Do you know the word for sitting quietly before the Lord? It's a very old word: *meditation*. Don't be afraid of the term. I think somehow the eastern mystical religions of the 1960s co-opted the word, because so many Christians have a tendency to think of meditation as something done by Buddhists or New Agers. That's a shame, for meditation has a rich Christian heritage. "Oh, how I love your law! I meditate on it all day long," the psalmist exults in Psalm 119:97 (NIV). Other verses in this psalm speak of meditating on God's wonders, precepts, statutes, and word. In Psalm 1 we are told the blessed man meditates day and night on God's law. Joshua instructed the nation of Israel to meditate on the Scriptures day and night: "Then you will be prosperous and successful" (Joshua 1:8, NIV).

Meditation is similar to a cow's rumination. The Scripture encourages a person to meditate on the Word the way a cow chews on its cud. Most of the nourishment from the grass is not gained in the initial teeth-chopping of the cow but as it is chewed and re-chewed. Similarly, much of the benefit in meditating on the Word is gained as a person "chews" on God's truth, rolling it over in his mind and bouncing it against his thoughts, actions, motives, and desires. Meditation can be an act of obedience to openly and deliberately allow the sword of God's Word to pierce the depth of our soul and spirit, exposing the thoughts and intentions of our heart (see Hebrews 4:12). It has become a vital part in replacing my thinking with His. As the Scripture sets out in 2 Timothy 3:16 "All Scripture is inspired by God and profitable for teaching, for reproof, for correction, for training in righteousness."

A careful review of Christian history will reveal that *nearly every significant Christian thinker or minister spent considerable time meditating*: John Wesley, Jonathan Edwards, Martin Luther, Augustine, St. Francis, Billy Graham—the list goes on and on. If meditation helped those men become mature, I want to follow their lead.

What are the practical steps to meditation? It's really not very hard. After you spend some time reading Scripture to know God's mind, stop and sit quietly, eyes closed, and ask the Lord to speak to you. Ask Him to teach you. If you really want to be bold, ask Him about the situations and decisions you are facing. Imagine the assurance built into the heart of a believer able to put God's wisdom into action! Some people choose to write down the thoughts that come to them in meditation. It helps them focus their thoughts and often clarifies a truth or a teaching. These certainly are *not* to be considered as equivalent to Scripture, but they can help us to concentrate on the thoughts of God as we meditate.

I will often outline passages of Scripture in my meditation time because it causes the Word of God to soak into my life if I write them down in an organized way. I'll also meditate on the words of the Bible while I'm running or exercising, letting "heaven fill your thoughts," as Paul put it (Colossians 3:2; New Living Translation). Don't be afraid of meditation. In a busy world, it helps us slow down and listen to the voice of the Father.

By the same token, there are many forms of prayer we can use to bring vibrancy to our prayer lives. Scripture speaks of praising the Lord (Hebrews 13:15), giving thanks for all He has done and will do (Ephesians 5:20), offering confession for our sins (Psalm 38:18), remembering others' needs (1 Samuel 12:23), and asking for Him to meet our own needs (James 1:5). You can help your Timothy learn to pray by praying with him. Assist him in putting together a prayer notebook to keep track of requests and answered prayers. This will help build his faith as he begins to see God is really at work in his life.

A well-organized prayer list or prayer notebook is a real benefit to a growing Christian. You can divide it into sections, leaving room not only for the request but also for the answer. Make sure to date each request so you know when you began praying for it. Chip MacGregor likes to put a short phrase at the top of each page to get him started each day. Some of the sections Chip has in his notebook include:

Praise: Lord, help me to see you as you are. . . .
Confession: Lord, change my life in these areas. . . .
Love: Lord, help me to love these people. . . .
Thanksgiving: Lord, thanks for these things. . . .
Supplication: Lord, please do these things for others. . . .
Petition: Lord, please do these things for me. . . .
God's Will: Lord, what is your will concerning. . . .
Intercession: Lord, please bring these people to a saving knowledge of you. . . .[3]

On each page Chip lists the current concerns he is praying about. This allows him not only to be focused when he goes before the Lord in prayer, but it also creates a beautiful record of the role of God in Chip's life. What a wonderful encouragement it must be to pull out that notebook and see all the times God has intervened to answer his prayers. And what a great tool to show to a Timothy, to help him get organized and know how to pray effectively.

Another useful tool I've come across is the "Ten Most Wanted" list, first created by CBMC years ago.

New Christians are some of the most effective evangelists on earth because all their friends are unsaved. They haven't hidden away in the "holy huddle" yet, so if you are discipling new believers, by all means help them prepare a similar list and pray with them that those people would come to know Christ. On my "Ten Most Wanted" card, I have written down the names of ten people I'm praying will give their lives to

---

3. The genesis of this format came from *Praying,* by Bobb Biehl and Jim Haglelganz, Gospel Light Publishing, 1975.

TEN MOST WANTED

1.
2.
3.
4.
5.
6.
7.
8.
9.
10.

These are the ten people I'm praying will come to a saving knowledge of Jesus Christ.

---

the Lord Jesus. I used to avoid naming names for fear of embarrassing someone. Then it occurred to me I'd rather be embarrassed here on earth by having somebody see my list than be embarrassed by having somebody turn to me on the day of judgment and ask, "Phil, why didn't you pray for my soul while I was still alive?" I want to be sure I'm talking to God about people before I start talking to people about God.

THE PROBLEM OF TIME

Those who most greatly benefit from a person's quiet time are often his greatest inhibitors. In other words, your family will be enriched by your time in God's Word, but they also may inadvertently do everything possible to keep you from it. Our wives or husbands may often keep us up too late talking about their day so that it's impossible to get up early the next morning to have devotions. Our children greatly benefit from our devotional time in the morning, but may keep us up long into the night discussing problems instead of getting a good night's sleep and taking the problems to the

Lord early in the morning. And everybody has activities throughout the week they want us to attend, so it's tough to take any time in the evening, get quiet, and go before God. Of course, I love talking to my children, and I enjoy attending their activities, but I have also found that it's possible to give them so much time I have none left for the Lord. Then they all wonder why we've come home *on* our shield as opposed to *wearing* our shield! If you're trying to establish a more consistent pattern of personal devotions, I encourage you to *tell your spouse and kids exactly what you are doing*. Make them part of your team so they can encourage you and help you get going. Many won't do this in the fear it will make them look like failures for not establishing this pattern earlier. You will have to swallow your pride and trust your family to support you in your new commitment. Rather than being disappointed in you, most Christian wives or husbands will be thrilled you're making an attempt to walk closer to the Lord.

Another pitfall of quiet time is that people watch TV, scan TV, gaze at TV; and then when they're finished, they watch more TV! They choose to follow people's view of the world on TV news and forsake an opportunity to talk to the Creator about all the challenges ahead of them for the day. In my view, nothing serves to corrupt a disciple's quiet time more than the boob tube.

Brother, a man can send his kids to the finest schools, attend the most Christ-centered church he can find, wash his car to set an example of cleanliness, mow his lawn so he's a model for the neighborhood, and then go out and hire a pack of thieves, prostitutes, and drug addicts to come entertain his family in his living room. Not only does most television programming fill our hearts with the smut of the world, we also become unusable vessels as we are shaped by the culture, and we demonstrate to our children what is most important to us. When you are glued to the TV, watching a scantily dressed actress wooing over her male companion, your daughter receives deep and lasting signals about the appropriate attire and conduct to attract and please men. Your son sits there feeling lust welling up in his heart, then looks over at you and assumes either such feelings are good or that you're dead. Your wife passes through, sees the young babes on TV and, having borne children, realizes there is no way she can compete with the 18-year-old models enrapturing her husband. This maims her self-esteem and makes her less likely to want to reveal herself to you in bed anytime soon.

Who has ever gotten anything positive from the television? Sure, there is breaking news, though it always comes from man's perspective. And there are sports, though many of us have probably felt the twinge of having totally wasted hours in front of the tube *after* a game. Occasionally there is even a movie or an educational program the whole family can enjoy together. But if we're really honest with ourselves, most of the things on television are total rot. Time is short, and we ought to be redeeming it. As a spiritual man, set an example for your family and your Timothys to follow. Cut the garbage out of your life. Turn off the tube and help them do the same. Sister, if your husband is willing to do this, do your part. Don't be a discouragement to him by turning the television on "for company."

Businesswomen and homemakers vary greatly with regard to when time may be available, and the working mom seemingly never has free time. So often Susy is counseling women who are trying to do everything—advance in a career, be a loving wife, be an attentive, nurturing mother, take care of the home activities and needs, be a loving daughter, sister, etc., etc. One friend told her, "I don't enjoy life any more, and I just feel used." A quiet time would give greater access to the Lord's power, peace, and provision and therefore is totally essential for such a busy life. But also, we humans expect more out of ourselves than God ever intended, and it is during these times with the Lord that His will and relief from overcommitment can be found. Try saying "yes" to God so you have the courage, commitment, and insight to say "no" to men and women who continue to push for more.

DOING THE HARD WORK

When I was a trial lawyer my goal was to win my cases. I would interview as many witnesses as I could, research my case and other related cases, scout out my opposition, then prepare, prepare, prepare. There were times I had to stay up late, put in long hours, and fly to other cities to do the best job possible. It was hard but necessary work if I was to succeed.

My goal as a disciple is to become a clean and willing vessel for the Lord. I want Him to work through me so that I can be the husband, father, worker, leader, and man in ministry He wishes me to be and so that I can achieve His goal of having me make disciples. Being that sort of Christian requires hard work. To help somebody else achieve it also requires hard work. At times it has meant getting in the face of a Timothy and holding him accountable. I know of one spiritual parent who used to get up at five every morning so he could call one of his disciples and read Scripture over the phone with him. It may sound like he was treating the young man as a baby, but he *was* a babe—a babe in Christ. My friend was willing to do the hard work required to get that young guy on the right path.

One of the new men I was meeting with recently, a very bright, young graduate from an Ivy League school, met me at the door with a delightful glow on his face and blurted out, "Phil, I've been reading Psalms! Did you know these Psalms are really great for business practices?" It was a thrill to see him discover the truth of the Scriptures, having gleaned principles for his business from his daily quiet time. Another friend told me that the eruptions and torrents of his life have been smoothed out by his daily Bible reading, gaining God's perspective on the challenges, temptations, and opportunities of his day. Both men have seen significant change come over their lives; it never would have happened if they hadn't gotten out of bed each morning to spend time with the Lord.

When I married Susy, I was a night owl, ready to rock 'n roll until two every morning. I didn't even get fired up until ten or eleven at night! But Susy has always been a morning person. She begins to fade about nine o'clock, and by six the next morning she's wide awake. The phrase "sleeping in" isn't even in her vocabulary. She drove me crazy on our honeymoon, wanting me to get up and get going in what I considered the middle of the night. I wanted to stay in bed— I still would prefer taking it easy in the mornings.

But to walk with God I have had to change my habits and get an early start every day. The result has been an unwavering commitment to get up early in the morning, which I achieve by setting no fewer than three alarms, every morning, every day of the week. I found out my days simply go better when I get up and have a quiet time, so I started doing it five days a week. Then I found my Saturdays were sometimes a struggle because of all the family activities and expectations, so I started getting up early with the Lord for a quiet time on Saturday morning as well. Soon I discovered Sunday mornings were just as difficult, with all of the social commitments at church, the options of activities Sunday afternoon, and the inevitable Sunday night realization that Monday morning was upon me. So eventually I made the commitment to start getting up early seven days a week and spending time in the Word. *Nothing* has contributed to my spiritual growth more than this decision. No book, no seminar, and no worship service has made more of an impact than my daily devotions.

God wants a one-on-one, in-your-face, honest and growing relationship with each one of us, and for me that means I will not do preparation for a speech or Sunday school lesson during my quiet time. My morning quiet times aren't for anybody else but me. I try not to start with any agenda, except to sit and soak up the Lord, read Scripture, work on memory verses, and meditate on what I'm learning. I'm devoted to God's phone number, 333—"Call to Me, and I will answer you, and I will tell you great and mighty things, which you do not know" (Jeremiah 33:3).

As a mid-life convert, my greatest hazard seems to be the time I spend alone. When I'm by myself in bed, I find those old sensual tapes of years gone by start playing in my head. When I'm alone on the road, the insecurity of my upbringing and the feeling of being a failure in my early years are vivid, pointed, and destructive to my thinking. I often arise in the morning with a deep sense of emptiness, loneliness, anger, fear, or lust. So my time with the Lord is not an option but a life-or-death struggle over my spiritual walk. I have to face the fact that I will choose each day whether I'm going to walk as a disciple of Christ.

My devotional time is what drives me toward Him, what gets me out of bed in the morning and brings meaning to my life. I often joke with the kids and say, "Hey, kids, I slept in a little bit late this morning. I think I'll skip my quiet time and we'll just go ahead and play baseball in the backyard." At that point, all the kids will turn to me in unison and say, "No, Dad, that's okay! We'll wait . . . you go ahead and get your time with the Lord." They've learned after all these years if I don't take some quiet time with the Lord, my day doesn't go as well. I get temperamental and short with my family. My children need to see in me the gentleness and grace of the Lord, as opposed to the old Phil Downer. My Timothys need to hang around a spiritual man, which means I have to get up, get out of bed, and go read my Bible. It's hard work, but I do it.

FOCUSED ON THE LORD

As I get up with the Lord, I find reading my Bible gives me God's perspective on my day. My goal is to get lost in the Scriptures and in God's view of me and my world. It is only then I can begin to set out my prayer requests with any wisdom. I want to be focused on the Lord, not on myself or my day. A disciple is someone disciplined in his modeling of the Lord. We model the Lord by letting Him live through us, and if I don't get a healthy dose of Him every day, then my old thinking takes over.

Romans 12:1 says, "I urge you therefore, brethren, by the mercies of God, to present your bodies a living and holy sacrifice, acceptable to God, which is your spiritual service of worship." That's really my goal in having a quiet time. I desire to present my mind, problems, desires, needs, guilt, ambition, words, and deeds to the Lord as a living sacrifice. I focus on Him and surrender every part of myself so He can conform me to His way of thinking. I don't want to be conformed to this world but "transformed by the renewing of [my] mind, that [I] may prove what the will of God is, that which is good and acceptable and perfect" (Romans 12:2). That transforming process occurs during my quiet time. That's when I can think about what God is doing and when the Lord can work on shaping my thoughts. It is as though the Holy Spirit were an artist and I a piece of stone. There is a continual, lifelong chipping away of the old man and a renewing by the Holy Spirit as He conforms me to the image of the Son. If I skip my quiet time, that process can't take place. I won't be focused on the Lord.

A man once said to me, "Phil, I think I've been too legalistic with my morning devotions. I've been adamant to the point of driving some friends away by talking about my extensive Bible memory and study time early in each morning. Frankly, after five or six years, I find I can just walk with God all day. I communicate with Him and stay in a constant state of prayer, speaking about my day and walking with Him, so I really don't find my daily quiet time all that essential anymore. What do you think of that?" With my usual propensity for understating the obvious, I said to him, "Kevin, I think that comment is straight from the pit of hell!"

Then I told him the men I've seen who can really change the world are the guys who meet with God every morning in prayer, Bible reading, Scripture memory, and meditation. The fact they remain focused on the Lord is the very reason God can use them.

I've had to face some pretty crushing blows in my life. Each time, I have chosen to draw apart with the Lord and actually write down the issues and picture the process of giving them up to the Lord. For example, for many years I would write down my sins on one side of a 3x5 card, and on the other side I'd jot down 1 John 1:9: "If we confess our sins, He is faithful and just and will forgive us our sins and cleanse us from all unrighteousness." Then I would begin to pray through the list and picture in my mind giving each sin to the Lord. When I was finished with the list, I would burn the card. It was as though I needed a visual picture of how Christ on the cross, blotted out all my sins. Doing that little activity kept me focused on the grace of God during the difficult moments of my life.

I did the same thing with a list of fears, writing them on one side while keeping Philippians 4:6-7 on the other: "Be anxious for nothing, but in everything by prayer and supplication with thanksgiving let your requests be made known to God. And the peace of God, which surpasses all comprehension, shall guard your hearts and your minds in Christ Jesus." As I prayed through the list and pictured surrendering all my fears to the Lord, it kept me focused on Christ during even the hardest times.

I often found the courtroom similar to the jungles of Vietnam—a dangerous place with a well-armed, hidden enemy. We would often be confronted with ambushes of various types and it required a strong faith to survive. During one such trial, early in my new life as a Christian, I was in the Fulton County Superior Court trying a very difficult case against an experienced lawyer. As I walked into the courtroom, I had a number of concerns on my mind. The other lawyer, probably seeing me as a greenhorn at the other counsel table, jumped up and began ridiculing me about my case, my client, and my firm. I could feel a wave of anxiety overcome me, replacing the peace of Christ I'd had that morning. Wanting desperately to pray, I did not feel the client would understand if I bowed my head and began talking to God in open court, so I started searching for a place I could be alone with the Lord. No place seemed right. I thought about just praying silently to myself, but sometimes my mind thinks so loudly and my heart feels so deeply my prayers must be said out loud. On this particular day, I just wanted to get away from that crowded courtroom and talk to the Lord, committing to Him both the pressures and the outcome of the case.

The lawyers' lounge was packed, the halls and corridors were full; there wasn't even an unoccupied stall in the men's room. The only place I could find to be alone was a public telephone. So I went over to the pay phone and, without putting in a coin, picked up the receiver and began a long, audible conversation with God. I admitted I was anxious, told Him I knew I'd been called to the role of lawyer, and asked that my performance would bring credit to both my client and our firm, as well as bring honor to Him. Then, as I stood there pretending to listen to a voice through the receiver, I sensed the Lord encouraging me. It was as though He was reminding me nothing would happen outside of His control, and He only wanted what was best for me. I told Him verbally how much I appreciated His love and encouragement, then asked Him to help me not act out of fear but out of legal competence. Faith in Him filled my heart, and I returned to the courtroom with a new attitude. I could feel the peace of God wash over me. By simply taking a few moments to focus on the Lord in the middle of a hectic day, I was able to regain what I'd had that morning in my quiet time. And best of all, the call was free!

Each of us should focus on the Lord in such a way that we know He is with us, regardless of where we are or what we are doing. We should share the confidence that comes from daily quiet time with our wives or husbands, our children, and our Timothys. If you'll begin your day by spending time with Him, you'll find this much easier to do. A missionary friend of mine puts it this way: if you were suddenly tossed into an African jungle, you'd want to rely on a local tribal chief to help you survive. The chief is the one who can tell you what fruit to eat, what paths are dangerous, and what natives are restless. As a spiritual parent, you do something very similar; you take your Timothy by the hand and lead him along a path toward God. Nothing can foster his spiritual growth more than spending time every day with the Lord, so you teach him how. Over time, as God works in his life, that man will emerge from spiritual darkness into the bright light of maturity.

QUESTIONS FOR DISCUSSION

1. At what point in your life did you feel closest to God?

2. Describe the "ideal" quiet time. What do you do in your quiet time?

3. What has the Lord been teaching you as you read His Word?

4. Name one of the most significant answers to prayer you have experienced.

5. Who is on your "ten most wanted" list?

CHAPTER 11

Developing CHARACTER

$\mathcal{T}$he life of Joseph serves as a wonderful example of the difference *character* makes in a man. Joseph was thrown into slavery by his own brothers and disappointed by fellow prisoners yet put into a position of power because of his faithfulness and integrity. He knew what it was like to say no. When the wife of Potiphar, his master, attempted to seduce him, Joseph put his principles into practice and ran away. It had to be pretty obvious what would result, yet Joseph was more interested in being a man of character than in seeking his own pleasure or protecting his role. He understood that, while men meant it for bad, "God meant it for good" (Genesis 50:20).

Joseph built character and maintained purity by being loyal, patient, and steadfast in his convictions. He acted with great courage, and when speaking he gave credit to the Lord, who gave him his wisdom and character. Joseph was even able to forgive and embrace his brothers, the very men who got him into the whole mess in the first place. His life is an incredible example of how a man with character can overcome his circumstances. Joseph lived out 1 Thessalonians 5:18: "In everything give thanks, for this is God's will for you in Christ Jesus." *Circumstances* did not dictate his principles— God did.

A FOUNDATION FOR CHARACTER

Character defines who a person is when he's all alone in a hotel room, far away from home. Character is reflected in one who will not let his circumstances dictate his principles. You don't turn to somebody else to ask what to do; you must simply do what is right. I've always liked the way Charles Swindoll put it: character does the right thing when nobody is looking and when everyone else is compromising. One of the goals of discipling another person should be to instill character in him so he will live by strong principles.

To understand character in the modern context, we must first understand the philosophy of our modern culture. Historically, mankind believed God was the source of everything. To communicate with man, He used both general and special revelation. *General revelation* means that mankind can see the existence of God in nature. Just observing the complexity of the universe, the design of our world, and the perfect balance of chemicals on the earth, we see evidence of a divine creator. More and more doctors and scientists have come to the inescapable conclusion that there must be a God because there is so much evidence of design in our world. As Paul put it, "Since the creation of the world God's invisible qualities—His eternal power and divine nature—have been clearly seen, being understood from what has been made, so that men are without excuse" (Romans 1:20, NIV). People who claim not to believe in God have had to work hard to be atheists, for everyone knows in his heart that there is a God. He has revealed Himself through general revelation.

Special revelation is the Bible, God's very words given to mankind as a special message about how we can have a relationship with Him. The Scriptures are God's specific message to mankind, and they reveal who He is and how we can have a relationship with Him. Men used to have high confidence in the Bible as God's truth, but our modern culture has replaced confidence in God with confidence in science. We have given up the supernatural to embrace the natural, abandoning God's wisdom in favor of man's. Consequently, when we left the mooring of God's truth, we were set adrift on a sea of relativism. "For although they knew God," Paul continues, "they neither glorified him as God nor gave thanks to him, but their thinking became futile and their foolish hearts were darkened. Although they claimed to be wise, they became fools and exchanged the glory of the immortal God for images made to look like mortal man" (Romans 1:21-23, NIV).

General revelation has given way to a secularized version of truth, which places human understanding above supernatural truth. That has led to a generation of people who have been raised almost completely apart from God. The answers to questions like "Why am I here?" "Where did I come from?" and "What is the meaning of life?" are now being answered by people *with no knowledge of God*. We used to believe, because it said so in Scripture, that certain actions were sinful and wrong. Now we have rejected this truth and embraced a theory of godlessness. Since there is no God, there is no truth. Everything is relative. What is wrong for me may be right for you—sin no longer exists since there are no absolutes. Few have any idea what "character" means any more, except perhaps those who holds to quaint traditional values. Without God, character ceases to be important to a culture.

That is exactly what Paul said would happen. Any culture that rejects truth will soon embrace a lie. The result of that decision will be the necessary collapse of morality:

> *"Therefore God gave them over in the lusts of their hearts to impurity, that their bodies might be dishonored among them. For they exchanged the truth of God for a lie, and worshiped and served the creature rather than the Creator, who is blessed forever. Amen.*

> *"For this reason God gave them over to degrading passions, for their women exchanged the natural function for that which is unnatural, and in the same way also the men abandoned the natural function of the woman and burned in their desire toward one another, men with men committing indecent acts and receiving in their own persons the due penalty of their error.*

> *"And just as they did not see fit to acknowledge God any longer, God gave them over to a depraved mind, to do those things which are not proper, being filled with all unright-eousness, wickedness, greed, evil; full of envy, murder, strife, deceit, malice; they are gossips, slanderers, haters of God, insolent, arrogant, boastful, inventors of evil, disobe-dient to parents, without understanding, untrustworthy, unloving, unmerciful; and, although they know the ordinance of God, that those who practice such things are worthy of death, they not only do the same, but also give hearty approval to those who practice them."*
>
> (Romans 1:24-32)

A lack of truth leads directly to a lack of morality. The loss of morality leads to all sorts of immoral practices, even to the approval of wickedness by society. Eventually, of course, it leads to the destruction of society and eternal separation from God. As our world has rejected the Scriptures and turned away from truth, it has begun to embrace lies. Our cultural acceptance of perversion, sexual promiscuity, and selfish hedonism, and our lack of regard for life are direct results of rejecting God's absolute truth. As a spiritual parent, one of your jobs is to help your Timothys understand that absolute truth does exist, that we can trust God's Word to be true, and that character is established by putting His principles into practice.

THE STUPIDITY OF SIN

It is amazing how the lack of absolutes has caused men and women to live in a dream world. They think they can escape the certain consequences of sin by denying its existence. But sin is a bad deal; no one sins and gets away with it. Every sin you commit impacts your character.

One of the illustrations I use, which might at first sound simplistic and silly, is that of gravity. In the middle of cautioning a man about the consequences of sin, I'll toss a pen into the air. No matter how much a man might deny gravity exists because he can't see it or feel it, we can be certain that gravity really does exist. How do I know? Because the pen I throw in the air falls to the floor. I've thrown all kinds of things in using that example: glasses, forks, books, even breakable items. "You can't see gravity, but it has impact," I'll say to the man, amidst the crash and bang of objects falling. "No matter how much you deny it or how you hope it won't happen, gravity exists everywhere." Sometimes I'll carry this on until the other person is at the point of embarrassment! But then I'll say, "Like gravity, sin has consequences. You can deny it and hope that it's not true, but that doesn't change the facts. God is holy, and He isn't going to make any special exemption from justice for those who find the consequences of sin too inconvenient to believe."

In this world of cocaine, infidelity, and abuses of every magnitude, however there remains a healthy percentage of women who, as Susy says, "don't see themselves as sinners and don't contemplate the kind of unrighteous lives others are seeking." They go to work, they love their families, they are faithful to their husbands, and sure, they may blow the budget with a new dress and enjoy the attention of people bragging about their success, but these are people who aren't desperately looking for answers. They simply are going the wrong direction. Having a strong relationship before talking to them about Jesus Christ is particularly important because the need for Christ is not something they ever think about. Build a relationship with her, encourage her, ask God to give you patience to see a need or open up a discussion where spiritual things can be broached.

I've seen men do some of the most stupid and sinful things imaginable. My own father once sat me down and listed a bunch of things he claimed he would never do, and then I saw him, over the course of time, violate virtually every one of the items on that list. I'll never forget the day my father, though a well-educated, confident, and successful businessman of great acumen, did one of the dumbest things you could ever imagine. He picked me up at the Dallas airport in late November and said, "Your mother checked herself into the hospital today. Said she couldn't cope with Thanksgiving." I was surprised by that news because Mom had been pretty strong recently, although she'd had emotional problems in the past. But Mom and Dad were having marital difficulties because of my father's affair with another woman, Darlene, so I thought things might have come to a head. But when I asked my father what had pushed Mom over the edge, he said, "Oh, it's because I invited Darlene to join us for Thanksgiving dinner." Absolutely incredible! My father had asked his mistress to join us all in celebrating a holiday—and it somehow made sense in his darkened mind.

I spent night after night telling him it wouldn't work, sharing Christ with him, encouraging him to find peace in a relationship with Jesus Christ, and trying to get him to recognize that feeding the flesh would only bring destruction to everything he held dear. Dad listened to everything I said but simply responded by saying he "did what men and women are doing today all over the country." He was more right than he knew. People are lying to themselves about the results of their actions, but one day they're going to have to give an accounting. Dads think they can look at pornography and have daughters who walk in purity. Husbands think they can neglect their wives yet have marriages filled with love. Businessmen think giving the cold shoulder to one another will help resolve their problems, but all that happens is they grow hard-hearted. The actions, attitudes, and atmosphere we convey rub off on those around us. Tragically, six months after the Thanksgiving crisis, my father put a pistol to his head and took his life.

Christians too often sneak around and think we're "keeping secrets." Who do we think we're kidding? Not only do we have a God who is omniscient and omnipresent, but He also lives inside us through His Spirit. So how do we think we're fooling the Lord? One young man I was discipling thought it was okay for me to believe that he was not sleeping with his girlfriend. I believed him—but God knew it wasn't true. It is accurate to say he got away with sin for several months without anyone knowing, but his conduct of deceit overcame his desire to walk with God.

Once you're trapped in sin you're a fugitive, and fugitives continue to break the law simply by being in the position they got themselves into. I've always thought it ironic that Lee Harvey Oswald was first brought to the attention of the Dallas police not on suspicion of killing the president but because his conduct looked suspicious to a policeman who didn't even know the president had been shot! The man in prison for blowing up the government building in Oklahoma City wasn't stopped for bombing anything but because he didn't have a license plate on his car. The Christian lawyer who went to jail for skimming money from his client's firm was not exposed because of his crime but because of his shoddy legal work. A man involved in secret sin is a fugitive, continuing to sin until he's caught. Who do we think we're kidding? Who do we think we're hiding from? God loves us even though we're sinners, but He hates our sin. And God will not be mocked—the Bible is clear that every man will reap what he sows (see 2 Corinthians 9:6, Numbers 32:23).

CHARACTER AND CHANGE

I was speaking one day in the Northeast. After my testimony a man came up and said he had come to Christ in a similar meeting some months before. He described his situation: a bitter divorce had cheated him out of his money and kept him from his children. He was angry at the judge, the lawyer, and everybody involved with the case. He even told me he had begun making plans to kill those who had hurt him: "Every time I drove by that lawyer's office, I advanced a plot to kill him. I stalked the courtroom and devised my plan to have the judge murdered. I had every intention of taking out the two men who had separated me from spending time with my kids."

As he described this, his eyes were piercing, his face taut, his lips stretched tight. But then he told me how he came to know Jesus Christ as his Lord and Savior and how he was being discipled by a man who had also been through a bitter divorce. He said to me, "I have actually been able to forgive those people, and now I recognize God was wanting to get my attention through all this so I would follow Him and not chase after my old ways of vengeance. My life was changed because I had someone show me how to live a new way." That's the power of discipleship. By sharing your life, you offer another person not just a new idea to believe but a new way to live. You help him develop a new character in the Lord Jesus.

CBMC produces and sells a video training series on discipleship entitled *Living Proof 2: Lifestyle Discipleship*. In one of the tapes there is a discussion about the challenge of making "right and left turns" in your life. When you've been deeply hurt by someone, you can use your own strength, grit your teeth, and find a way to channel your anger. But you won't be able to find forgiveness. Choosing to rely on your own strength is like making a left turn. The other alternative is in exactly the opposite direction, the way of humility. You can admit your pain, brokenness, and need for Christ, and you can seek the Spirit-led discipline to do the right thing under God's control—taking a right turn. One or the other will dominate your life.

Either God will control you, or you will try to control yourself. You see, the Holy Spirit, not your own strength of will, is the source of all character. We've all started exercise programs where we've gritted our teeth and done it. We've all tried making New Year's resolutions to act better, be more patient, or take more time with our families. But if we try to do those things in our own power, we're sure to fail. Christ came to die because men were not able to make those lasting changes and therefore save themselves. Either you will turn to the right, or you'll turn to the left. The choice you make will reveal who controls you.

One time I was storming around the house, overwhelmed with my leadership responsibilities, my caseload at work, and my list of things needing to be done at home. "I can't do all this, Susy," I yelled to my wife. "I can't please all these people. I can't do it!" Susy, patiently praying for me and trying to offer counsel, couldn't be heard. Finally, I shouted, "I've got too much. I just don't deserve all this!" And my wife replied softly, "That's right, Phil, you don't. You deserve the cross." She was right, of course. I'm actually getting much better than I deserve— through the forgiveness of Jesus Christ. My complaining about the pressure was just immaturity.

Too often I tend to grit my teeth and struggle through the challenges, as opposed to yielding my will and letting Christ *live* the challenges. The difference is incredible—and vital to a disciple. One builds character; the other builds self-sufficiency. If you want to build character into your Timothys, help them choose to let the Spirit lead.

When I was meeting with Dave Hill, one of the men who mentored me, I would often have a huge lunch, then a hot fudge sundae for dessert. Dave would just smile at my overspending and overeating, not offering criticisms but talking with me about spiritual principles. Finally I got to the point when both my budget and my waistline were out of whack, and asked Dave if he thought I was overdoing it. He smiled and said to me, "Phil, I have seen a lot of growth in your life. I've seen you get hold of some solid scriptural principles, and one of them is moderation in all things. If the Spirit is urging you to change, my suggestion would be to listen to His voice." Then he shared with me some biblical principles for budgeting and staying in shape. God regularly used those sorts of encounters to shape my character. A mentor can influence a protégé in important yet subtle ways.

MAKING NECESSARY CHANGES

When I first became a Christian, I thought just shining up the old character would be good enough for God. I was wrong. The "old man" is described in Scripture as a dead, rotting corpse. Putting on a little makeup and a fresh suit of clothes isn't going to make that old carcass any more acceptable. God wanted to change me from the inside out and make me wholly committed to His ways.

When we were new to Tennessee, we moved to an area that's not exactly rural but certainly out in the country where the houses are far apart, surrounded by woods. The possum inhabiting this part of the world was a new creature to us. We had never been in a place that had so many possums. I was driving down our street one day and noticed a dead possum about 100 yards from our house—fresh roadkill. I thought about stopping and burying it, but the press of my day was upon me, so I went on my way. When I came home, the possum was splattered all over the road; I figured it would be well-worn and dried up in short order. But after about three days, we started to smell the possum in our yard. At the end of the week, I could literally smell it inside my house. I finally got out a shovel and scraped what was left off the road. The spot continued to smell even after I buried the carcass. You don't live with an old corpse; you bury it.

The Scripture is clear. We are to change when we meet Jesus Christ. Our character will change because everything we know to be true changes. If there is something dead in us, we need to get rid of it, bury it:

> *"Therefore, consider the members of your earthly body as dead to immorality, impurity, passion, evil desire, and greed, which amounts to idolatry. For it is on account of these things that the wrath of God will come, and in them you also once walked, when you were living in them. But now you also, put them all aside: anger, wrath, malice, slander, and abusive speech from your mouth. Do not lie to one another, since you laid aside the old self with its evil practices, and have put on the new self who is being renewed to a true knowledge according to the image of the One who created him"*
>
> *(Colossians 3:5-10).*

Sometimes we're just too lazy to deal with sin, so we leave it for later. But eventually sin begins to stink, and the stench permeates one's whole life. Better to bury it immediately and take on an entirely new life.

I didn't learn my first possum lesson very well. One morning a few months later I was out running, not very far from that same place, when I encountered another dead possum. I almost tripped over the thing in the dark—a great big, fat, dead possum. This time I decided I needed to get rid of it, so I grabbed it by the tail, hurled it around, and slung it deep into the woods. I thought to myself, "Great, I got rid of that one." But I hadn't taken care of the possum; I'd simply hidden it. Sure enough, about three days later I was driving by and smelled a stench from the woods. I could smell it in the front yard of our house. Hundreds of yards from our house, that possum still stunk. I finally had to dig through the woods to find the decaying carcass and bury it.

I've done the very same thing with sin in my life. For years I struggled with my thought life, so when I came across Job 31:1 in my quiet time one morning ("I made a covenant with my eyes not to look lustfully at a girl." NIV), I decided to emulate Job's words. That meant I promised the Lord I would not set my eyes upon any questionable material such as fleshly or ungodly movies, magazines, or photographs. The eye is the gate to the heart, and the heart is the seat of intentions, so I committed to shield my eyes to protect my heart and actions. Then the Victoria's Secret catalog was sent to our home, even though Susy had never made a purchase from that store. A woman can argue it is simply an underwear catalog, but to a man it's a purveyor of pornography. It's insidious because in our culture it appears innocent to women and is pronounced blameless by men willing to lie to themselves and their wives. Many men have actually convinced themselves they can peruse the catalog, even visit the store, yet keep their focus on the Lord. I believe that is a lie. If you think looking at this catalog is the same as men looking at a Sears catalog for sporting goods, you need to see your doctor for a check-up!

Too often, men like to look at those pictures and act as though it doesn't impact their thinking. That's like taking a guy in the midst of a diet and letting him saunter through a candy factory, taking a few bites of the things he likes best. Men need to stay away from those sorts of tempting visual images—and they need to inform their wives what that stuff does to them.

After the third time I found the latest Victoria's Secret catalog in the living room, I realized Susy had not remembered to heed my plea to stop its garbage from coming to our house. I picked up the latest copy, sat her down, and started pointing to the pictures, telling her in graphic terms what men see. Susy's face became red, and she teared up. Then she jumped out of the chair, grabbed the catalog out of my hand, slammed the bedroom door, and called the Victoria's Secret 800-number to make it very clear they were to drop our name from their mailing list. She didn't speak to me for thirty minutes. You can say I wasn't very gentle, but until we get a focus on the fact we're in a battle and Christians are dying all over the place because of the sin in their lives, we need to speak frankly about our weaknesses and flee from the things that cause us to fall.

Men and women are wired differently. Women will never understand the seemingly insane attraction men have to the outer surface of females, but it's a fact that needs to be discussed and dealt with openly. Like the possum on our road, we need to bury the parts of our lives that are old and dead—the habits and practices that can stink up our whole lives.

Recently I was running down that same road and came across a third dead possum. This time I knew what to do. I charged back to the house, grabbed what I needed, and came running down the street singing the Marine Corps hymn with the shovel at port arms—Corporal Phil Downer on possum patrol. I dug a hole and buried that rodent about two feet under. This time there was no stink. That's what we need to teach our Timothys to do. You can't dress up your old sin; you have to get rid of it. That means you have to admit it to a brother, pray about it with him, and be held accountable to defeat it. You have to allow the Holy Spirit to work in your life to empower, change, and develop the character of Christ in you. Bury that old man or woman and start living a new way. If you compromise by pretending it's not there, you'll still be left with the stench of sin.

SHAPING THE CHARACTER OF TIMOTHY

When he first met Paul, Timothy was a sickly, weak young man. But Paul loved him anyway. He looked for Timothy's good qualities, set an example for him, and offered encouragement to help him grow. Paul gave Timothy jobs to do, jobs that grew in responsibility as his character could handle them. He didn't just tell him what to do, he did it *with* Timothy. As a spiritual parent, you can do the same thing.

My friend Patricia is a great discipler of women and her first meeting with Barb was a real delight. Patricia knew Barb lived a racy life and melted in the face of temptation, but she also saw that this weak-charactered young woman could, with Christ, become an Esther. When I asked Patricia why she knew this, she said, "Because God said so, and because I've seen it happen in the lives of many other women." As the two ladies met in a discipling relationship, Barb struggled with the assurance of her salvation. She would commit herself to Christ, break her commitment, confess her sin, then start the process all over again. She never sensed a power over sin, so she continued to fall into temptation at work because she said she "felt helpless under the pressure of a man's attention." Patricia focused in on Barb's relationship with her heavenly Father and her natural father, seeking to rebuild Barb's self-esteem in Christ. But the road was long. It occurred to Patricia she should counsel Barb to quit her job and look for another place to work, but outside of a convent there were few places without men. It didn't seem that the workplace was the problem; it was the poor character of her young Timothy that needed to change.

One day Patricia had the idea she and her husband should go with Barb to her office and spy out the land. She told Barb she and Gary would stop by to pray that God would fill the place with His angels. Barb was absolutely elated Patricia would actually be willing to "go with her to her place of biggest temptation." So the day came that Patricia, Gary, and Barb did the following things: First, before anyone else was at work, they met at the business site and prayed for God to put to death the immorality, passion, and evil desires that were hampering Barb. Second, they drove around the parking lot and prayed over the grounds where Barb worked. Third, they asked the Lord to put a hedge of protection around Barb and fill that place with His presence. Fourth, they prayed for the other people working there, particularly the men in question— that they would be convicted of sin and come to Christ. They also prayed that either the men would leave Barb alone, or God would remove them from that place. Fifth, they prayed Barb would be able to see these men's comments and their intentions as filthy rags for which Christ paid the penalty.

When the office opened, Barb took Gary and Patricia to meet all her co-workers. They went from office to office, cubicle to cubicle, and Barb introduced her spiritual parents to everyone in the place. Gary made a point of getting close to each man as he shook hands, looking him in the eye, and saying, "Oh yes, Barb's told me all about you. I'm very glad to meet you. Since she became a Christian, Barb tells me this job has become very important to her."

In other words, Barb's spiritual parents announced to her world that she was under new ownership. She was now a daughter of the King. That was the last time Barb ever had any problem in the office. Temptations did not cease 100 percent, but Barb's ability to fight them improved 98 percent. She now understood she could live differently, that God would take ownership over her if she would take steps to bury her sin. And Patricia saw firsthand how going with her Timothy was like taking a legion of soldiers to help in the fight. To this day, Barb walks faithfully with Christ.

Since I was a trial lawyer, people often asked me questions about their cases. I enjoyed my work, so I usually found discussing their cases interesting. One of my Timothys was involved in a very difficult suit with his partners; they had committed acts that breached their contracts and given them substantial liability. But his business partners wouldn't admit the problem, deal with it, and face the inevitable blight on their reputations and blast to their pocketbooks. After giving advice to him over and over again, I finally decided what I needed to do was simply go and talk to his partners about the case. So he arranged a luncheon where he introduced me as his personal lawyer, familiar with the case. His partners were surprised and even irritated as we began talking about the case, but after about thirty minutes they seemed relieved to finally be directly confronting issues that kept them awake at night, interfered with their concentration on the golf course, and caused a fearful stirring in their stomach every time a lawyer called.

After about two hours, it was agreed they would try to settle the case. My friend—who was mostly to blame for the problem—agreed to bear a disproportionately larger part of the financial settlement. The case was settled within thirty days and the impact on their reputation and customer base was minimal. The financial settlement wiped out two quarters of their profit in an extremely profitable year, but the partners saw their junior partner in a new light. He was someone who had courage, conviction, and conscience. He was a man of character.

Going with your Timothy can sometimes be the most powerful thing you can do. My oldest son Paul was only five years old when he was invited to memorize and present the Christmas story at our church Christmas pageant. Paul was very reluctant, but I thought it would be excellent experience for him to have to stand before a large crowd and talk, so I encouraged him to give it a try. It meant Paul had to recite more than a dozen verses from memory, and have the confidence to present it four times to large crowds of people. The problem for me was that I had to assure Paul I would help him memorize the verses and be comfortable with the process, but I was going to be gone quite a bit for a large out-of-state trial. I would not even be around for the first three performances to offer moral support. But the week before the pageant, after practicing the verses several times with the family, we drove to the church and walked around the stage, praying about every aspect of the performance. We stood where he would stand, sat where the people would sit, talked to the men putting up the lights about how bright they would be, and looked at the sound system to see how it worked.

On opening night Paul walked out in his red shirt, went right up to the microphone in the center of the platform, and, with the large crowd looking on, flawlessly delivered his verses. At age fourteen, he went to Africa as part of a team to present the gospel to business and government officials at outreach meetings, conduct follow-up meetings in men's offices and couples' homes, and help establish new CBMC ministries. Paul believes the fact that his father walked with him nine years ago and helped him face a great speaking challenge not only marked his life forever but also was the basis for his confidence that he could be used by God as a missionary speaker. God goes with us, and we need to go with our Timothys.

CHARACTER AS SALT AND LIGHT

Bill and Dee are both owners of their own businesses— writers and professionals in their own regard. After Bill's first wife died, Bill and Dee were married, became involved with CBMC, and were discipled into maturity through *Operation Timothy*. They moved to a large city in the west and bought a home in the heart of one of the most difficult cities in which to operate as a Christian. Their spiritual parents challenged them to become salt and light in a dark world. "If we are going to become men and women of character," they were told, "we must be willing to tell others about the Lord." So Bill and Dee prepared to make disciples. They were established, equipped, and mobilized as people of character in a city of moral relativism.

Their first goal was to reach their neighborhood. Bill and Dee invited Christian couples to their home to watch the

Living Proof 1 training videos, which dramatically explain the concepts of lifestyle evangelism. Out of those meetings flowed a great desire to reach people in their neighborhood with the message of Jesus Christ. Then this team of Christians started hosting home dinner parties—each would invite people to come to their home for a progressive dinner. The people arrived at the home at 5:00 p.m., were split into teams, and each team received a shopping list. One team would have a list for the hors d' oeuvres, another for the main course, another for the dessert. They had to design the meal and purchase the ingredients, staying within a limited budget. When the women realized all they had to do was dream up recipes, go to the store, and buy stuff, they were thrilled. The men were responsible for the actual cooking. At the end of the evening they'd vote on who had served the best course.

At the start of the evening some of the men looked like they were about to jump out the window. But after they overcame their initial fear, it turned out to be one of the most fun evenings those couples had ever experienced. Throughout the evening they were building relationships, which later became springboards for sharing the gospel. Bill and Dee have seen a number of these people come to Christ and start their own "Living Proof" groups all over the city. Bill also helped encourage a local CBMC group there and moved the men to his own office building to give them a regular place to meet. Now they have what's called the annual "Good Friday Breakfast" in their city, which five hundred people attend so they can hear the gospel. If this is possible in their city, it's possible anywhere. All it took were some men and women of character willing to stand with one another for the cause of Jesus Christ.

At a CBMC outreach meeting, two of Bill's guests prayed to receive Christ, and he began to disciple them. That's what happens when you build disciple makers—the vision keeps on growing. You move them from the crib of immaturity into a close relationship with God. Not even one of the most sin-filled cities can stand up to the power they have in Christ. They become examples of salt and light in the world.

Steve Sanders was a fresh graduate from a great school with a successful new career working for a local company when he came to a CBMC meeting and became involved. I had the privilege of taking him through *Operation Timothy* and watching him grow in the faith. Many others have had great input into his life as well. I'll never forget the day he told me he was thinking about starting a business of his own. After much prayer and study, I gave him the sage advice that, because of his age and lack of business experience, he needed to stay with a place that offered security. I felt he needed to remain with a well-established company and not take the risk of going on his own.

Thankfully, however, Steve ignored my great advice, went out on his own, and grew his company to 150 employees working for him in five offices across the country. Steve talked about the gospel with everyone in his company. People came to Christ and lives were changed. It is amazing to see how he changed and what God has done through him. But that's what happens when the Spirit of God shapes the character of a man.

You can see the same thing happen by helping shape the character of someone else. Come alongside another person and teach him the truth. Then spend time with him so he can see how he ought to live. You'll soon begin to see the power of God at work, through you and other people, in the life of another.

QUESTIONS FOR DISCUSSION

1. How does a lack of truth lead to a lack of morality?

2. In what ways do our attitudes and actions influence our families?

3. Identify the character quality described in each of the following verses (all NIV):

1 Corinthians 15:58 – "Therefore, my dear brothers, stand firm. Let nothing move you. Always give yourselves fully to the work of the Lord, because you know that your labor in the Lord is not in vain."

1 Thessalonians 5:18 – "Give thanks in all circumstances, for this is God's will for you in Christ Jesus."

James 2:8 – "If you really keep the royal law found in Scripture, 'Love your neighbor as yourself,' you are doing right."

Romans 13:8 – "Let no debt remain outstanding, except the continuing debt to love one another, for he who loves his fellowman has fulfilled the law."

Matthew 7:12 – "So in everything, do to others what you would have them do to you."

Colossians 3:13 – "Bear with each other and forgive whatever grievances you may have against one another."

1 Peter 5:5 – "Young men, in the same way be submissive to those who are older. All of you, clothe yourselves with humility toward one another, because, 'God opposes the proud but gives grace to the humble.'"

Matthew 5:8 – "Blessed are the pure in heart, for they will see God."

1 Corinthians 6:20 – "You were bought at a price. Therefore honor God with your body."

Hebrews 12:14 – "Make every effort to live in peace with all men and to be holy; without holiness no one will see the Lord."

CHAPTER 12

Surviving
ADVERSITY

*O*ne of the toughest things parents go through is watching their children fail. When my son Paul was twelve, everything came together for him with his Little League pitching. Early in the season, most of the batters not only couldn't hit the ball, but many would back out of the batter's box because of his great velocity. He threw with confidence, speed, and accuracy that carried him to the All-Star team. Paul was the starting pitcher in the first game of the playoffs, and the coach hoped that once again Paul would hold the other side to a scoreless three innings, letting our team get ahead. But it didn't turn out that way.

The first pitch hit the batter right in the chest, the loud thud stunning the crowd. The batter got up off the ground and walked to first base. Paul proceeded to walk the next four batters. He had obviously lost both his confidence and his control. All I could do was pray and try to study his motion to see if I could spot anything that would help. Paul's next pitch hit the batter in the elbow, making it 3-0. Now it's 3-0, the bases loaded, and nobody out. Paul, working like mad to get out of this jam, sent a blistering fastball at the next batter, which careened off his helmet, sending him to first and scoring yet another run. With that the umpire leaped from his crouch, pointed at Paul, and gave him the heave-ho. "I want a new pitcher," he cried, as if to say "before somebody gets killed!" Paul left the mound feeling defeated, his team in a big hole. We actually came back to win that game, moving on to the second round of the playoffs, but you can imagine how discouraged my son was.

On the way home, I battled with my own sense of embarrassment and disappointment and really was not sure what to say with everybody sitting in the car in silence. Finally I said, "Paul, I want you to check on how you did tonight against the four goals we have with sports. Number one, did you do your best, even if you don't think it was very good?" Paul nodded. "Number two, were you a good sport?"

"Yes, sir."

"Number three, did you honor the Lord with your thought, word, and deed?"

"I believe I did, Dad."

"Paul, our fourth goal is to have fun, which I could see you were trying your best to do. Am I right?"

After a pause, Paul said, "Well, it certainly wasn't fun. I've never before had the experience of doing the right things and having everything turn out wrong!"

"That may be true, Son, but according to our goals, you had a perfect game!"

At home, we walked around in the backyard together, both of us trying to think of what to say. I didn't want to minimize it but did want to show my support and let him know he was a winner in my eyes, no matter how he pitched. I wasn't going to forsake him or be embarrassed by his performance, just as God will never forsake us or deny us. Suddenly a thought came to me—possibly the world's greatest idea! I turned to my son and said, "Paul, did you know I once lost a case so big they put my picture in the paper?" His head shot up and he said with surprise, "Really? When?"

"Yes, it really happened. I lost a court case so big they put my picture in the paper as the losing attorney, and underneath the photo they described in great detail how I had blown it." Suddenly he laughed and asked about the details, and we went on to talk about how the Lord loves us despite our failings. As a matter of fact, He loves us so much He allows some of those failings to strengthen our character and expose our need for Him.

When you start discipling people, you can expect some similar experiences. Your disciples are going to make mistakes or go through tough times, and you'll want to bail them out. But keep in mind God brings tough times to create tough people. Everyone who has ever accomplished anything significant for God went through adversity. A quick check of any American history book will tell you our greatest presidents, Lincoln and Washington, went through the most difficult experiences. I believe all great men became great only after they were refined by the fires of testing.

I once discipled a man named Roger who had all sorts of ability. He was a good-looking, articulate young man, with a gifted mind for business. Everything he did for his company was going great. Then something happened. Someone above him, a man who I believe was jealous of Roger's success, started putting roadblocks in his way. That man purposefully made it impossible for Roger to meet his goals, and suddenly the shine came off his career. Through nothing of his own doing, Roger could no longer achieve what he had been hired to do. Within a few short months he was let go by his firm. Devastated, Roger called me up, and we arranged to get together.

"Why?" he asked me. "Why would the Lord allow something like this to happen to someone He loves?"

I sat and stared at my coffee cup, wondering if Roger was ready for the answer. Deciding he was, I said, "Because He loves you."

"What!? If that's love, God has a funny way of showing it!"

"Roger, do you think God only wants us to have success? Did He allow His own Son to experience only success? Would you say any of the twelve apostles, or any of the early church founders, were marked as being successful in this world?"

That stopped him. Roger sat for a minute before replying, "I never thought of it like that."

Then I said, "Sometimes bad things happen in this world, Roger. I don't know why, but I *do* know God is in control of the circumstances. Sometimes He wants to toughen us up. Every Christian goes through hard times—that's what helps us mature. But I'll tell you something: it is in the tough times you learn to rely on God. Those are the times when you can really grow spiritually, for those are the times when you need Him most. If all our times were easy, we'd forget all about the Lord and take all the credit for our success. God's allowing some hard things in your life right now, but that means He is going to use them to help you mature in Jesus Christ."

When I said those words, Roger's very countenance changed. Suddenly he saw new purpose in what was happening. "That's right," he said. "So that means God has something better for me. Phil, that's great! Thanks for reminding me Who's in charge." Then he proceeded to move into an incredibly successful new career with an even better firm. But he was also more prepared to appreciate the presence of God after that and he became a real dynamo in sharing his faith with colleagues going through hard times. Of course, if we had not established a discipling relationship, I never would have had the opportunity to say those words to Roger.

TOUGH PEOPLE FOR TOUGH TIMES

Every Christian can expect to go through some tough times. As a matter of fact, the Lord Jesus told His disciples, "In this world you *will* have trouble" (John 16:33, emphasis added). (NIV) So we know we'll face some struggles along the way. But the good news is that Jesus completed His statement with the words, "But take courage! I have overcome the world." Nobody gets through this life unscathed. God uses tough times to mold tough people. I have experienced many easy days and many hard days, and I can say without question it has been the hard days that caused me to grow spiritually.

So when you disciple someone, be prepared for some hard days. Be ready to see him, offering comfort and encouragement when the tapestry of his life begins to unravel. Think about the times you have grown most and make sure you can articulate your own faith in God through tough times. You will be handed a marvelous opportunity to help this person take big strides in his maturity, but it can only happen if you have already established the relationship and built up trust in one another. Then the growth potential is almost unlimited.

One of the men I discipled was in commercial real estate and was caught holding when he should have been selling. When the bottom fell out of the market, he saw eight years of work and all his reinvested profit washed away like leaves in a fast-moving river. I went to see him, to let him cry on my shoulder. But that man surprised me. Familiar with 1 Thessalonians 5:18, he spoke in terms of thankfulness for the Lord's sustaining him and had a gentle recognition that God was in control of his circumstances. He was willing to cry out to the Lord through his pain and express his emotions honestly as he struggled with fear over sustaining his family's provision, but he knew the Lord would supply all of his needs. Having that sort of confidence is half the battle.

I was impressed as I watched that man deal with a difficult situation. He stayed close to the Lord. His mind was renewed, and he took comfort in knowing God was in control. He decided to get counsel, to trust God and not panic, and not to inflict harm on himself or vengeance upon a business partner who was instrumental in this predicament. But he still struggled with his emotions. He relied on his spiritual parent to see him through the hard times. So often Christians will dutifully recite Romans 8:28 ("God causes all things to work together for good to those who love Him, to those who are called according to His purpose") (NIV) and blissfully go through the first part of adversity, then wear out their self-control and explode because they are unwilling to let the Holy Spirit minister to their emotions. "Blessed are those who mourn, for they shall be comforted," Jesus said in the Sermon on the Mount (Matthew 5:4). My friend was mourning, but because of his faith in God and the support of his friends, he found comfort. We prayed for him, encouraged him, and allowed him to express his fear, anger, and emotion in prayer as we stood with him.

One particular morning he was going off to a meeting from which he would very likely come back financially destitute. As some of us gathered around him, one individual recited some Scripture, and then we prayed for him. He later told me he went into the meeting feeling a sense of deep peace and trust that God was in control because he had brothers who would stand with him—not for what he had, not for what he had achieved, but for *who he was in Christ*. He knew Jesus was standing with him. During this time, this young man had no idea his business colleagues and fellow commercial real estate brokers were watching him to check out his faith. His neighbors, club members, and unsaved family were all keeping an eye on him as he went through desperate financial straits. These adversities opened up door after door for him into the lives of men who were going through similar problems and challenges.

SIN: THE SOURCE OF PAIN

Adversity can be authored by the Lord, ourselves, our fellow human beings, or the devil (with permission from the Lord). Often the adversity we bring on ourselves is simply caused by blatant sin. While we can be forgiven of our sin, living through the consequences of it is wearisome, humiliating, and painful. King David was certainly forgiven for having an adulterous affair with Bathsheba, but he had to live with the consequences of his sin for the rest of his life. Sometimes in our culture people equate "forgiveness" with "fantasy"; God can forgive you of the most heinous sin, but it's fantasy to believe your life will go on as though the sin never happened. God declares you justified and takes the *penalty* of your sin away, but the *natural consequences* of your sin may still be evident and can bring some tough days.

It all started for Jerry by watching nighttime situation comedies and other network TV programs. Those programs got his mind going, so he started going to hotels and renting pornographic movies he paid for as a part of his business expense. Happily married to a beautiful, godly wife, and holding church and parachurch ministry leadership positions, Jerry started struggling with the visual images the movies left in his mind. One day he stopped his taxicab in a bad part of town and visited a massage parlor. Feeling horrible, he swore he would never do it again, but he was unwilling to share his deep weakness with his friends, his wife, his pastor, or his spiritual parent. He thought he could handle it on his own; besides, the chance of the information getting around if he shared it was too high a risk. The very next week, on a business trip, he spent two out of four nights in a similar setting. After three months of an increased frequency of this kind of sin, his office manager discovered charges on the company credit card that looked strange. Upon investigation, the office manager found Jerry had been to eight massage parlors in the course of just under four months. He was summarily fired, and soon everybody knew why.

As we sat in a cafe drinking Diet Coke, tears ran down Jerry's face as he shook his head and repeated, "I've ruined everything. . . . Oh God, please forgive me. I've ruined everything." It would be more comfortable for us to say Jerry was not a Christian, but I believe with all my heart he was a believer who tried to be a spiritual Lone Ranger through a deep canyon of weakness. He gave in to areas of the flesh one step at a time—with regret, but without sincere mourning and repentance, not seeing the sin as God saw it. He had a small view of God's omniscience and omnipresence and acted as though he could hide from God because he was hiding from people. Jerry fell into the trap many men fall into—he forgot God hates sin more than He wants us to keep our reputation. He will expose us even if it hurts His name and ours. God will expose our sin because He loves us, regardless of what the consequences of our sin may be. He wants us to grow, and sometimes we don't grow until we're caught red-handed.

To overcome the sense that "God won't see," or "I might get away with it this time," or "Everybody's doing it," or even "It's worth the risk" in my life, I practice the principle that a good defense is an aggressive offense. I often pray for purity in my life: "Dear Lord, if I fail you and my family tonight and fall into sin with a woman, I would ask You that my actions would be totally exposed, that I would receive every known disease into my body, and that my picture would appear in the front page of the paper. Lord, I even pray that when I wake up in the morning I would find my private parts safety-pinned to my forehead! I pray that I would have no ability to get away with sin and that You would never let me go to the left or the right without exposing what I have done." I have some friends who have received the challenge of that prayer with me. (One has even traded safety pins with me as a reminder!)

It's tough to pray, "Oh God, expose my sin" and then sneak off to do in darkness what we would never do in the light. Numbers 32:23 says your sin will find you out. Nothing is hidden from God. If you plan to sin, plan to have pain. I'd advise you to carry a safety pin.

WHEN OTHERS HURT YOU

Sometimes we suffer adversity because somebody else brings great pain into our lives for their own selfish motives. My friends Tom and Eileen are godly people with a very active ministry in their city. They've raised their children in a good church, offered a great family environment, and given their kids every opportunity to grow as spiritual people. However, their oldest son began to pull away from the Lord in his teenage years. Their whole life was shattered when their son was arrested and later admitted to murdering a woman in a holdup.

As they went through the shock of the arrest and the facts came to light, they chose to stand by their son. They reached out to the family of the young woman who died. During his time in prison, their son came to Christ and actually became a great testimony for the Lord Jesus Christ with the other inmates in his cell block. Prisoner after prisoner began to describe how he had come to Christ through the testimony of this young man charged with a felony who met the Lord only after going to prison. Even though the son had fully repented, fully confessed the crime to the authorities, and had many people writing letters to the court, the judge gave the boy the maximum sentence for the charge: imprisonment for life.

As I read a recent letter from Tom and Eileen recounting the outcome of this case, there was a gentle sweetness evident from parents who made no attempt to justify the crime or explain away the sin, and showed no anger toward the judge for assessing the maximum sentence. They only affirmed in brokenness, humility, and faith that God was still in control, and that they would continue to stand by their son as he faced a lifetime in prison. Some of the most difficult pain we can ever go through is the adversity brought upon us by those we love the most. Through a single act of stupidity, a mistake, or blatant sin, families across the country are being dragged into torment by one of their own. The choice we have is between bitterness and belief. As a spiritual parent, you have to pray for people and remind them God uses tough times to create tough people.

There was a story in *USA Today* about a Christian couple traveling with six of their children on the interstate when their car suddenly hit an object and burst into flames. Before the fire could be stopped, all six children in the car were consumed by the flames. The article was an astounding evidence of the power of God in adversity to demonstrate love, faith, and forgiveness. The father was quoted as saying, "I think that God was in control, and although this was a tragedy, He has a plan." He even described how he and his wife had put a favorite toy on each of the kids' coffins, choosing to respond to the tragedy with love rather than bitterness. Both the husband and the wife talked in terms of forgiving the truck driver, who had not only caused the accident by having a part fall off his truck, but who had actually ignored a warning about the dangerous condition.

What an opportunity to hate a man who was negligent in the maintenance of his truck! What an option it would be to hate God for taking their precious children. Yet this godly family, in a world wracked with bitterness and revenge, returned grace, forgiveness, and love in a situation that would test the faith of even the strongest saints. Who knows how many people's lives will be saved eternally by the testimony of this godly Christian family *willing to understand* that God allowed the taking of their children in a way no one foresaw, desired, or could reverse.

What do you say to Timothys who have had adversity thrust upon them? You pray. You stand by them. You don't lecture about all things working together for good, but you let them know you love them and God loves them, even when this love is hard to see because of the circumstances. Sometimes sitting in silence is the best ministry you can offer someone who is grieving.

THE ATTACK OF SATAN

Sometimes adversity is caused by the devil. Job was a man who loved God but had everything taken from him by the power of Satan. All of his family, possessions, and wealth were gone in one afternoon. But it's important to keep in mind that nothing was taken that was not permitted by the Lord to be taken. God *allowed* Satan the opportunity to test Job.

The devil asked for permission to afflict Job's body; the man was given sores to the point that he cursed the day he was born. The most interesting thing about the book of Job is that in the end, after God cross-examined him with a bunch of questions, Job admitted he was not in control. He humbled himself to the Lord and admitted all this pain had been allowed by God. One of the Lord's purposes in sharing this story with us is that we learn about the suffering of the righteous. Even the most righteous man was allowed to be absolutely crushed through Satan's permitted conduct against him. If I were Job, it would have helped me if God had at least said, "Job, I've done this to you to be an example to all of creation as to how you are supposed to live through adversity." But Job never knew that. He knows now that he is in God's presence, but he didn't know it when he was on earth. Sometimes the Lord allows bad things to happen so He can shape our character; sometimes He may be planning to use us as an example to someone else. Sometimes, we simply never know.

There is no doubt in my mind the toughest job any American president ever had was given to Abraham Lincoln in 1861. There were thirty-three states in the Union the day he was elected; by the time he took office, the number was down to twenty-seven. Elected largely because the other political party was divided, Lincoln didn't ask for such a tough role. As historians have said, some seek greatness while others have greatness thrust upon them. Lincoln was one of the latter. It is doubtful he ever realized how significant his life and his presidency were to our country. God took Abraham Lincoln and this country through a very difficult time, but it brought out the greatness of God in this man.

The man who discipled me came to breakfast for our meeting one morning with a pained look on his face. He had just found out his supposedly Christian financial counselor, whom he had met through the church, had squandered all of the investments entrusted to him. These had been set aside for my friend's retirement and the education of his children, and he was hesitant to tell me because he thought I might say something like, "Stupid doctor, lost all his money." But he loved me enough to share it, and he had such a great faith in the Lord and a wonderful focus on discipleship that he knew I needed to go through this with him for my own learning. So he told me all about his pain, struggles, anger, and resentment. Then he walked me through Scripture to show me how to handle financial struggles as well as the thoughts, actions, and emotions that come with them. He was seeking to live out his faith in this circumstance in front of me so I would grow.

Not many months later, when something happened to me and I was greatly distressed over a problem at the office, I went through all the Scripture my spiritual father had walked me through and experienced it as I had never before. As disciples, we must be transparent with our problems, challenges, fears, and temptations in order to teach our Timothys how to apply faith to life.

I came home from work once extremely hurt by a man who had called me and been critical and insensitive. Instead of taking it to the Lord, I stewed on it. I was supposed to lead my family in devotions the next morning but really didn't feel like it. The Scripture we were studying was about peace, and I had no peace. So I asked my children what was wrong with a person who has no peace, and my son Paul suggested, "Maybe that person isn't a Christian!" Steaming, I resolved that one, but then he added, "Dad, maybe that person without peace is in sin." Just what I needed—to be corrected by an eight-year-old boy. But as I thought about it, it occurred to me that he was right. I had to confess to my son that, yes, I thought I had sinned. I had not been willing to take this to the Lord, even though I knew all the Scripture about forgiving one another and maintaining unity in the body. I had acted on my feelings, which had resulted in anger—and sin. That morning my kids prayed for me, and I prayed about forgiving this individual, trying to see things from his point of view and receive his comment as correction. I went to work that day with peace, having been ministered to by those I was discipling in my home.

The very next Sunday Susy told me a friend of hers said her husband had been torn by anxiety and was desperately upset about a work problem. Would I be able to see him? I asked if this man was a Christian; she said she thought so. I sat down with him that evening, and he told me all about his anxiety. He'd had a tough childhood and was a man racked with doubts. I asked if there had ever been a time when his faith in Jesus Christ had cut through this anxiety and he'd had peace. I wanted to take him back to the time that he felt peace at the foot of the cross and understood God was in control, but he said, "No, there's never been a time." I told him what had happened in our family devotions the week before and said, "Well, according to my children, that may mean you're not a Christian." The man thought for a moment and replied, "Maybe there's never been a time I've surrendered to His will in my life." That very night he became a Christian by praying to receive Christ. We started a discipling relationship a few days later.

Brothers and sisters, if we will be transparent with those we're discipling then, as we pass through adversity, we can see great growth. Having been transparent and honest with my boys about my temptation to be angry, I had a wonderful platform to interact with them when they became angry and frustrated with somebody and wanted to strike out. During times of adversity we have the greatest opportunity to see God impact another person's life and the greatest opportunity to foster maturity.

The man who discipled me was an obstetrician. He told me doctors never learn from routine cases. They always learn from the complications of their cases. That's true of those of us in discipling as well. We can look back over the road map of our lives, and if we walk in faith through adversity we will notice great times of teaching and growth.

GOD DOESN'T WASTE PAIN

Every couple faces pain and suffering and that has certainly been true of Susy and me. We have lost a baby, clients, the sale of a house, a job, and friends. We have even lost relatives through violence. During one of these times, Susy was sent a book, *God Meant It For Good*, by R. T. Kendall. It discusses with biblical clarity and in practical terms the principles we can learn from the life of Joseph. Susy called it "my guidebook for God's taking me from pain to victory."

The Lord develops character in us through suffering. So when your Timothy is going through a difficult time, God is working in his or her life. Many people will try to minimize their suffering. They'll ignore it or stuff it inside and pretend it doesn't bother them. But the longer we fail to deal with pain, the more of a problem it becomes. Paul went through some incredible suffering, but he said, the "God of all comfort" was with him, comforting and supporting him (see 2 Corinthians 1:3-4). If you can't deal with your own pain, you can't help others deal with their pain. When you open up and admit your pain, telling the truth about how you're feeling, others will be willing to share their pain. This can be both cathartic and healing. You see, suffering can produce both despair and hope. Satan will try to drive you to despair, but God is always there with you, even in the most difficult circumstances.

Shortly after I came to Christ, Susy started going to Bible studies and prayer times with other Christians. I thought things were going great and that coming to Christ had solved all our problems. But one of the most painful things that ever happened to me was dealing with the recognition that I had not only been unreasonable, verbally abusive, and totally selfish with Susy—I had actually crushed her love for me.

A few years later, after our marriage was restored, we were asked to speak at a CBMC conference and give our testimonies. I had written mine out or shared it with groups of men before, but Susy had never actually put hers down on paper and shared it with anyone. That afternoon we set to work with our yellow legal pads, I pruning mine, and she writing hers out for the first time. About two hours before we were to share our stories she gave me her pile of yellow pages to read. As I went from page to page, reading the description of how my selfish anger had tormented her and torn our marriage apart, I wept. I kept saying, "I didn't know that. I didn't know I had done that to you. I'm so sorry."

As I continued reading, I marveled then at the faith Susy had, to begin praying, "God, I can't imagine living with Phil the rest of my life without loving him. Would you please make me fall in love with Phil again?" In God's grace, and because of Susy's obedience, that's exactly what happened. We fell in love all over again, and we have a glorious marriage today.

We still have some painful memories, and I still have some deeply ingrained habits of occasionally being less than gentle with my wife. I don't ever want to justify what I did, but we recovered through God's grace and forgiveness. As Susy often tells people, "If God can heal our marriage, there is no marriage beyond His healing touch." I had destroyed our relationship through my own sin and didn't even know I had done it.

Frankly, that's the condition I find many marriages in today, particularly among those who struggle with anger and selfishness. We don't realize we are not just hurting our spouses, we are destroying love and therefore hurting ourselves. I used to always say I was sorry and resolve to do better, but then I would repeat my selfish and outrageous conduct day after day. The "sorrys" and the "I'll do betters" simply couldn't heal the pain Susy was suffering. You can't keep kicking a dog and saying, "I'm sorry" without consequences. Pretty soon the dog will feel pain even if you don't swing your foot, and shudder with fear at the very sound of your footsteps. I meet men all over the country doing this precise thing to their wives, children, and even business partners and co-workers. They are causing pain and need to mature in Jesus Christ, ask forgiveness, and change.

I've seen people try to numb their pain through drinking, eating, pornography, or keeping themselves so busy they don't have time to think. Even ministry can be an excuse to keep from having to deal with pain. But the Lord allows pain to come into our lives for a reason: to cause us to grow. God doesn't waste pain. So when your Timothy loses his job, is diagnosed with cancer, or is in anguish over a son in trouble, remind him God is in control. He allows tough things to occur so we'll draw closer to Him. "Draw near to God, and He will draw near to you," we read in James 4:8. God just keeps looking after us. Painful experiences change us, like pressure and heat refine a lump of coal into a diamond. The process is hard but necessary. God reveals our fears, negative attitudes, and secret sins as He takes us through the refinement process.

However, *hard experiences don't guarantee change.* Just the fact that your Timothy goes through a tough time doesn't mean there will be a life change; that depends on the response. Your job as a spiritual parent is to help your Timothy have the right response, trusting God and believing in Him no matter what. Without God's Word, your Timothy won't be able to make sense of his experiences, so make sure to integrate Scripture with experience.

Having said that, the "right answer" is not always the solution to suffering. Your disciple must still go through the struggle of deciding how to respond. He still needs to feel the emotions, for that's one of the reasons God made us with emotions. There is suffering, and in the suffering we become open to change. There is a tension between one's personal will and God's will, and this struggle provides the context for growth. All of life is making decisions, so deciding to follow God's will, no matter how difficult it may seem, is the essential step in growing through suffering.

We can reject the truth and preserve our independence, or we can say yes to the truth and obey God. The attitude of the believer makes all the difference. That's why I'm always reminding my Timothys about the importance of humility. God wants us humble before Him. The very word "worship" literally means "to bow down." When we worship God, we bow to His leadership over our lives. God leads, and we follow. The more we understand this truth and surrender to it, the more we'll grow. I've discovered that humility is the key to seeing my life change, yet I seem to fight it all the way.

I want things my way, and I want to be in charge of them. My self-will keeps me from maturing in Christ. But if, in the midst of struggle, I will go humbly to the Scripture, I find the Holy Spirit moves in and brings peace and a whole new understanding of self-control.

The problem with humility is that it does not come naturally. Taking control, extolling my own opinion, and reading my own press clippings are temptations I fall into too often, and the Lord has frequently had to humble me. One time I walked into an executive staff planning meeting with everything nicely bundled up as to what we were going to do, ready to leave for the airport for my next out-of-town travel assignment. The agenda I planned was a bit too long, but I thought if I could carefully guide the conversation away from the less productive chatter and avoid other people's rabbit trails, we could accomplish all I wanted in the meeting. I'd even prepared the devotions to speed right along.

As I sat at the table, very confident—or perhaps what the Lord would call "puffed up"—I casually leaned over to my right-hand man and asked, "On a scale of one to ten, where would you say the team is right now?" Fully expecting him to talk about eights and nines, my jaw dropped when my best guy said, "Oh, about a three."

Surprised by Bruce's lack of his usual enthusiasm and figuring he was just having a bad day, I threw the question to the rest of the group. That was a mistake. Fred gave us a one. Dave scored it a two. I found, on average, the executive team members all thought we were about a three. That's when chaos broke out. We spent the better part of the day with various members of the team expressing frustrations, miscommunications, and lack of direction—all stemming from the president. Me.

During this time my thoughts went from disbelief and humiliation to anger and self-pity. It just wasn't fair. Did they have any idea how hard I was working? But when I shared that thought, they said I wasn't allowing the gifts of the team to be used by the Lord in coordination to accomplish God's purposes, and the guys were pretty frustrated. We spent most of the day talking about the problems in the organization, and I felt there was very little said of any constructive nature. Yet somehow I had managed to restrain my expressions of frustration and disagreement with much of what was being said, so I didn't stifle the free exchange of thoughts. The worst part of the meeting was I really didn't think anyone was reacting out of bitterness or some other sin. They were simply expressing honestly where we were; it was my fault, and it didn't feel good.

But the funniest thing happened at the end. Dave stood up and said, "Phil, great meeting. This one was really worth coming to—not nearly as boring as the other ones." I had to admit Fred looked better, having been able to get some stuff off his chest. And Bruce, who is highly relational, appreciated people being able and willing to share. So as I sat there, with my pride and ego battered, it occurred to me I really needed that day. In fact, the team needed that day. And if I had any sense at all, I would take a part of that day home with me in prayer and find out what God wanted to teach me through my executive team. The Scripture says that even though Christ was perfect, He still "learned obedience from the things which He suffered" (Hebrews 5:8). If the Lord had to learn through suffering, how much more does God need to teach me through hard times? God doesn't waste pain. He uses it to help us grow.

OBEDIENCE IN HARD TIMES

One of the hardest things I've had to learn is to trust God when everything seems to be going wrong. Yet that's exactly why God allows things to go wrong. Only when we're at the end of our rope can we sense the Lord's assistance. If we can become obedient in hard times, revealing that obedience to those we are discipling, the Lord can greatly use us to change others.

I used to be in bondage to my own will. Now, by the power of the Holy Spirit in my life, I have been set free to choose to follow the Lord. There's a new pattern established in my life, surrendering control so God can guide me toward a new way of living. I can trust Him rather than trusting my own judgment. Whenever I disobey Him and insist on doing things my way, it seems I always fail. When I try to do God's job my own way, it always ends in disaster. I'm utterly unqualified to take God's place. That's why He tells us, "Apart from me, you can do nothing" (John 15:5, NIV). But if I trust in the Lord, coming before Him in humility and obeying Him in all things, I find the Spirit works things out. And in the process He changes my life.

You and I have grown up in a world that demands performance and perfection. We've been schooled, trained, and paid for being right and producing results. People measure our worth by our success. In short, we live in a society that values not humility, but success. And most people have accepted this measuring stick. Unfortunately, it's a trap from Satan. He wants us to measure ourselves by the world's standards, so we keep striving after the shifting image of success. However, as I study the Scriptures, I'm more and more convinced God hates independence above all. It leads to selfishness, probably the root of all sin. Our independence authors and fosters innumerable acts of rebellion, disobedience, and sin. God hates independent attitudes but loves a dependent, obedient spirit. Dependency on Him is fostered in humility, fathered through pain, and brought to complete fruition in Jesus Christ. That's why God allows circumstances we would never choose for ourselves. He wants to teach us to depend upon Himself. He wants us to learn obedience in hard times.

FOLLOWING THE PATTERN

A man came to talk with me recently who was unhappy with his job, having some struggles at home, and drowning in debt. He told me he couldn't see how the pieces of his life fit together. He'd been a Christian about a year and had been hoping to have conquered a lot of these problems by now. So I told him he was not alone. We live in a time when it takes all of our energy just to hold things together each day with our families, careers, and personal goals. Living like this does not result in the abundant life Jesus talked about in John 10:10 or the peace referred to in Philippians 4.

But the fact remains that, even in difficult circumstances, God is there with you. Even when you feel abandoned, the Spirit of God is at work on your behalf. As a Christian, you will be with Him forever. So I looked at the man and said, "I know you feel you are in a difficult situation, but in reality you have a tremendous inheritance. Ephesians chapter one tells us you have been bought with a price, you have been redeemed, you are forgiven, loved, and a child of God. You're going to inherit eternity one day. That's your position in Christ, and the challenge we have is living out that position in Christ through our daily walk."

His eyes brightened at the thought that he wasn't alone, so I continued: "What I've found essential is to spend time with a coach. The Bible says it is not good for man to be alone (Genesis 2:18), so He gave us woman, and encouraged us in Hebrews 10:24-25 to stimulate each other to love and good deeds and to get together with other believers. Maybe you're going through hard times just so you can grow. Maybe you've come to me because God wants *me* to grow. I've found a great benefit from meeting with other men who are ahead of me in the spiritual walk, so if you'd like a one-on-one relationship where you can go through this with a brother, I'm all yours." He readily agreed, and our sessions enriched both our lives.

Friend, God wrote the Scripture for our training. It's there to help us through the hard times. While I was in Vietnam, I learned the importance of training. I stayed alive in Nam largely because I'd memorized the manufacturer's handbook for my machine gun. I probably knew more about that weapon than anyone else in my outfit, except for the man who trained me. There was a time I could take my machine gun apart blindfolded. That's because in training one night, I had to take it apart, put it on my bunk, then crawl onto the bunk and sleep on all those parts. You get to know the parts of a machine gun pretty well when you sleep with them all night! I knew what to do with the gun when it jammed. The manufacturer taught us how to do that.

One day on the side of a mountain, when we engaged an enemy column, I had to do just that. My buddy Ralph and I were on the side of the hill, blasting away with the machine gun, firing 550 rounds a minute, when the weapon jammed and stopped working. I'll never forget that feeling. Ralph and I stood together with machine gun fire coming in on us and AK-47 fire hitting all around us, risking our lives to get the weapon working again. We'd been trained well; in the heat of the moment, in probably 50 seconds, we cleared the gun, took the bent cartridges out of the breech, and got it running again. All the while bullets were pelting the dirt nearby as we stood on the side of this burned-out mountain, wide open to enemy fire. But we had learned the manufacturer's handbook. We knew what to do when the crisis came, and we stuck together as men trained and committed.

That's what men and women need to do today. They need to spend time in the Manufacturer's Handbook with one another, to understand what the Maker said about what to do when our life jams. What happens when our rapid fire is so strong the barrel gets too hot to project the rounds properly and accurately? What happens after a battle, when we need to maintain this machine gun? What are the sensitive parts, and why do we always carry an extra firing pin? That's exactly the sort of nitty-gritty details God addresses in His book. He talks about marriage, money, and what's really important in life. If we'll read it with a brother or sister in Christ, we'll both learn how to survive the tense moments.

When I was in the Marines, not only did I have the manufacturer's handbook, I also had a man to walk beside me and help me understand it. His name was Ralph Crossley, a big-city African-American guy who had flunked out of the University of Michigan and joined the Marines. I was a white guy from suburban America who had flunked out of Ohio University, so we had a little in common. Ralph trained me. He showed me what to do when the gun jams. He was the best gunner around; when I came along, he helped me become the best so he could go home. The truth is, we stayed alive with one another.

Discipleship is simply two people pairing up to study the Manufacturer's Handbook together and apply those principles to their lives, especially when life is jamming. It's changed the way I deal with my children, the way I interact with my wife, the way I spend my money, and the way I view my job. Reading God's Handbook has given me the principles; seeing them at work in the lives of people has given me the confidence to put them into practice. When everything is starting to explode, I know I can always rely on God's Word and my mentors. Nothing in my life is the same now that I know Christ, and nothing has helped me more than to go through tough times with tough men. Of course, that didn't happen overnight. The Lord used those difficult circumstances over time to shape me into the kind of man He wants me to be.

QUESTIONS FOR DISCUSSION

1. Why does God allow Christians to experience hard times?

2. What hard things have you endured?

3. Were they brought about by your own actions, or did they arise from circumstances outside your control?

4. What helped you get through those hard times?

5. What have you learned from your tough times?

CHAPTER 13

Knowing GOD'S WILL

*J*ack was sorting through business problems in his mind as he drove along the interstate. He was just wasting time between two appointments, trying to decide with which contractor he should do business. Suddenly he noticed he was in front of one supplier's office. He thought to himself, "Hey, that must be a sign! God must have put me here."

Ron, sitting in his office, pored over the latest episodes in his marriage. "I know God wants me to be happy. He loves me more than anything. But I'm not happy; I really think I need to make a change. Maybe it's all right if I divorce Janie— if it will make me happy."

Clete was trying to decide which job offer to take. Nelson Investments had made him a good offer, but The Stronghold Corporation had also made a play for his services. He had spent a little time praying about it, but had not been able to decide. Now he was being pressed for an answer by both companies. Picking up his Bible to read for inspiration, Clete noticed it fell open to Psalm 27:1: "The Lord is the *stronghold* of my life." (NIV) Taking that as a message from God, he accepted the position at The Stronghold Corporation.

It may sound funny to you, but these are all true stories. I've seen all three of those situations take place as Christians have begun their search for "God's will." But believers often use the term "God's will" when they talk about the future, but few ever define it. Because of this, some Christians become downright superstitious about the role God's will plays in their lives. In doing so, they fall into an ancient trap: trying to divine the mind of God.

Men have always wanted to be able to divine the mind of God. They have studied the stars and tried "reading" the entrails of sheep, searching for some way to get in touch with a supernatural being to guide them. As Christians, we already have direct access to God, so any sort of divination is pointless. More than that, the Bible warns us not to be involved in those sorts of practices. Yet when you talk to Christians today, you will often hear people speak of God as though He is some sort of magic genie they just need to find the right incantation to contact. That's why they'll use a "promise box" or let the Bible fall open to a page and take that as a "sign." In my view, God rarely uses signs. But He is there, guiding and speaking to us through His Holy Spirit. Since it is important we understand what the will of God is, it is also important to help those you disciple know how to follow His will.

The three guys I mentioned in the above illustrations were all believers being discipled, but all had some room for growth. When Jack talked to me about his inspiration regarding his business suppliers, I tried to describe the concept of God's will. The Lord's will isn't some sort of secret that's hidden from us. Ephesians chapter one tells us God "made known to us the mystery of His will according to His good pleasure, which He purposed in Christ to be put into effect when the times will have reached their fulfillment" (verse 9). That passage goes on to say God "works out everything in conformity with the purpose of His will" (verse 11). In other words, God is concerned about the details of our lives, and He is at work in history, arranging things in ways to bring glory to Him. It doesn't make any sense for God to hide the very thing He wants us to accomplish.

I explained to Jack that he should make his business decisions based on prayer and the commands of Scripture, not on the simple circumstance of accidentally passing by a supplier's office. After our discussion, Jack decided to search the Scriptures for God's principles of decision making. He found Matthew 6:33 gave great guidance: seek the kingdom of God, not simply financial reward in this life. Jack realized in relying upon an accidental circumstance, he was taking the easy way out rather than the best way. He was making the decision based on self-interest rather than on competency or price. After more prayer and study, he decided God had really given him the answer on this issue.

When Ron asked me about his marriage, I told him his happiness was not God's first concern. Ron's *holiness* was what the Lord was most concerned about. We are to seek God's righteousness, whether it makes us feel happy or not. Then I showed him Malachi 2:16, where God gives the very clear message, "I hate divorce." We then looked at Bible passages that offer instruction on divorce, I told Ron I didn't think he had any biblical grounds for divorcing his wife; instead, he had a commitment to remain married, and within his marriage God could provide the fulfillment and happiness he sought. God is more concerned about the condition of our hearts and our obedience than He is about our feeling good.

"If you love Me, you'll keep My commandments," the Lord said. He wants our obedience ahead of our good pleasure. Ron admitted he had not spent much time in the Scriptures looking at God's commandments regarding marriage. In talking it over, he came to understand his role in the marital relationship and he realized he had not loved his wife "as Christ loved the church." As he confessed this to the Lord, he resolved to try again, this time with the Spirit's power.

Likewise, when Clete told me how he had come to his decision, I suggested the Bible was not a book of spells to be used like Aladdin's magic lamp. The Bible is God's Holy Word. We are to read it thoroughly so the Lord's voice can speak to us through it. I recommended he spend more time studying his Bible and praying over his decision, and he agreed to do so. Sometimes as a spiritual parent you'll have to help people think through God's will.

GOING MY WAY

The real problem in determining God's will is that most people aren't in very close contact with the Father; consequently, they rely on their own selfish desires. Before I became a Christian, my favorite activity was doing what I wanted to do. As I began to study the Bible and befriend godly people, I found doing my own thing was really treason against the King. After confessing my sins and coming into a relationship with God through Christ, I realized the wisdom of going His way and chose God's path for my life. But after having been saved by faith, I slipped right back into my old habits of trying to be sanctified by works.

I set out in the Christian life trying to do what I thought was needed to impress the Lord, to impress people around me, or to accomplish what I thought would make me look good. However, I soon discovered this "works" mentality ignored God's will for my life. His will for me involved a plan by which He could use me and gradually conform me into the person of the Lord Jesus Christ. He would bring things to me to encourage that process, the "working out of my salvation," as Paul put it. But every day I seemed to struggle with the option, "Am I going to do it my way, or am I going to seek God's will for my life?"

Every Christian has to make this choice. Do we follow our natural leading or the supernatural leading of the Spirit? Do I do what I want to do or what the Lord tells me to do? Will I be going my own way or following the way of the Lord? That's the first issue we have to face in discussing the will of God. He wants us to die to ourselves and be born again in Him, relying totally on His guidance. But this means giving up what I want. It's a tough choice, and I have to get reminders time after time that the Lord's way is always better than my own way. It may not be easy, but it is best.

Ken and Karen were wonderful Christians, and there was a time when their home was at the top of the heap. Their kids were sweet and involved in Christian activities and there was always something exciting going on at their place. Ken, a very competent lawyer from a fine school, had a strong practice with a large firm demanding more time than he thought should be devoted to work, so he took the big step of going out on his own to reduce his long hours. The problem was that Ken, while involved in many ministry efforts and a very competent lawyer, was generally inattentive to his family's needs. He was an excellent provider, wasn't involved in any secret sin, and always spoke highly of his wife and children, but he didn't seem to connect with them. Karen was a conscientious, loving mother who had an excellent education and was always interesting to talk with. However, after a few minutes of conversation I would always hear a few barbs about Ken's long hours, his involvements away from home, and all the time he gave to help with things at church.

You see, Ken wanted to do what Ken wanted to do. He was always first to arrive at ministry functions and the last to leave, and his wife was getting tired of it. Pretty soon Ken was volunteering to do *pro bono* work for Christian causes, which meant he was busy in the courtroom but making no money for his work. He was getting pats on the back from the Christian community that boosted his self-esteem, but I don't believe he was really doing what God wanted him to do.

When the financial pressures increased, Karen finally started putting her foot down, demanding he get untangled from his ministry involvements. But Ken didn't want to give up the one thing he enjoyed most. He wanted to keep doing the things he enjoyed—and he could fall back on the excuse it was all "work for the Lord." Their Christmas card came back this year because Ken and Karen, longtime Christians, are divorced. It wasn't adultery, alcoholism, or abuse that caused the breakup—but an unwillingness to give up doing things his own way.

GOD'S PROGRAM OF GUIDANCE

In one sense, following God's will is really a matter of trust. If you trust that God loves you and wants what is best for you, you will find it easy to follow Him. The primary purpose in God's plan is to make you like Jesus Christ. This is the work He's doing in my life; my part is to get to know and better follow the model. God's will can be made clear through reading, hearing, studying, memorizing, and meditating on God's Word and through talking with God and His people. As the great man of faith, George Muller, once said, "through prayer to God, the study of the Word, and reflection, I come to a deliberate judgment according to the best of my ability and knowledge, and if my mind is thus at peace and continues so after two or three more petitions, I proceed accordingly."

Chip MacGregor worked on a book some years ago entitled, *Finding the Will of God*.[4] In it, Chip and Dr. Bruce Waltke put forth the idea that we don't "discover" the will of

God. If God really loves us, He won't hide what is best for us. A loving father doesn't hide his desires from his children, then hope the kids can somehow search in the right places to find them or discipline them when they guess wrong. But that's how many people in the church think about the will of God. We talk about it as though it were a giant game of "find the penny," searching everywhere in hopes of discovering some lost treasure God is keeping from us. That's the wrong perspective.

I've known men who flipped through the pages of their Bibles, stopped and pointed to one page, and claimed the word to which they were pointing as God's command to them for the day. I know a woman who decided to become a missionary to the Philippines because her car broke down by the Philippine embassy and she took it as "a sign from God." We've all known people who have used promise books, signs, and all sorts of gimmicks to "find" God's will. "If I could only discover God's will," they say, sounding suspiciously like someone who has been duped by the enemy. God isn't a manipulator, nor is He a genie. We don't do something magical to make Him appear and tell us His will. The New Testament offers no command to "find" God's will, nor can you find any instruction on how to go about finding His will. There is no mysterious secret for getting a glimpse of the Almighty. In fact, in Acts chapter eight, Simon Magus was severely criticized for doing just that.

The New Testament deals with the issue of God's will. We are told that as we walk close to the Lord, it becomes clear (see Romans 12:2). Paul says nothing about trying to magically determine God's will. Instead he points out that people who walk close to the Lord will recognize His guidance.

The "will of God" refers to His immutable decrees and His plan for each of our lives. The things that are His will are

---

4. *Finding the Will of God*, Drs. Bruce Waltke and Chip MacGregor, Gresham, OR; Vision House, 1995.

those that are pleasing or right to the Lord. We generally refer to the will of God when we're looking for help in a particular situation, but that's just one small part of the larger picture. Rather than praying to "find" God's will, which is really just a search for some greater authority, we ought to help our disciples understand God's program of guidance. The Lord has put together several specific steps for leading His people.

First, we have His Word, the Holy Bible. The Scriptures are given to us to help us know the Lord, so that is the first place to look. Paul said to Timothy, "But as for you, continue in what you have learned and have become convinced of, because you know those from whom you learned it, and how from infancy you have known the Holy Scriptures, which are able to make you wise for salvation through faith in Christ Jesus" (2 Timothy 3:14-15, NIV). In the next verse he goes on to tell us that Scripture is "God-breathed" and that it equips us for "every good work." None of these benefits can be reaped if we don't read our Bibles. It is God's tool for shaping your life, the special method God chose for revealing Himself. There is no better way to experience God than by reading His living Word. If the person you are discipling struggles with knowing God's plan, encourage him to take out his Bible and start reading.

"See that no one repays another with evil for evil, but always seek after that which is good for one another and for all men. Rejoice always; pray without ceasing; in everything give thanks; for this is God's will for you in Christ Jesus," Paul told the church at Thessalonica (1 Thessalonians 5:15-18). Does your Timothy want to know God's will for his life? It is to rejoice, pray, give thanks, and seek that which is good. We come to know the Lord and His will when we spend time in the Bible. Teach your Timothy to read, interpret, memorize, and meditate on the Scriptures. Help him to obey the commands of God in Scripture. That's the best way to be in the will of God.

A HEART FOR GOD

One way to know God's will is by the desires of your heart. The Holy Spirit puts desires in your heart so that by doing what the Spirit would have you do, you please God. Too many people are waiting around for God to show them a sign when all they really need to consider is the desires of their hearts. Again, it doesn't mean God is some sort of genie, granting your every wish, but He is in control of your life. The things you long for in your spirit when in agreement with God's principles are often put there by the Spirit of God. That's what the psalmist means when he says, "Delight yourself in the Lord and He will give you the desires of your heart" (Psalm 37:4).

Many of your disciples will live with the mistaken notion that following their hearts is somehow sinful. But Paul regularly talks about his desires: "I long to see you," he says in Romans 1:11. If a man or woman loves God, the primary desire of that person's heart is to please the Lord. Make sure your desires line up with your faith and with the Bible, but then assume that the desires of your heart are also the will of God.

A third method God uses to guide us, besides the Bible and one's desires, is the wise counsel of mature believers. Many times I have been in situations in which I wasn't sure what to do, and the Lord spoke to me through the counsel of my spiritual parent. Once, when I had to face several decisions about my career, home, and taking care of my family, I became more or less "frozen" with options. That's when Dr. Jim took time to read the Bible and pray with me, talking over the various alternatives. I didn't want Jim to make the decision for me, but I needed him to help walk me through it. He did, and the Lord used Jim to move me down the right path.

Sometimes just listening and letting our Timothys sort through the issue at hand helps them discover God's will. I wish I had Susy's listening ear. Just the other day, she told me about Francis, who called her with a desperate need—a decision had to be made immediately—and she just had to have Susy's advice. Dropping everything for her dear friend, Susy met her at a restaurant where Francis poured out the details of her husband's job and location change, which would change everything for Francis. As Susy listened to Francis over a lunch that grew into an afternoon, except for an occasional "Oh" or comment of sympathy, Susy's "advice" was primarily, "What does John say to that?" or "What do your kids think?" or "What does God's Word have to say?" The day after the long meeting, Francis called, thrilled that Susy had had the right words of questioning, wisdom, and support and repeatedly thanked Susy for her great counsel.

"Wisdom is found in those who take advice," Solomon says in Proverbs 13:10 (NIV). He also noted, "Listen to advice and accept instruction, and in the end you will be wise" (Proverbs 19:20, NIV). Tell your Timothy to read the Bible, consider the desires of his heart, and seek counsel from mature Christians. Instead of waiting for some sort of miracle to happen, instruct him on how he can already tap into the miraculous love and power of God.

CIRCUMSTANCE AND LOGIC

As I said earlier, God has never spoken to me audibly, but He has spoken to me through the Scriptures, the counsel of other people, and the impressions on my heart. He has also sometimes arranged circumstances in a way that they speak so loudly it is as if the Lord were screaming His message over a loudspeaker. I have prayed about problems over a series of days, gone off for periods of prayer with Susy, and brought things before other Christian friends. As I sought God's will, He communicated to me in such a way that a skywriter inscribing the answer across the sky would not have been as plain as what I "heard" God say to me.

There have also been times when I felt a sense of total silence from God and, because of the enormity of the decision or the fact Susy and I did not have oneness of mind, I decided to take no action. I hadn't "heard from God" on the issue yet. Perhaps God wanted me to spend the time in prayer and Bible reading to force my focus back to Him, or perhaps He was waiting for the perfect time to reveal Himself. In our market-driven society, with its emphasis on long-range planning, we sometimes forget that God doesn't have to tell us what He is doing. Paul did not always know where the Lord would lead him, though he tried to make plans based on the guidance he had received. I'm not saying we shouldn't plan, but we should remember God doesn't always reveal the entire plan because then we humans would get lazy and lose our motivation to remain close to Him.

Sometimes my great ideas really are great, but sometimes they're stupid ideas and I just haven't figured that out yet. Susy has a wonderfully gentle way of sometimes saying nothing when I share my latest "great idea." That causes me to wait on the Lord, collect additional information, and give her a chance to sift through the issues. Together we'll take the time to seek the Lord in prayer before making the decision. We probably have not always done what we should have, and undoubtedly we've run ahead of the Lord a few times, but I think we've avoided a number of disasters because we were willing to wait for God to make known His plan in His time.

I firmly believe one of the ways God guides us is through circumstance. There are times He puts us into situations specifically to teach us lessons. For example, the Bible tells us Ruth "chanced" upon the fields of Boaz. God arranged for the circumstances to be right so He could take care of Ruth. Moses "chanced" upon the burning bush because God arranged his circumstances so he would be the right man, in the right place, at the right time. If Moses had arrived earlier, the people of Israel might not have listened. God's power would not have been on him. When the

Scriptures talk about the "fullness of time," they refer to the fact that God brings about our circumstances at just the right moment. We have an unlimited God who can superintend those sorts of things, so remind your disciples nothing happens to a Christian by accident.

While there were many years early in our marriage in which Susy was convinced she had married the wrong man, we now know, having experienced God's handiwork in our marriage, we were made for one another. We didn't get together by accident, and our differences are not the problem. Our differences are really opportunities for God to work through our circumstances and change us to be more like His Son. My weaknesses fit well with Susy's strengths. We are both working together in the Holy Spirit. The day we met in economics class at Southern Methodist University, the last thing on my mind was marriage. I was just back from the Marines, ready to make up for lost time. When I left for Vietnam, hair was short and skirts were long; but upon my return, hair was long and skirts were short and I was living in the flesh. There were lots of pretty girls at SMU besides Susy, and she didn't appreciate what I considered "the finer things in life": alcohol, cigars, dancing, and my brand new GTO. From the time she was in the ninth grade she had wanted to be a lawyer, a goal from which she would not allow herself to deviate for any man. I got good grades to get ahead; she got good grades because she loved school. We were extremely different, but when she walked into economics class that first day, the very first thought that came to my mind was, "Wow! I wonder what kind of a man it would take to marry a woman like that."

Accidents don't happen to Christians. God arranged for us to meet in that classroom at SMU. Our marriage was made in heaven, broken on earth by me, then healed by our heavenly Father as a result of our obedience to Him. God arranges our circumstances in such a way that they will cause us to mature.

QUESTIONS TO ASK YOURSELF IN DETERMINING THE GUIDANCE OF GOD

Have I prayed about it?

What does the Bible say about my situation?

If I am walking close to the Lord, what does my heart tell me?

Have I talked it over with wise Christians I trust?

How has God arranged the circumstances?

Does this make sense?

These questions were inspired by Dr. Bruce Waltke seminar on the will of God.

Wise old Solomon once said, "the race is not to the swift or the battle to the strong, nor does food come to the wise or wealth to the brilliant or favor to the learned; but time and chance happen to them all" (Ecclesiastes 9:11, NIV). I like to map things out and make goals, but I know God has a way of rearranging circumstances so things don't always work out the way I planned them. Still, I know God is always at work on my behalf, and I trust Him regardless of the circumstances. Bad things happen occasionally and I don't always know the reason why, but I trust that the circumstances are for something good.

Don't put your circumstances ahead of the Word of God, but don't ignore them either. God has you in a certain place on purpose. Encourage your disciples to remember, too, that God gave them brains for a purpose. Sometimes we make a decision because it just makes sense. God's will can work through our logic as much as through our circumstances. I hesitate to say that, however, because Scripture is replete with examples where logic failed. It made no sense for

Abraham to sacrifice his son, so by logic he should have refused. But in that case God's specific instruction took precedence over logic. Still, God doesn't expect us to check out mentally when we're making a decision.

Some people have done that. They wait around for some sort of divine intervention, but that rarely occurs. God shares His will with us through the Bible, His providence, mature believers, and our circumstances, but He rarely shares His will through miracles. Paul's Damascus road experience and Peter's escape from prison are the exceptions, not the norm— so rare, they were made part of the New Testament record! God doesn't often have the stars line up to tell you which way to go. He usually guides in more direct and normal ways, and He expects you to follow them.

This pattern ought to be passed on to those we are discipling. Instead of casting lots, our Timothys can make progress in the guidance of the Lord by drawing close to Him. To expect God to somehow supernaturally intervene in the life of a person who refuses to walk close to Him is wrongheaded and anti-biblical. God has already intervened supernaturally in giving us His Word and His Spirit. To ignore these primary interventions in our lives is folly.

SHOULD THINGS BE EASY?

Andy, a new Christian, was struggling in his position of senior officer with his company. As we met for discipleship he expressed his dissatisfaction and decision to leave the firm. He worked for a group of three men who could never agree on important future investments to carry out its vision; virtually no planning had been done in the last two years. The company was floundering from a lack of leadership, and Andy knew his role as vice president of manufacturing would be impossible to fulfill without the product changes that were needed.

As we met to go through *Operation Timothy*, Andy said, "I've been interviewing with other firms and really believe God is leading me out of this company." However, as we talked longer, Andy admitted he had great anxiety about interviewing and no idea, really, what God wanted him to do. He was also concerned about his daughter, who had been diagnosed as diabetic, and the pressures already on his wife.

As we talked, he reasoned that one more change would be hard on his family, so I asked him if he had spent any time alone talking with the Lord for longer than ten or fifteen minutes, praying about this issue. He answered he had not but thought it would be a good idea. I also asked him if he had spent time reading his Bible, to capture God's wisdom on the topic. He and I decided to each spend a week reading Scripture passages dealing with conflict and business issues.

Andy was quite concerned about sharing his troubles with anyone, including his wife, who had enough problems to think about. But after some prayer, he decided that while his wife was busy with special concerns for their daughter, she was also concerned about his future employment and always had great insight into people. He set up a time the two of them could leave their daughter with her mother and get an afternoon off to talk through, pray through, and analyze the position he had in his firm. At our next meeting, we discussed his life purpose and how God was using him.

I asked Andy some tough questions: "Does God necessarily want us to be comfortable in our jobs? Do we expect Him to give us easy jobs while we're on earth? If God is in the process of changing us, will He give us challenges that require us to seek Him and His Word in our daily lives?" As we chatted, we were both struck again with the fact that God never said being a Christian was going to be easy.

At our third meeting, Andy outlined his thoughts and what he had learned from his study of Scripture. He and his wife realized he had made a lot of mistakes in his role with the company. His first step needed to be to go around and apologize to some of the men he worked with to whom he had not listened. He told me he realized God had placed him in that business as a tool to be used. Andy's job was to obey the Lord, not to set himself up with an easy life. He stayed, and it turned out to the best solution imaginable.

WHEN BAD THINGS HAPPEN

Unfortunately, things don't always work out. Sometimes terrible things happen in the lives of believers and we just want to scream out, "Why, Lord?" Knowing accidents don't happen to Christians doesn't make it any easier, though they can eventually draw us closer to Christ. Our friends Brett and Wilma were concerned about taking their two-year-old son Jamie to his grandparents' house because of the party atmosphere they kept. The TV always seemed to be tuned to some lousy movie, and there were beer bottles around the house, but Brett really wanted a date with his wife. Also, his parents had asked for more time with their grandson, promising to be on their best behavior. So after some prayer and consideration, they dropped Jamie off for the evening.

Two hours later, as Brett turned onto his parents' street, he passed an ambulance heading in the opposite direction. Brett pulled into the driveway to find a hysterical group of family and neighbors, who blurted out Jamie had fallen into the pool, apparently unnoticed, and was pulled out by a neighbor. By the time the rescue people got to him, he wasn't breathing. Brett and his wife couldn't get information from his mom and dad, who were hysterical, his father reeking of liquor. Added to the horror of the news was the realization that, once again, his parents had partied with his two-year-old son in the room.

As Brett sped to the hospital, his wife sat sobbing beside him, saying, "Oh no, oh no, it can't be, it just can't be." They had a deep sense they would not see their two-year-old again alive, and their fears were confirmed by the emergency room physician.

What do you say to a man who sits with you at breakfast and asks, "Why did God take my two-year-old boy?" The minister did a tremendous job at the funeral, explaining the sovereignty of God, the creation of life in the hands of the Almighty, and the time the Lord gives each one of us here on the earth. He talked about how we could get to heaven, and where Jamie is now, but I think everyone there—especially Brett and Wilma—continued to ask the question "Why? Why would God allow such a thing to happen?" Since then the relationship with Brett's parents has obviously been strained, but he and Wilma have worked hard to forgive them. They understand that without Christ, his parents don't share the spiritual perspective Christians have. As nonbelievers, Brett's parents have not received power over sin. People without Christ have a harder time keeping their promises, especially with regard to a weakness.

I would like to be able to say the grandparents are now Christians, that many people have come to Christ as a result of God's allowing this tragedy in the loss of Jamie—but that has not happened. Perhaps it will. I imagine many people have watched the husband and wife walk through this incredible pain and not lose their faith, but I don't really know of anyone who has come to Christ as a result of it. His parents still drink. There is still an empty bedroom in their home. It seems the only real result of the entire ordeal has been a terrific amount of pain and many people wanting to know "Why Lord?"

Where was God when this happened? I think the answer has to be He was right there, allowing the events. It doesn't seem fair, but it doesn't negate my faith either. God is God, and the Bible says His ways are not our ways; He has a perspective on eternity we simply cannot comprehend. God's trying to explain all of His decisions to us would be like explaining a computer to an ant—it simply would not be understood. Sometimes bad things happen, without any apparent meaning. We can hurt and ask, "Why?" but we can continue to choose to trust Him and believe He is good.

Job, one of the most righteous men of all (see Job 1:1), became angry with God when he lost everything. He told his friends he wanted to ask God, "Why?" But Job did not lose his faith. He continued to say, "Though he slay me, yet will I trust in him" (Job 13:15, KJV). Sometimes God lets us know exactly why things happen; sometimes He does not give us clear, tangible answers to the pain we've gone through. But He is still God, and I trust He knows what He is doing. Perhaps bad things happen to Christians so the world can see the difference in our response.

Undoubtedly, people have been touched by this family's faith, but Brett says he does not think he will ever be the same. Every time he goes by a playground and sees kids Jamie's age, he thinks about his son and it hurts. I don't think he has received an answer that totally satisfies him. However, he has made a choice to continue on with the Lord and stay faithful to Him. He has a quiet willingness to say, "Yes, Lord, I will follow You." God may choose not to answer all our questions on earth, but God is still God. The best thing we can do in a bad situation is to stand by the people who are hurting and let them know we care.

Bad things will happen to your disciples. At times they will happen to you. Sometimes there will be no apparent reason. The proof of your faith will be if you can look at your Timothy and say, "I don't know why it happened, but I trust God just the same."

QUESTIONS FOR DISCUSSION

1. What would you say to a friend who told you, "Whenever I need to know God's will, I let my hand flip through the pages of my Bible. Wherever it stops, I read and use that as my answer."

2. How do you go about getting guidance from God?

3. Why is prayer and Bible reading essential to understanding God's will?

4. What can you say to someone who has experienced a tragedy and asks, "Why?"

5. How can you help your Timothys as they seek God's guidance in their lives?

PART THREE

Making a
DIFFERENCE

*Y*our job as a discipler isn't over when your Timothy becomes strong in the faith. One of your roles is to make sure the *discipled* becomes the *discipler*. You want to make sure that the Timothy eventually turns into a Paul. A new Christian will have an entire network of non-Christian friends he can lead to the Lord and disciple. Instead of pulling him out of that network, put it to use for the Lord. Typically, when people become Christians, the first thing the church tries to do is pull them out of their social groups, work relationships, and neighborhood groups in order to protect them. We'll throw them into a Christian culture filled with Bible studies and Sunday school groups, hoping to somehow "improve their character." That might make us feel better about the person's character, but it isn't a pattern given to us in Scripture.

The Lord calls us to flee from sin and recognize that our home is with Him, but we are never told to withdraw from this world. As a matter of fact, the Bible says that we are to be *in* the world but not *of* the world. The problem is we get so worried with appearing to be of the world that we forget about being in the world. Even short glances at the lives of Jesus, Paul, Timothy, and Peter reveal that they remained very much in the world, in spite of dangerous and sinful territory. They took their holiness with them as temples of God but remained insiders in their communities. God's plan is to change this world through the use of His ambassadors— and the most effective ambassador is the one who is planted inside a foreign country, not one who separates himself from his represented country. As insiders we have relationships, positions, and reputations that God has given us, and we are to use them to reach people for Him.

Please don't misunderstand what I'm saying. Our lives will certainly change when we meet Jesus Christ. There will no doubt be a few places we no longer visit. Some of our habits and friendships will change. But most of us can continue to be insiders with non-Christian friends without compromising our faith. Seek to leave your Timothys right where they are in their bowling leagues, baseball tournaments, and with boards of directors, so old friends can notice the new life.

Encourage your disciple to begin sharing his faith at work or in his neighborhood. Help him learn how to raise the flag for Christ, tell short stories of how God has worked in his life, and offer his testimony. If your disciple is married to a non-Christian, help him learn how to reveal the love of God to his wife or her husband. All of our disciples ought to know how to multiply their lives. If your Timothys feel like part of a team and get involved in God's work in the world, you'll soon see your spiritual child give birth to others for the family of God.

CHAPTER 14

Taking Your Faith TO WORK

*I*t has been my experience that most people want to be in control of things. They want their work to go along perfectly, ignoring the truth given to us in Genesis 3—that men are cursed to work and toil by the land, and there are going to be thorns and thistles. We think of ourselves too often as purveyors of peaceful success at work when we are actually managers of thorns and thistles. There will always be problems. How are we going to handle them? Will we act as God's ambassadors? Are we willing to work in a way that sets an example to others? If you can teach your Timothy to manage crises in a godly fashion and therefore steer the enterprise in a way that honors the Lord, as well as impacts those around him, you will soon find you have a new group of spiritual babies who need loving care.

A friend of mine, Steve, came to Christ as an adult. He had already built a successful business and was well-known in his city. But when he met the Lord, his life changed. Rather than hiding that change or pulling away from people so his old friends would no longer see him, Steve let everybody know his life was different. He uses his platform as a successful businessman to impact thousands for Christ. His enterprise is operated on godly principles, and his employees and managers know what is different about his life. Steve sets an example to those around him by doing outreach meetings right in his own building. He shares the love of God with the people who work for him. He is helping win and disciple people up and down the halls, and it's largely because he was told by his spiritual parent he'd be most effective for Christ if he *kept his friends and showed them how he had changed.* Like Steve, we need to learn how to take our faith to work.

As I mentioned earlier, before the Lord called Susy home to disciple and teach our children, she was an attorney and Assistant Corporate Secretary for Delta Air Lines during the airline "glory days." This was her mission field, and her job was her pulpit. Susy did not make passing out tracts, taking on Christian issues, or doing public Bible studies her focus at work. Her goal was to work hard, achieve a position of credibility, and let the Lord open doors. In addition to discipling a number of women one-on-one, away from the office, she found one of the most effective ways of impacting her colleagues was to increase their spiritual sensitivity by "raising the flag" of her faith in front of fellow workers with "faith stories."

For example, after Susy had said at lunch that she had prayed for God to give guidance on a particular buying decision, one of the men from the Personnel department said, "You did what?" She explained that God was the best fashion designer and time saver. She explained she prayed about what store to go to and exactly what she needed on a day when little time was available for a working mom for such activity, and how God had led her to exactly what she had been seeking. To this day when she sees that man he says, "I'll never forget that God is even a fashion designer." She also invited some of the men and women to attend outreach meetings put on by the Christian Airline Pilots Association and CBMC.

On the day she left her job, out of concern for the eternal destination for one of the senior officers of the company, she mustered the courage to go to his office. While thanking him for the opportunities afforded by the company over the last ten years, she said she couldn't leave without asking him where he stood eternally with his relationship with Jesus Christ. The conversation went deep, and as she left his office she felt that she had been faithful to share the hope that was in her (see 1 Peter 3:15).

WILL GOD SUPPLY?

You have no doubt seen the bumper sticker that reads, "I owe, I owe, so off to work I go!" You may be able to identify with this. You have a house payment, car payment, college loans, taxes, and you'd like to set something aside for retirement. Everything takes money, and the last time I checked there still was no free lunch. Sometimes we think money runs everything and we have to work to pay for it all. But God owns everything and has promised to take care of those who love Him. Did you know God is the one who established work? In Genesis 1:28, He commanded the man to "fill the earth and subdue it," putting mankind in charge of this world. Verse fifteen of Genesis 2 goes on to say God placed man in the Garden of Eden "to cultivate it and keep it." In other words, the Lord knew man needed a job. God ordained work for man. It didn't show up solely as a result of the fall; it was around even when our relationship with God was perfect. Work was supposed to be a blessed opportunity to participate with God in His enterprises. However, after the fall, work became more difficult. Fatigue and hardship resulted from man's rebellion against God.

To reject God's plan meant man was going to come up with his own plan, which required hard work. Most men I know are simply sick and tired of the "work-to-pay-the-bills-so-we-can-buy-more-stuff" mentality prevalent in modern society. That's why it is sometimes hard to balance the *blessing* of work with the *difficulty* of work. God worked, and so do we. But Jesus said in John 6:27, "Do not work for the food which perishes, but for the food which endures to eternal life, which the Son of Man shall give to you, for on Him the Father, even God, has set His seal." In other words, we don't work solely to feed and clothe ourselves, but because God has set an example of work for us to follow. Work is both a blessing to us and a way to honor God. Philippians 4:19 says God supplies all of our needs, that He is not dependent upon us. With that in mind, help your Timothy recognize there is another purpose to work besides going through the motions so he can pay the light bill.

Actually, God intended work for several reasons. First, our work is a reflection of our relationship with Him. In Romans 12:1, Paul talks about our "spiritual service of worship." That word "service" is more commonly translated "work." When you give your life to the Lord Jesus Christ, everything you do becomes a sacrifice before Him. All of your work—all of your effort—is a form of worship toward the Creator. Therefore the way you perform your job is a reflection of your walk with Christ. That's why Paul exhorts the Corinthians to be "abounding in the work of the Lord" (1 Corinthians 15:58). We are to give our all, trying our best, for this is what the Lord wants us to do.

God also intends for us to work so we can use our provision to help those who cannot work. Ephesians 4:28

reads, "Let him who steals steal no longer; but rather let him labor, performing with his own hands what is good, in order that he may have something to share with him who has need." The blessing from your work should allow you to bless others. That's a great jumping off point for beginning to teach your Timothy about the importance of tithing, sharing, and ministering to others. God has blessed each man and woman with a job; they ought to thank Him for the opportunity and use the proceeds to care for others' needs as well as their own. That "other-centered" concept is a key to helping new believers grow in Jesus Christ. In a selfish world, God promises to take care of our needs, and He commands us to take care of others.

NO PAIN, NO GAIN

Occasionally you will disciple someone who is naturally lazy. Helping him gain a biblical perspective of work can help motivate him. Paul told the believers at Thessalonica that God's people should work and take care of themselves (see 2 Thessalonians 3:12), and he exhorted them to "work in quiet fashion." Paul himself was a tent-maker, moving from city to city working on tents so he could pay his own way in ministry. He understood he had to endure the pain of working if he were to enjoy the pleasure of God's prosperity. We've largely moved away from that model in recent years, so a "part-time pastor" is viewed by the Christian community as not quite being on a par with "professional, full-time" ministers. That's a shame, because Paul set an example for us of earning his own way in the church.

If a man won't work hard, he is in rebellion before God. Our ambition should be "to lead a quiet life and attend to your own business and work with your hands, just as we commanded you, so that you may behave properly toward outsiders and not be in any need" (1 Thessalonians 4:11-12). A Christian who is always in need sets a lousy example. It suggests God won't really take care of all our needs, leading people to conclude Christians are more con artists than converts.

Of course, there are times when a Christian loses employment. God often uses these circumstances to put him through a tough time to help him mature or cause him to demonstrate his faith to those around him. The testing of our faith produces patience, which leads to maturity (see James 1:2-4). Pray for your Timothys who are out of work, and offer encouragement, support, and financial assistance when necessary. Being out of work can take a terrible toll on a man's self-esteem, but remind him that the basis of our worth is not our great accomplishments in this world but the fact that God lives in us.

If one of your disciples feels under-employed or under-challenged, help him remember to view his role as a ministry from God, whatever his role is at the time. The Lord has used some incredibly gifted people in some very simple roles. We aren't working to pay the mortgage. We aren't working to have others tell us how wonderful we are. We are working to bring glory to God. Remember what Paul said to the church at Colossae: "Whatever you do, do your work heartily, as for the Lord rather than for men" (Colossians 3:23). When a man works hard, God establishes for him a platform that can become a pulpit to teach, win, and disciple those with whom God has given him strategic position. We are the church, so let's assume our responsibilities.

YOUR WORK IS A SERVICE

Not only have we elevated "full-time servants" but I think we have also abdicated the true structure of the New Testament church. We have, in effect, gone back to the Old Testament concept of a theocracy, in which it was the priests, on behalf of all the people, who had access to God. We have forgotten that the veil in the Temple, separating people from God's presence in the Holy of Holies, was torn from top to bottom at the time of Christ's death, symbolizing the access each of us has into the presence of God. There is no more need for a priest to act on our behalf because by Christ's act, we have all become priests in our own right, with full faith and authority to represent the King in His work. Many Christians have elevated pastors to the point of making them feel separated and apart from the body, overwhelmed with unrealistic expectations. After all, pastors exist in the institutional church to teach, exhort, and encourage all the priests—that is, *all Christians*—to win and disciple the world for Jesus Christ.

In 1 Peter 2:9, Peter writes, "You are a chosen race, a royal priesthood, a holy nation, a people for God's own possession, that you may proclaim the excellencies of Him who has called you out of darkness into His marvelous light." When we rely on pastors to do all the "spiritual tasks," we become a body of spectators, as opposed to the body of Christ, each one fulfilling a God-given role as a part of His plan to win the world. We hand our friends invitations to meetings and tapes from prominent people when God has actually given us entry to our friends' lives through which they will listen to the truth of the gospel—if we simply will share it.

Your work is a service to God. Whatever job you have, you can be sure the Lord has put you there for a reason—and has put others around you so you can share the truth with people on the path to hell. Your work is your pulpit. It's important for Christians in the 21st century to regain the biblical idea that our work matters to God; whatever we do is done for His glory, and we are to be used at work to reach others. Any concept of work less than that goes against the pattern our Creator instituted in the Garden of Eden.

Jim was a man who had a great mind but little education, having had to drop out of school at an early age. He wasn't a big man so he probably would not have been the first picked for the schoolyard ballgame, and I doubt if he were ever accused of being the life of the party. He had a job that paid a modest salary with the United States Post Office and decided he would redeem his time for the Lord.

Jim had a conviction that God put him at his job for a reason. So instead of complaining, getting into sin, or wasting his time with trivial pursuits, he set upon the goal of learning the Scriptures. He did his job and did it well, pleasing his employer. In his spare time he read his Bible. As well as any man I've ever known, he mastered God's book to an extraordinary degree. He became a purveyor of Scripture. Being with Jim was like being with a Bible junkie, his briefcase and pockets filled with tapes, outlines, and treatises he had written himself that dealt with different aspects of the character of God. Everywhere he went, you knew Jim had been there. You could find a trail of tapes and verses—and, most of all, impacted lives.

When he came to our hometown, we would have him over to meet several couples or share a meal with him and let him teach us something from his study of God's Word. He was a great one to ask questions such as, "Why does God allow pain?" "When is the Lord coming back?" "Why was David called a 'man after God's own heart'?" or, "Who was it that appeared in the Old Testament as God?" He knew the Word of God the way Vince Lombardi knew football.

I remember one morning at the First Baptist Church in Atlanta when Dr. Charles Stanley was dealing with a most difficult subject in one of his wonderful sermons, carefully threading through a thicket of Scripture. I looked over at Jim and he was crying huge tears. They were dribbling down his chin, soaking his tie. I couldn't decide if he was moved by the illustrations of suffering or by the worshipful tone of the service. When I asked him about it, he simply said in a quiet voice, with a smile on his face and tears still streaming from his eyes, "He got it right. He got it all right." God's truth was everything to Jim, and he became an ambassador of truth on the job. He may not have impressed people with his public speaking, but men up and down the west coast of the United

States, throughout Texas and Colorado, in Atlanta, Detroit, Pittsburgh, and Boca Raton, Florida, are involved in the warfare of reaching people for Christ because of Jim Brady.

LIFE AS A TV DINNER

I think one of the biggest pitfalls Christians can fall into is believing the mistaken notion that our work life is somehow separated from our spiritual life. That sort of thinking causes us to leave our values at the door when we leave for work in the morning, then pick them back up when we get home. Many men are not involved in ministry in their communities because, they admit, their work life and reputation do not bring credit to Christ. Too many think about life as though it were a TV dinner: his job is in one neat little compartment, with a divider to keep it from slopping over into his spiritual life, and both are separated from his recreational life, just like the aluminum tray keeps the meat from merging into the potatoes. Christians cannot live that way. Life isn't a TV dinner. Who you are at church ought to be reflected in who you are at work.

I have a friend who is vice president of sales in a large company. About every two weeks he'll call me seeking counsel about something he's being asked to do in his business. The practices are always rationalized on the same basis: everybody does it, we've been doing it for years, no one really cares, it's the only way to get business, and if we don't do it this way we're going to lose business. There's subtle pressure that if you don't comply, you could be "outta here." This particular friend, Nathaniel, has been able to stand up to his business and insist, "I'm not going to do it that way, because that is not the right way to do it"—and God has continually brought in the sales for him. People around Nathaniel are now beginning to trust him because they see his integrity. They're working harder and are more motivated, and now he has a team of men and women working together in righteousness. Even though some of them are not Christians, they are excited about being on a team that stands for something good, one that will not compromise. He has used his integrity to honor the Lord, in the process of building a team of people who admire and want to work with him.

However, it is not always so easy to take a stand for God. Malcolm, who worked in the accounting department of a large firm, noticed his office had regularly been double-billing clients for a particular type of work. When he raised questions about it, he was fired. Maintaining his integrity cost him his job; the Lord allowed him to experience a tough time before enabling him to find another job at a similar salary. However, he now has a tremendous ministry with men who are between jobs, offering hope and encouragement that goes far beyond a career choice. Malcolm has had the opportunity to share his faith in Christ with many men in crisis, and he has seen God use him in a mighty way.

Don't encourage your Timothy to change jobs just because things become tough. We're called to bloom where we are planted. God can use a person willing to take a stand for integrity in the face of opposition. The Old Testament prophet Daniel set a great example for anyone who wants to be a Christian in a non-Christian world. As a young man, his nation was invaded and he was carried off to serve in the court of King Belshazzar. He served faithfully, doing his duty to God and setting an example for others to follow. But when an order was given banning prayers to the Lord, Daniel didn't hesitate to do the right thing. Knowing he had to obey God rather than man, "he went home to his upstairs room where the windows opened toward Jerusalem. Three times a day he got down on his knees and prayed, giving thanks to his God, just as he had done before" (Daniel 6:10, NIV). Daniel knew it would cost him dearly; he was thrown into the lion's den as a penalty. But God honored Daniel's obedience by shutting the mouths of the lions and protecting Daniel from harm. In a hostile environment, your Christian character needs to stand out clearly.

SHARING THE FAITH

When I first became a Christian, I was so overwhelmed with the majesty of the Lord and the incredible peace of the forgiveness of my sins, I wanted to share it with everyone. But I did it in a way that irritated many around me and caused me to be ostracized from the normal routine at the office of going to lunch. It soon got around that "Phil is a fine lawyer, but don't get alone with him because he'll dump Jesus on you." It wasn't long before I figured out I had to find another way to talk with people if I was going to be effective in sharing my faith.

Some of the men from CBMC taught me the principles of lifestyle evangelism presented in the *Living Proof 1* video series. These principles helped me learn how to share my faith through the context of relationships, making the gospel a normal part of my conversation. An old saying points out, "People don't care how much you know until they know how much you care." My colleagues at work didn't know I cared for them; they just thought I wanted to convince them. So I decided to change tactics. Rather than dump the gospel at every chance, I determined to begin developing relationships out of my sincere love for my friends and associates. As I went back to the office with this new training, realizing what I really wanted was to show my love for these people, I found the men in my office grew interested. It became very natural for me to get involved in the lives of people I cared about at work, to let God allow those relationships to develop over time. He wanted me to share the truth of His love with people, but only after I had *shown them His love.*

One of the men at the office was a fine young lawyer who had a great future with the firm but who appeared more interested in nightlife than he was in law practice. I went into his office one day and began to talk about my perspective on success. He was a little taken aback by my conversation. Because I was a senior partner of the law firm and he was one of the "low men on the totem pole," he was noticeably tense, waiting for me to get to the point.

I simply said, "You know, Allen, you are potentially one of the best lawyers ever to have worked for this law firm. There's nothing any of the other partners around here are doing you couldn't do someday . . . but there are probably three or four principles you need to understand if you really want to find success. If you ever want to discuss those with me, give me a call." Then I thanked him for his time, went back to my office, and waited for the knock on my door. Sure enough, moments later Allen was in front of me. "Say, Phil, you know those principles you were talking about? Well, how would you like to go to lunch?" I told him that was a great idea, and we had a chance to develop a mentoring relationship soon after. It began by simply talking to him about the things he would need to know if he wanted to become a competent lawyer; it led eventually to his giving his life to Jesus Christ.

RAISING THE FLAG

Part of the discipleship process is getting our Timothys to the place where they share their faith. You can't really make disciples without involving them in evangelism. As we travel, go out to dinner, and attend business conferences, a lot of lives cross our paths, and we need to see them as divine appointments. God has brought people like this into your life. When this happens, we need to pray, "God, show me what I need to do to reach out to this individual." We all want to be involved in a lasting work—to have a significant impact on the lives of others. Sometimes I'm on a boring flight or trying to enjoy a terrible meal, and I can salvage an otherwise difficult moment by being a part of God's plan for eternity by reaching out to one of the individuals that comes across my path.

Because I spend a lot of time with my natural or spiritual children, it's always a good model to let them see how naturally I can share my faith in Christ. The most effective way to share your faith, I believe, is to wrap it around a personal testimony. When you preach at people, you basically sound like you're telling them what to do. But when you share your testimony, you simply tell the truth about what has happened to you. The focus is on you, your problems, your decision, and your changed life. You aren't telling how they ought to live but explaining about the decisions you've made in your life. Jesus Christ made a difference to you. Rather than telling them what to do, you're showing them what you did, letting the Holy Spirit speak to them regarding conviction of sin and righteousness. Every Christian needs to develop a testimony to present at opportune moments. Actually, I believe every Christian eventually ought to create a one-minute, five-minute, 15-minute, and 30-minute version of his testimony. Sometimes you only have time to give a brief description, while other times you'll be asked to go into great detail. This is very difficult for most people. You can convince a businessman to fly across the country for a million dollar business deal, but when it comes to sharing his testimony, he gets sweaty palms.

An easy way to think about sharing your testimony is to determine that there are different goals depending on the situation in which you find yourself. Sometimes you just want to raise the flag—that is, you want to let people know you're a Christian in an honest, non-judgmental way. For example, it's natural for me to say, "The Lord has been working in my life," or to tell other people about what He has been doing. I'm not asking anyone to repent of sin or turn his life over to Christ, just raising the flag for my faith. I was sitting next to a man on an airplane recently, not engaged in conversation, but occasionally making a friendly comment about things. When he told me he was heading to Atlanta, I said, "Great city! That's where I met the most important person in my life: Jesus Christ." That was all. I didn't whip out a "Four Spiritual Laws" booklet or try to press him for a commitment. I simply dropped a seed, and I pray the Spirit will allow somebody else to water that seed and another person to harvest it one day.

I really try to raise the flag with my neighbors. Christians in this country have a tendency only to focus on *confrontational evangelism*, using surveys, tracts, and cold calls to press people for a spiritual decision. That strategy worked well when we were dealing with people who had been raised with a religious heritage. Half of Americans today were not raised with religion, thus cannot be reached the same way. Many of them don't even speak our language—words like "sin" and "righteousness" are foreign to them. Since confrontational evangelism does not work in many circumstances today, we shouldn't be confronting people so much. Confrontation will probably turn people off unless God has been cultivating His Word in their lives, preparing them for a gospel message. To be more effective, we ought to be focusing on *relational evangelism*, using flag-raising stories to introduce spiritual things. I often rent a car from the same Avis dealership, and I have become friendly with the man working the counter. A few weeks ago, I was rushing to get to an appointment and in his hurry to serve me he made a mistake on my bill. "Whoops!" he said. "I made a mistake. It'll take me just a moment to fix it."

"No problem," I replied. "At least those are the kind of mistakes we can easily fix. In my line of work, I often meet men who have made huge mistakes and nothing can fix them."

"What line of work are you in?" he asked as he typed on the computer.

"I tell people about the Lord Jesus Christ. And if a man dies without knowing Him, nothing can ever correct it."

"Really?" he asked, rather interested.

"Yes. He actually changed my life and has given me a peace I never thought possible in this pressure-packed world." But then the man at the counter was done, so I just smiled, thanked him, picked up the bill, and headed out the door. I didn't have to press him for a decision. I'm establishing a relationship, so I know the Lord will give me or someone else another chance to share with that man further. All I was doing was raising the flag.

TELLING FAITH STORIES

Another aspect of sharing your testimony with others is to tell faith stories. Encourage those you are discipling to begin sharing their new life with their old friends. Some people will reject them, just as they reject Christ, but others will be attracted by what Paul called the "aroma" of the gospel. They'll see a life change that is positive and peaceful, and become interested in knowing more about the Lord Jesus. To help bridge the gap between Christianity and culture, help your Timothys develop one-to-five-minute faith stories. For example, last night a waiter mentioned he was in the army, so we started to talk. He mentioned he was unmarried but had met a girl he really liked. I said, "You better be sure you know a lot about her before you marry." When he looked at me in surprise, I added, "My wife thought she knew a lot about me before we were married, but on the second night of our honeymoon she was ready to divorce me." That was a perfect hook to catch his interest, relating to him as a single man concerned about marrying the right person. People today don't want to divorce, so there I was, explaining how I had destroyed our marriage and how I came to Christ and was changed, thus saving our relationship. A man who probably would never have stepped into church sat for five minutes and heard a clear presentation of the gospel. But the reason it worked was because I wasn't telling him how to change, *I was telling him how I had changed.*

A non-Christian can argue against my theology, but it's really hard to argue against my life experience. Rather than trying to convince him of the facts about Jesus, I simply tell a short faith story that illustrates how Jesus has worked in my life. Since people enjoy stories, they'll usually listen. Remember, the goal is to move a man or woman a little closer to Christ, not to get him to commit his life (yet). The decision to accept the Lord Jesus as personal Savior isn't always one big spontaneous step a person takes, where he hears the gospel message and realizes he has been going the wrong direction for forty years. The decision to follow Christ is often made following a number of small steps, starting with simply becoming aware of God and the fact He is at work in men's and women's lives today.

MOVING TOWARD THE LORD

It was while traveling on airplanes that I discovered something important: most people are usually concerned about at least one of six issues. A person either has a problem with his marriage, kids, business, finances, spiritual walk, or health. Remember, this is a fallen world and everyone is struggling somewhere. When I'm talking with a man on an airplane, I'll just ask him those questions: "Tell me about your business."

"Oh, my business is going great. We've doubled our profits."

"That's good. So, are you married?"

"Yes, she's a wonderful woman."

"How's your health?"

"My health is great. I run three miles a day and do fifty pushups."

Having covered most of the other possibilities, I'll say, "Do you have any kids?"

There is a long pause...and then finally, "Yeah...in a way."

That's when I know I've hit the right button. "Tell me about your kids."

"Which ones do you want to hear about: hers, mine, or ours?" Soon I'm into a tremendous discussion about the life needs of that man. As he pours out the story of his rebellious son who's doing stupid things, I'll say, "Look, I was once a stupid son. Did stupid things. I almost got a bunch of teenagers killed in a car, driving drunk one night. But I finally found the answer I was searching for. That answer totally changed my life." The man will often put down his drink and ask, "What was that?" Then I tell him a faith story about what Jesus Christ has done in my life.

TELLING YOUR STORY

Every person needs to be able to explain why he is a Christian and how he came to know Christ. The value of doing this with your Timothy is that he begins to see how a conversation about the Lord can be as natural as a conversation about his work or his family. The most effective way is to wrap it around your personal story. First, *tell what your life was like before you met the Lord.* Second, *tell how you met Him.* Third, *tell how your life has changed since becoming a Christian.* Anyone can use this outline to create his own story of meeting God.

If you were raised in a godly Christian home and accepted the Lord at a young age, praise God for His protection! Never feel sorry you don't have the dynamite testimony of being saved out of some heinous sin—instead, rejoice that God kept you from having to experience that sort of degradation. For you, a better way to think about sharing your testimony is to *focus on a key issue*. Chip MacGregor became a Christian at a young age. Rather than telling a story about being saved from drugs or being turned around in mid-life, Chip talks about two things: purpose and loneliness. Usually he will share his testimony by talking about purpose. All men desire a purpose for their lives, and only Christ can give life real meaning and purpose. They'll try to find it in success, in causes, or in material pleasures, but they always end up feeling empty. Chip's purpose in life comes from knowing Jesus Christ.

If the person he is talking with seems focused on feeling lonely or friendless, Chip has another version of his testimony to deal with loneliness. His father committed suicide when Chip was young, and he struggled with the feeling of being left alone. But Christ moved into Chip's life as his best friend, and he no longer worries about loneliness. These two stories present the gospel and describe how Chip came to know the Lord. If you came to Christ at an early age, think about the key issues involved in your decision and base your story on those issues. You never know what issues are going to impact another.

A lawyer I worked with was never interested in attending a CBMC luncheon because he felt he couldn't connect with the speakers. He was a real academic and didn't have any interest in hearing captains of industry talk about their faith. However, one time we had scheduled a Navy pilot who was going to speak about being shot down over Vietnam and how his survival later resulted in his coming to Christ. I figured the speaker's life and my friend's life did not coincide at all, since they were vastly different kinds of people and their life experiences seemed totally unrelated. But in simple obedience, I invited this lawyer just as I had every month. To my surprise, he agreed to go with me. After the luncheon, I went back to his office to see what he thought of it. He was almost jumping up in the air with enthusiasm. "That man's life was *exactly like my life*," he told me. "I can't believe you invited me to hear a speaker whose problems and issues would so mirror mine." Of course, I was stunned, realizing my plans never seemed to succeed but God's always do. His ways are certainly not my ways. That very day the lawyer prayed to receive Christ.

When my daughter Anna was ten, she gave her testimony and said, "I became a Christian when I was five years old. Before that, I remember I used to tell lies. I had a hard time speaking the truth. I would make up things because I didn't like myself. Now I know that my poor self-image was caused by my not knowing Jesus Christ. When I gave my life to Him, He changed me completely. Now my confidence level is high enough for me to speak to groups and talk about my faith because I understand God sees me as being valuable. The God of this universe loves me enough to die for me, and knowing that has changed even my young life." Having been raised in a Christian home is not a handicap when it comes to giving a testimony. Think through why you believe, and talk about your reasons.

LEARNING TO LOVE PEOPLE

The Lord said, in essence, "If you are ashamed of Me, I'll be ashamed of you" (see Luke 9:26). In my view, too many Christian men and women act like they are ashamed of their faith. They hide it at work, refusing to talk about it for fear of what someone else might think. But we ought to desire others to think about our faith, for it offers people the only real hope they'll ever have in this life. In Romans 1:16, Paul says, "For I am not ashamed of the gospel, for it is the power of God for salvation to everyone who believes." We don't share our testimonies to get another notch in our spiritual guns but because we love people. Those men and women you work with who do not know the Lord are headed toward an eternity apart from God. Only a hardened man cannot be moved by that thought. We are to be lights in the darkness, spreading both the love and the words of the gospel to a dark world. If you are going to be a discipler, you need to talk naturally about your faith and regularly raise the flag, tell faith stories, and share your testimony. But more importantly, you have to *love people*, or none of your words will mean anything.

One of the first things someone learns about me when we first meet is that I love my wife. Susy is a wonderful gift from God, and I want everyone to know that. I also think it is very natural in my social relationships for people to understand I love the Lord and that He has changed my life. People I've known a long time have seen a change in me. They know I wasn't always this way. But my long-term friendships have posed some of the hardest challenges for me to talk spiritually because I tended to damage relationships trying to persuade the person of the truth of the gospel. Long-term relationships have lots of history and often lots of baggage. So as I drop comments about Jesus Christ into my conversations with old friends, I sometimes feel as though I'm coming across like a hammer instead of a loving hand. I have to make sure I am honest but not too eager to change others. I have to make certain my love comes across stronger than my reasons.

One of my close friends, Brent, was known as a congenial, life-of-the-party businessman who came to Christ when he asked for help in overcoming an addiction to alcohol. One of the many nice things about Brent is, that after becoming a Christian, he didn't turn his back on all his non-Christian friends. I've seen Brent in all different kinds of settings—one-on-one lunches, large groups, board meetings. He is always the same. He has absolutely no fear of groups that hate Christ. He is not put off by "wretched sinners." He still loves a good laugh, and he is loved by scores of people who do not know Christ. When they're around Brent, they feel friendship, acceptance, and warmth without condemnation or judgment. People can tell Brent loves them, and it's because he hasn't forgotten he went down the same road those folks are traveling.

Brent and I went to dinner one time in an area I thought would be new to him. In fact, I'd hoped to introduce him to a man I thought Brent could help. But as soon as we hit the door everyone from the owner to the waiters came up and slapped him on the back, greeting him warmly. Everybody already knew Brent—as a matter of fact, some of them had been to a Bible study in his home. No one noticed we didn't order a bottle of wine and we didn't make any big thing about praying before the meal. Brent is an insider all over town with businessmen and those in the restaurant industry. He ministers to God's lost sheep—those who are hopelessly entangled in sin. His easygoing manner causes people to open up to him and hear the message that Jesus Christ is the answer to their problems. His testimony flows out of his mouth and life as easily as a famous football player would tell a story about catching a game-breaking catch.

But the most amazing thing is that people just want to be around Brent. They want to have what he has. He is one of the best advertisements for the new life in Christ I've ever seen. While he hates sin, he exudes love in every way for sinners. He avoids speaking about eschatology, predestination vs. free will, or any other theological argument. I'm sure he has deep convictions about politics, abortion, and other issues, but I've never heard him publicly debate them. His central purpose is to represent his homeland—the kingdom of God—to lost friends and business associates. Brent has kept his insider status because, as he told me one time, "I have a burden for those I love to know the One who loves them." He takes his faith to work and is willing to see people the way God sees them. Brent is an insider making a difference with all who know him.

That's exactly what Christ is calling us to be. We are insiders—working at our jobs, loving people, and sharing our faith so we can lead others to the truth. You have to love people, and you have to be able to talk about the Lord. If you find you really don't have a heart for others, it's time to get down on your knees and spend some time in prayer, asking for the Lord to fill your heart with love. If you find you can't talk about your faith, it's time to get out a pencil and paper and begin putting some thoughts down so you'll be ready when the opportunity presents itself. As Peter put it, "Always be prepared to give an answer to everyone who asks you to give the reason for the hope that you have" (1 Peter 3:15, NIV).

Christian, set an example for those you are discipling. Proverbs says people perish without vision so share with them your vision for leading colleagues, friends, and family members to the Lord. Show them how you raise the flag and share your testimony, and help them to do the same. Until a person sees and begins to develop a hunger to reach people for Christ, he will not be a disciple.

WRITING YOUR TESTIMONY

1. Speak to God, and ask Him to speak through you.

2. Follow a three-point outline: life *before* Christ, *how you met* Christ, and life *after* receiving Christ.

3. Start with an interesting sentence and offer a good conclusion.

4. Include relevant, thought-provoking personal experiences. Give enough detail to arouse interest.

5. Use some Scripture verses to help you explain the gospel clearly.

6. Avoid negative statements about others and Christian jargon like "sanctified" and "redeemed."

7. Build your testimony around a theme—something characteristic of your life.

8. Lift up Christ as the only means of eternal life.

CHAPTER 15

Bringing Your Faith HOME

A friend of mine has a sign in his office that says, *"Success in marriage consists not only in finding the right mate, but in being the right mate."* I realize that not everyone reading this is married; but if you are, you should realize that most married people who accomplish great things for God have successful, fulfilling marriages. A bad marriage will drain your physical life, your spiritual life, and your emotional life. It is absolutely imperative for you to instill in your Timothy the hope that his marriage can be fulfilling and give him a vision for impacting his family. You can do so only by modeling this fulfillment and impact.

BUILDING A RELATIONSHIP

You don't build a house overnight, and you can't expect to build a solid marriage immediately. But even a damaged, hurting marriage can be healed by the holy love of God expressed through the attitudes and action of a Christian man or woman. Scripture offers a beautiful picture of what marital love should be like in Ephesians chapter 5, where Paul says the marital relationship ought to mirror the relationship of Christ and the church:

> "Husbands, love your wives, just as Christ also loved the church and gave Himself up for her; that He might sanctify her, having cleansed her by the washing of water with the word, that He might present to Himself the church in all her glory, having no spot or wrinkle or any such thing; but that she should be holy and blameless. So husbands ought also to love their own wives as their own bodies. He who loves his own wife loves himself; for no one ever hated his own flesh, but nourishes and cherishes it, just as Christ also does the church . . . and let the wife see to it that she respect her husband"
>
> (Ephesians 5:25-29, 33).

How did Christ love the church? Sacrificially. He *gave* Himself. He put the needs of the church ahead of everything, even His own life. He protected the church, kept it holy, and made sure to keep Himself holy, too. Paul says Christ loved the church as if it were His own body. Men today should be able to relate to this imagery. In our culture, we take great pains to take care of our bodies and make them look good. You should have that same pride and concern for your wife, making every effort to help her grow in godliness.

As you look through all the practical commands Paul gives men and women in Ephesians chapters 4 and 5, you will find a number of things that apply directly to marriage. For example, Paul says to speak the truth in love. Don't be harsh and don't lie, but lovingly communicate with your mate. He says to be angry but not to sin. Allowing anger to fester gives Satan an opportunity to invade your life, so learn to focus on the problem in your marriage without attacking your partner.

Near the end of chapter 4, Paul says to use your words to build up rather than tear down your mate. He urges us to be kind and compassionate and forgiving, getting rid of all malice and slander. Our mouths ought to be tools of blessing in a marriage, not weapons of destruction. We are to be holy, imitating God and living a life of love. There ought to be not even a hint of impurity or immorality. In short, Paul is telling us to live like Jesus Christ if we want to live godly lives and experience great marriages. The actions he encourages are building blocks for a successful marriage.

Paul tells husbands to love their wives and the wives to respect their husbands. Both of those are hard to do in our selfish society. For a man to love his wife means he will put her needs first, rather than his own—not a terribly popular activity these days. For a wife to respect her husband, she will have to submit to his authority—something every feminist group in America is preaching against. It's hard to put these ideas into practice, but without them the marriage can never be what God intends it to be.

SELFISHNESS AND HUMILITY

The core issue in a strained marriage relationship is usually this: *Who will win?* If either person is intent on *winning*, the marriage is in trouble. Each will fight to get his or her own way, to achieve his or her own successes. But if each person wants to please the other and honestly desires for the *partner* to "win," the relationship can grow into maturity in Christ. That may be the hardest task in the world, especially in American society. Everything in our culture stresses the importance of selfishness—even advertising:

"You deserve a break today" and *"You're* worth it." Looking out for number one is the philosophy of our society, and greed has become god. In the midst of this sort of a worldview, God's Spirit says to us, "Do nothing out of selfish ambition or vain conceit, but in humility consider others better than yourselves" (Philippians 2:3) (NIV). Our culture rejects that sort of teaching. Our urban areas are caught up in the message everyone needs to earn "respect," so the notion of humbly serving others and treating them as better than ourselves isn't very popular.

Yet that's exactly what Christ has called us to do. Without humility in a marriage, you will have two people demanding their own rights. Without humility, you will have two people wanting their own ways. Without humility, you will have *two people* when God's ideal for marriage is for the two to become *one*.

Brother, manifest humility. Set an example of service. Let your disciples see you considering others better than yourself. If they see your sacrifice, they will have a model to follow. And more than anything else, *let those you disciple see how you treat your wife or your husband*. I don't think anything I do has more of an impact on the men I disciple than to allow them to get an in-depth look at my relationship with Susy. Sister, show respect and forgiveness for your husband, not just in his presence, but when you are sharing with your Timothy.

Keep in mind that most people have not seen many good marriages. Many of their parents didn't model a good marriage, even if they came from "Christian" homes. Most of their family members, friends, and co-workers don't model marriage as God intended it. I'll even venture to guess that many of the people in ministry who have worked with your disciples have not set an example of a submissive, loving, fulfilling marital relationship. *So you have to do it.*

This doesn't mean that you are expected to model a perfect marriage. No couple has one of those. I sometimes still struggle with being sweet and patient with Susy when I am under stress, but all is not lost when you have an argument. Just model for others your steps of humble repentance and share with those you are discipling your commitment to continue growing in your marriage until you are with the Lord.

I can't think of anything else I've said in this book that has more life-changing potential than the simple act of modeling a growing marriage. A friend of mine is a successful youth pastor, and he tells me his greatest impact with teens has been simply opening up his home so young people can observe his relationship with his wife. It seems they seldom get to see good marriages any more, so by allowing people to see what a good marriage is like, he is taking a major step in the discipleship process.

THE NEEDS IN MARRIAGE

Everybody has different needs, but a good marriage is marked by two people each seeking to meet the partner's needs first. Some people need acceptance; others need affection. Some need security more than anything else, while others need respect or approval. Ask your Timothy what he needs most from you and what he needs most in his marriage. Sometimes the key to strengthening a relationship is simply asking the other person what he or she needs, then providing for that need. In *Unlimited Partnership*,[5] a workbook Susy and I wrote with David and Teresa Ferguson, we included a list of ten common intimacy needs:

see next page

---

5. *Unlimited Partnership: Building Intimacy and Teamwork into Your Marriage* by Phil and Susy Downer and David and Teresa Ferguson. Intimacy Press, Austin, Texas, 1996.

WHAT DO YOU NEED?

Acceptance – A deliberate and ready reception with a favorable response (see Romans 15:7).

Affection – Care and closeness communicated through physical touch and affirming words (see Romans 16:16).

Appreciation – Hearing words and feelings of personal gratefulness from your mate (see 1 Corinthians 11:2).

Approval – An expressed commendation; when your partner thinks and speaks well of you (see Romans 14:18).

Attention – Having another take thought of you and convey appropriate interest and support (see 1 Corinthians 12:25).

Comfort – Having someone come alongside with words, feelings, and touch, to offer tenderness (see 2 Corinthians 1:3, 4).

Encouragement – Being urged forward and positively persuaded toward a goal (see 1 Thessalonians 5:11).

Respect – Feeling valued and highly regarded; feeling as though you are of great worth (see 1 Peter 2:17).

Security – Having the confidence of harmony in a relationship, feeling free from harm or danger (see Psalm 122:6).

Support – Having someone come alongside and gently help carry the load (see Galatians 6:2).

Of course, for many people today the primary need seems to be for time together. Our busy lives and crushing schedules make it hard for couples to take time just to focus on one another. Yet that is exactly what most marriages need. For most of our marriage, Susy and I have taken one night a week to go on a date. This is not a time to go out with friends, but a time to encourage each other and remember why we chose each other to spend life together.

At the same time, we have found we need a weekly time to discuss the business of the household. What businessman operates a business without staff meetings? What military officer operates a war without a meeting of his officers? Too many Christian couples operate their marriages without staff meetings, not taking the time to discuss schedules, money, and priorities until a conflict forces the issue. Adopting a date and marriage staff meeting will probably mean cutting something else out of your life that is important but not as important as your marriage relationship. Help the person you are discipling commit to spending these times with his mate by modeling it for him. Invite him over to your home or take the couple with you when you and your spouse go on a mini-vacation. That offers the added benefit of letting them see your solid marriage in action in addition to ensuring that the couple will have time to focus on one another.[6]

WORKING THROUGH CONFLICT

The three issues couples fight about most often are resolving conflict, dealing with sexual needs, and handling money. It's amazing so few couples really know how to fight—that is, how to disagree over an issue without attacking one another personally. You can make a great impact on the marriage of your Timothy by holding him accountable to communicate with his mate and by demonstrating through your own life an example of positive communication with your spouse. Offer your Timothy topics and exercises to try, help him figure out how to come to agreement on issues, and get him counseling if necessary. Do all you can to help build his marriage into something positive and strong rather than something negative and weak.[7]

6. In addition to *Unlimited Partnership*, these principles are expanded in Susy's and my book *Optimize Your Marriage*, Christian Publications, 2003.

7. David and Teresa Ferguson's Intimate Life Ministries conducts four-day Marriage Intensives that the Lord has used to save many marriages. Please refer to Other Helpful Resources in the back of this book for contact information.

This will mean you are going to have to open up about your own weaknesses. Talk about your own shortcomings and the things you have fought (or still fight) over. If the couple is having trouble with money, help them work out a budget and create a plan for living by it. Show them your own budget and talk about where you struggle to maintain it. And, in the privacy of your relationship, honestly answer his questions about sexual issues. For all the sensuality in our culture, there are still very few directions an adult can turn to get straight answers on things like sexual tension. Your honesty and openness on the issue can bond your Timothy to you.

Often people are so swamped with their own responsibilities and struggles they don't see much beyond themselves. That's why it's critical to walk with men and women through their struggles with their felt needs until they begin to see God resolve these issues and bring answers. That in turn will cause them to begin looking outward, to reach others with the same kinds of needs.

As you assist your Timothy with resolving conflicts in the financial or sexual areas of a marriage, it's important to check for "ticks." Look for the hidden problems that are sapping his strength. Have you ever seen hunting dogs work together in flushing out prey? It's a joy to watch them team up, encouraging one another, pacing one another, and having fun as they work together. Unfortunately, the hunting dog has some enemies, including an unseen bloodsucker called a tick, which can keep dogs from being effective.

In Vietnam, going through the marshy jungle we would get leeches. Sometimes they were the size of 50-cent pieces, attaching to our legs and in our groin. Not only would they sap our energy by sucking our blood, but after we burned them off by touching a cigarette to their back, they would leave round circles of wounds that rapidly became infected. But at least we could very quickly discover them. Not so with hunting dogs who often get ticks in their heavy fur or under their ears. They often go undetected, and the bloodsuckers can continue with their parasitical destruction. A similar thing can happen in a marriage. When a man has a hidden money or sexual problem, it's bound to impact his marriage and his walk with God.

When I started discipling Frazier, it was clear his wife, Sally, was a confident, godly woman. She was doing her best as she juggled the demands of the children, struggled to keep the home operating, and submitted to Frazier's desire that she go to work to help supplement his decreasing income (the result of failing sales efforts). Sally was up and working at five, and rarely going to bed before 11:30 p.m. Even so, Frazier expected her to fetch his popcorn for the game, take the shirts back to the cleaners, and call his committee list for his church post every week. Frazier and Sally's marriage was composed of one dog and one tick.

When he came to me to complain about Sally's lack of desire in the bedroom, I suggested his wife might have more energy if he would look after her interests more than his own. A marriage isn't designed for a man to get what he wants but for two people to move each other toward Christ. We need to confront our Timothys in love to help them see their selfish ways and allow the Lord to humble them, teach them, and equip them to become giving, loving, complementary partners. Once we've helped them deal with their own selfishness, great progress can be made by helping them deal with common issues of conflict like finances and romance.

YOUR LIFE PURPOSE

Developing a life purpose statement is another tremendous tool that will help your Timothy's marriage. You need a life purpose statement to help you focus on the right things in life. A person without a clear purpose is lost in a fog, but one who knows why he is here on earth and what he hopes to accomplish has clear goals and strong motivation. In my experience, a couple who talks about their life purposes are comfortable and in agreement with each other, which makes for an open door to ministry. The couple can move toward serving others by focusing on their life purpose.

What is your life purpose? You can help the people you disciple to determine their life purpose statements by asking them the following questions:

First, what does God desire of you?

Second, who are you? How has God made you?

Third, what are your dreams? What has God given you a heart to do?

Fourth, what are your gifts and abilities?

Fifth, what impressions do you get through prayer about your life purpose?

Sixth, what do godly friends say you should be doing?

Encourage your disciple to spend time thinking through these questions and develop a clear purpose statement for his life. Suggest your Timothy pray about a life verse. It may take some time and several refinements before it fits him, but I've seen it make a great impact on a marriage when both people are crystal clear as to why God has them on earth.

Without a life purpose statement, it's very hard for most couples to determine their priorities. For example, one of Susy's and my life verses is Matthew 28:19-20: "Go therefore and make disciples of all the nations, baptizing them in the name of the Father and the Son and the Holy Spirit, teaching them to observe all that I commanded you; and lo, I am with you always, even to the end of the age." So we have purposed to be involved in making disciples, which included not only those outside our home but also our own children. When it came time to consider doing a home Bible study, we wanted to make sure we involved our children in teaching and sharing the Word with people who didn't know Christ. This was a very high priority for Susy and me, based on our life purpose, but it meant there would be other excellent opportunities to which we would have to say no. If we were going to show our children how to disciple others, we had to make them a part of the process.

THE HOME AS A MINISTRY BASE

If you are going to take your faith home and start discipling those with whom you live, you have to begin seeing your home as a ministry base. You don't want to live your faith just while you're at work; you want to live like Jesus Christ while you're at home, to influence those most important to you in the world. Make the decision to *disciple your children*, leading them to maturity, then inviting them to become part of your ministry team. Take the time to get them involved in ministry in some way. It will enrich your spiritual walk and set an example your family will never forget. If you want some ideas in this area, you should read my book, *A Father's Reward, Raising your Children to Walk in the Truth*, as described in the resource section at the end of this book.

As I've talked with other parents, they have generally used the same old excuse for not involving their children in ministry: "It takes too much time!" But in my view, you make time for the things that are most important. Susy and I have found that God, in His mysterious economy, finds time for His work. If we take a step of faith when presented with an opportunity that fits our life purpose statement, the Lord will provide the time. It always seems to work that way. When we schedule a meeting with our Timothy, a couples Bible study, or an outreach in the neighborhood, the Lord comes through.

Once we've made a step of faith to serve God in some way, it's always interesting to see the next step—a lot of opposition by circumstances, criticism, insufficient funds, or a lack of time needed to carry out the task. Just before we perform our act of service, whether it's teaching a Good

News Club in our home, going to speak, or doing a Bible study, it seems as though our flesh wants to quit. But as we continue in faith, armed with the belief that God scheduled the activity and therefore we must see it through, it's almost always something He uses dramatically in our own lives as well as the lives of other people. At the end of it, we can look back and marvel at how God accomplished so much through one ministry activity. In other words, it has been my experience that if we decide as a couple to serve God in ministry, God always holds up His end.

There is never time for ministry because it is a spiritual work. If we had the time, energy, ability, and resources to do ministry, we would likely do it alone, in the flesh, without God, because, after all, "We can do this!" But as God said in Hebrews 11:6, "Without faith, it is impossible to please Him." The apparent shortage of time should be seen as an opportunity for faith, not an obstacle.

Susy, home with our children, ages 8, 6, 4, 2, and 2, gained a new spiritual daughter and sister in Christ when she shocked herself and everyone else by being willing to step out and meet with the woman for whom she had prayed for many years who suddenly showed some interest in a Bible study. Of course her temptation at first was to direct her to a formal Bible study, but instead she offered to meet with Christy one-on-one. This young woman leaped at the opportunity.

You see most people have spiritual and biblical problems but aren't asking spiritual and biblical questions. She probably never would have gone to a formal Bible study, because it was to Susy that she was initially drawn, not to the Bible and God. It is to your peace and God-likeness that your friends are attracted, not to your church program or books that you read. Some would have said it was irresponsible for the mother of a young and growing family to take the time, and in human terms it seemed there was no time for these meetings! But more than anything else, Susy wanted our children to love the Lord and love others enough to share

Him with them. In other words, since before they were born, Susy and I have prayed that our children would become disciples and disciple makers. How could we expect them to disciple others if their primary models, their parents, couldn't find time in their schedules or space in their hearts to do it?

So on a weekly basis Christy would come to the house, and the kids would pray for "mommy's meeting with Christy and that Christy would accept Jesus." What a miracle, faith builder, and model it was for our children to learn of Christy's receiving Christ about four months later—they really felt a part of her conversion. And to this day, when they are with Christy, they not only have a sense that this godly Christian mom, whom they respect, is a sister in Christ, but they recognize that in spiritual reproductive terms, this is one of their spiritual daughters.

Susy and I were committed to building a team for evangelism within our own family. We met together, studied the principles of lifestyle evangelism, and at the end of our studies realized the entire family could get involved in ministry as a team. I minister by traveling and speaking, as does Susy, and we take our children with us when we can. However, we didn't have a ministry our kids were doing directly. So when our older children ranged from ages six to twelve, we decided to start a Good News Club sponsored by Child Evangelism Fellowship for children ages five to eleven. The Club met on a weekly basis in our home during the winter and spring months. Susy invited about 30 kids, and over three years we saw more than a dozen of them come to know Jesus Christ as Lord and Savior.

Each week, the family simply did not have time for this Good News Club. In fact, Susy often admits that an hour before the Club meeting she was thinking, "I can't ever do another one of these again; it's just too hard." She and the children cleaned the house, scrubbed the toilets, and made snacks, and each learned different aspects of the Bible story— and they watched thirty kids track mud all over the house.

They had to practice the songs, decide how they were going to divide into two groups, and work on the memory verses and missionary story. The whole thing was a lot of work.

But our family found that the Lord, through the faith and obedience in this activity, greatly blessed all of us. My kids saw God work in the lives of their friends from their baseball and softball teams as those kids came to know more about the Bible than they had known before. We built relationships with parents, and one of the fathers became one of my new Timothys.

One fall Susy was calling parents to see which children were coming back to Good News Club. She had a somewhat cool reception as she spoke to Cindy, whose boys had quit coming before the end of the last year, so she asked Cindy what she could do to make the Club better for her family. Cindy hesitated and then said, "I guess I just don't believe the way you do." Susy replied, "That's fine. Tell me what you believe." After a long pause she said, "I guess I don't know what I believe." Susy told Cindy that she had been in that exact position and that Liane had met with her to answer her questions. When Susy offered to do the same with her, Cindy's coolness turned to enthusiasm. "Oh, I've been wanting to ask you if we could meet, but I just didn't think you would have the time."

Susy and Cindy began *Operation Timothy*, and Cindy poured out years of questions to Susy—everything from dinosaurs to predestination. When Susy didn't know the answer, she would ask someone and get back to her. That didn't bother Cindy a bit. Some months later after she had accepted Christ, Susy gave her a *Life Application Bible*. Cindy wrote a thank you note that said, "Thanks to your wonderful gift, the Bible has changed from something I never picked up to something I can hardly put down!"

That is the reward of giving your life away to another. Turning my marriage and family into a ministry base has renewed my spiritual fire and brought great blessing to our home.

THE BLESSING OF SERVING

Our children have also learned the power of hospitality and the hard work of being servants. They've learned why we clean up the house and why we use it for fellowship and outreach opportunities. They've learned how to teach and train other children their age, how to reach out to people for Jesus Christ, and how to memorize portions of Scripture and Bible stories to present them to their peers. One of the greatest benefits of involving our children in ministry is that it encourages them to learn to talk naturally and comfortably about their faith, both one-on-one and in front of groups. The Good News Club has been much more valuable to our children in that way than the speech course I took during college.

My kids have, of course, deepened their faith as they have explored the tenets of God's Word and watched those principles change the lives of their friends. They've learned how to work together as a team for a common purpose and have also seen the value of their different gifts. Anna is a merciful girl—a joy to sit with and talk to for those who are lonely or feel left out. Abigail has great organizational abilities and gained substantial confidence as she took responsibility for teaching the missionary story and memory verse. My son Paul's ability to share his testimony so effectively on his trip to Africa was a direct result of his years of nervously sharing his portion of the Bible story in Good News Club. Joshua's enthusiasm made him a real team builder, and Matthew's people skills made him a magnet for young people to come to our home.

There was a time when we didn't think we had time for the Good News Club, but the fact is, the Club fits our life purpose and has been an effective tool for reaching our neighborhood and discipling our children into ministry. Rising out of our Good News Club have been opportunities for our kids to be involved in disciple making with their peers. Matthew, at twelve, began meeting with one of his friends in order to disciple him. Abigail began another

Timothy relationship with an eleven-year-old girl who came to the Good News Club and had a real interest in spiritual things. Paul began taking a fourteen-year-old friend through *Operation Timothy*. So through the activity we didn't think we had time for, we have seen God accomplish many of the goals and purposes we set out for our family.

Introducing our children to the service and work of the kingdom at this age has been teaching them to have God's view of the world. They understand that fellow members of the body of Christ, with different giftedness and different strategic positions, are all part of the same body and accomplish the purpose of reaching this world for Him. They see others as people God loves and with whom we are to share the good news of Jesus Christ through our thoughts, words, and deeds. In the years since, their commitment to ministry in general and discipleship specifically has deepened. Several of the people who have come to our Good News Club have been real bullies and troublemakers, but they've been touched by the Spirit of God and changed before our family's eyes.

When we started our first Good News Club in Atlanta, Georgia, in 1988, our children (then 7, 5, 3, and 1-year-old twins) were too young to help teach as they did later, but the older ones could and did invite their friends, helped get the house ready, and shared their faith in simple ways. One year we had a neighborhood carnival that offered popcorn, games, and cotton candy. We invited the neighborhood kids and used this event as a jumping off point to invite them to a Good News Club meeting. One of the kids Susy invited shocked us all: William, a neighborhood thug. Since I was a combat veteran of Vietnam, it seemed funny that I was afraid of a ten-year-old, but this kid was a bad guy. Susy invited him to come to our carnival as he walked by the house one day, but he proceeded to put cotton candy in the girls' hair, ruin Abigail's cake-walk, and go around the house picking up food and throwing it on the floor. Our children had a living example of why discipline is essential for the operation of a family, but they also were able to see God's love in action.

William could not read or write and his father and grandfather couldn't either. William acted out the pain of his life in the way he dealt with people. Susy knew our children could be kind to him and that if he came to Christ he would be radically changed; she knew our kids could be part of that change. Our family caught a vision—our mission was not to change conduct but to share the love of God and introduce people to Jesus Christ so *He* could change their conduct. We lost touch with William when we moved to Tennessee, so we can't say William has come to Christ. I think it's safe to say, however, that he will never forget our home, the love he felt there in the Good News Club, and the information he received about a loving God who died for him on the cross.

GOD STILL CHANGES LIVES

One visionary thing we need to share with our disciples is that you never know how your message will impact a friend. One of our friends went on a trip to Israel. While on the banks of the Jordan River, the man in charge of his tour group asked if anyone would like to be baptized. Our friend was surprised when one of the young girls in the group said yes. This friend of ours had been praying for that girl and was excited to learn she had come to Christ "while attending a Good News Club in a brick house in my neighborhood." It was our house she described, and our friend was able to tell our children that he saw the fruit of their lives thousands of miles away on the other side of the world. Our children were impressed with an important lesson: *"God uses us."* Christians never know completely how we are used until we get to heaven, but God does use us.

Many people who are discipled find not only a new life in Christ but a new marriage and family life. In fact, I routinely see improvement in the marriages and families of the *disci-*

plers; as they get involved in the lives of their Timothys, their own marriages improve.

Our friends Tommy and Carol had been active in church with committees and Sunday school classes. She had done a great job raising the children and was now working as a bookkeeper while trying to complete an accounting degree. His business had grown to the point where he was actually bored and looking at expanding into branch offices. But with all their success came one problem: they had grown apart over the years. It wasn't that they were insensitive to one another; they just didn't take the time to build and nurture a growing relationship. Then they decided to have a *Living Proof* group in their home on Monday nights with several couples from his men's group and her Sunday school class. As usual, they negotiated the division of labor and set upon getting their respective tasks completed for the study. But after watching the high-powered dramatic vignettes of couples struggling in ministry, they would inevitably get into arguments. It seems the video was far too real to keep at arm's length.

As the weeks went on, their arguments continued. Soon they asked someone else to host the group and then missed a few sessions. When they returned, during one of the sessions, one of the couples pointed out they didn't seem to be sitting together and they drove in separate cars. Janie and Stephen, younger members of the group, blurted out, "Hey, can we talk honestly? We don't see you as a couple ministering *together*. You tend to minister alone and compete with one another." It was sad but true. Their secret had been exposed; what started out to be a twelve-week evangelism training class turned into a much-needed confrontation in which the six other couples pointed out an area that needed work in Tommy and Carol's marriage.

It is true they were discipling Janie and Stephen, brand-new believers with a host of problems with their finances, children, jobs, and parents, but they were also struggling with ministering *together*. Janie and Stephen shared that they prayed together every night before going to bed, giving them a regular time of emotional and physical intimacy. Tommy and Carol started copying that practice. The young couple was modeling the very thing the older couple needed. And as Tommy and Carol began discipling together, their marriage grew and flourished. They got back the old fire as they began ministering as a team. God changes lives, even among mature couples who have been in the church for years.

THE EXAMPLE OF DAVID

If you doubt the importance of turning your family into disciple makers, consider the example of David. Here was a godly man who was never discipled. He obviously loved the Lord and is described in Scripture as "a man after God's own heart," yet he had no one to keep him accountable when he faced temptation. He blew it big-time at the age of fifty by sleeping with another woman (see 2 Samuel 11), by which age you might think a man would be wise enough to avoid such a stupid mistake. But I've seen plenty of men's lives go up in smoke at fifty. The Christian men who seem to head into their fifties strong for the Lord usually have a spiritual parent or two.

The Bible offers us an insight into the problem David faced, however. Back when he was a young man, he showed up at the battle line to bring some food to his brothers (1 Samuel 17). They basically responded by saying, "Scram, creep!" David grew up loving God but had no spiritual parent. That became evident later in life when Joab became his best friend. Joab was a great general, whom David could trust with his army, but Joab was not a spiritual man who could be entrusted with the king's innermost thoughts. Consequently, after David had a big fight with his wife, Michal, he had no one with whom he could talk. Nobody advised David to patch things up with his wife, and that led to his eventual adultery. Nor could David pass on to his children a deep spiritual legacy of discipleship because none had ever been passed to him. Thus, his son Solomon, the wisest man ever to live, ended up acting like a fool. Had David offered some spiritual parenting, perhaps his son would have made wiser choices in his lifestyle.

I guess we can't be too hard on David, since there are really few good fathers in Scripture. The Bible offers all sorts of good mothers—Hannah, Ruth, Mary, Eunice—but the list of great fathers is pretty short. The dads constantly seem to be blowing it, either falling into sin or alternately neglecting and indulging their sons. Obviously, being a dad is a tough job. So I encourage you to meet together regularly with another man to talk through the pitfalls of parenting. Have him hold you accountable to be honest with your wife, caring with your children, and the spiritual leader in your home. Disciple your children into the faith. Let them see you reading your Bible, and talk naturally to them about spiritual things. Go through a Bible study with them, and look for ways to involve them in ministry. Make sure to read the Word and pray with your wife, keep a good attitude toward church, and set the example of service for your children to follow. There are no guarantees a godly man will have godly children, but you will get better results if you lead them spiritually rather than wait for the church to do it for you.

DOING THE HOMEWORK

In meeting with a man and getting to know his family, you'll often see "homework" left undone. In other words, you will see that the disciple needs to work harder at his family life and his marriage. Most of the men I meet with, except for the very mature Christians, do not view their wives with the cherishing, nurturing admiration that Scripture calls us to have. So inviting a man to a bunch of new activities while leaving his wife with more responsibilities and more messes to clean up can really hurt their relationship. In my experience it is very difficult to have a great relationship with God while having a lousy relationship with your wife, so make sure the men you are discipling are building their relationships with their wives just as they are building their relationship with God.

In one of the groups I work with, all of the men were considering taking on new responsibilities with their businesses, their churches, and their communities, all at the same time. Several of their wives had said that they felt neglected. They all had small children at home, so I felt these men were forgetting about their "homework." I made the point three or four times that they needed to consider spending time with their wives and getting to know their kids. In giving such advice, I always try to offer men descriptions of what I mean, because if I just share principles, they think they're being lectured and they'll begin to resent me for saying it. So I told them how I had been very insensitive to Susy, talking only about how hard my day was and never listening to hers, and assuming when I left somebody would pick up all the stuff I'd thrown down. I tried to help them understand that our wives are in great need of three things: conversation, a godly leader in the home, and some practical, everyday, roll-up-your-sleeves help with the children and the chores. And the fact that these men were ignoring their wives' pleas was a warning sign to me.

A young Christian business leader called me one day to ask my counsel on whether he should serve on a board of directors. "It only meets one weekend a year," he said, then went on to tell me what a great experience it would be, what great exposure and training it offered, and how much he wanted to do it. So I casually asked him, "When's the last time you had a weekend away with your son, and when is the next one that you've scheduled?" I asked him the same question about his wife and daughter, and he started to get the message.

"Well," he said to me, "I'll go ahead and schedule those *along with* the board meeting." So I said to him, "Dan, if you want to know what a person *will* do, look to what he has *been* doing. Promises are cheap. My advice would be to spend a couple of years having getaway times with your wife and kids and consider a board of directors position later. There will always be opportunities for godly men to serve on boards. The problem today is that there are too few godly men to fill the available posts." He declined the opportunity and decided to schedule a weekend time away with his son.

I often ask men, "If your wife were to give you three suggestions for improving yourself, what would they be?" Something amazing I've discovered is this: the man's answers never match the wife's answers! The men always want to conquer new territory. We usually want to create new projects so we can stand back and say, "I did that. Isn't it great?" While the wife often wants to maintain what she has. Clean the windows, sweep the walkway, pull up the weeds—all the stuff we hate to do because we can't stand back and admire it. I try to communicate with the men I'm discipling that we need to be involved in helping things run around the home.

Years ago I realized that if I insisted on perfection in my projects, my kids were not going to be involved in what I did until they were adults—if then. It takes a long time to learn some of the things I know how to do; the result was that I was always doing them alone. So I made it my goal not to do anything around the house I couldn't do with my wife and my children. I hired somebody to work on the roof because I can't do that with youngsters. But I can work in the yard, do simple projects around the house, and even paint (if I can control where they put their fingers). Our family policy is that the kids help with all the projects. This builds teamwork in our family and allows my children to see me as their mentor.

Men, decide to do things your children can learn along the way, and let someone else do the other things. If you will submit yourself to your wife and kids in this way, soon, rather than a group of independent contractors living together, you will have a team. Train your children to work, show them how to be a part of a team, and teach them how to clean up—that's one of the greatest things a man can do for his wife.

One of the hardest parts of being a mom is the change of seasons. Very few men recognize that when a season changes and you have growing kids, suddenly there is a massive project waiting—finding out what fits, what doesn't, where the clothes are that were used last year, if any of it is still good, whether things will fit a younger brother or sister, and where to store what needs to be saved until next year! We men can use the orderliness and organizational skills we learned in business or the military to help our kids learn how to make a seasonal change. One way I've done this is to have my kids watch what I do in taking care of my things and ask them to learn how to do the same with their own.

Too many men act as if they married a maid. Mom was the first maid, a girlfriend the second, and now the wife is the third. If you sense that is the case in the life of your disciple, help him with his homework. When I went into the Marine Corps, I didn't know how to sew on a button, take care of my clothes, or even operate a washing machine. The guys with the round hats taught me quickly how to do all that. They used a great motivator called fear. In God's army, however, we use love. In your home, if you don't do well at those kinds of things, it's time to fall in and learn from your wife. You'll need to humble yourself, get in step with her program, and learn how to do some of the important things that make a house run.

There may also be some things your wife can learn from you. Maybe you grew up with a mom who had you help with the cooking, and you can help your wife learn how to cook, or maybe even do a portion of the cooking yourself. Twenty years ago young married women knew how to cook, sew, and clean; now many know how to operate computers, score penalty shots, and make money in the stock market instead. I've known some brilliant female physics majors who knew all about the natural world but who couldn't do household chores if life depended on it. Minister to your wife in some of these areas, and you'll find your relationship deepening and your ability to minister to others much greater.

I'll never forget the time I asked Susy how I could show her I loved her, and she said, "Well, you could be nice to me." I told her I wasn't sure what all that entailed, so she made me a checklist of 10 things I could do that would reveal my love to her. Brother, may I make a suggestion? Ask your wife to make a similar list, then ask her to rate on a scale of 1 to 10 how you are doing in each area. Next, ask her which are the three most important things on the list and have her describe in detail how you should and should not communicate with her regarding that need. Then commit to meeting weekly to discuss how you're doing. Wives, if you would ask a similar question of your husband, I guarantee you would both surprise and encourage him.

It is possible to have a great marriage, but it takes work. Fortunately, there is nothing more rewarding—and nothing you can do to impact lives more than loving your wife or husband and letting others see your love.

QUESTIONS FOR DISCUSSION

1. Who modeled marriage for you? For your wife or husband? How has that model helped to shape your relationship?

2. What do you and your wife or husband fight about most often? What could you do to resolve the issue?

3. What values are you passing along to your children?

4. What are the five most important character qualities you'd like to see your kids develop?

5. What ministry would you like to try with your wife or husband? With your children?

CHAPTER 16

Learning to Multiply YOUR LIFE

*M*any years ago, reading Genesis 14:14 ("And when Abram heard that his relative had been taken captive, he led out his trained men, born in his house, three hundred and eighteen. . . ."), I caught a vision for asking God to use my life to touch and disciple 318 men in my sphere of influence—to send trained men to go into the world and make disciples. That seemed to be an impossible prayer, as one-on-one discipleship takes so many tears and years before your Timothy is ready and willing to disciple another person. But once that multiplication process begins, the exponential result will change the world as God blesses your efforts.

I met a young man named Charlie who was a member of the single adult class at our church. He and I dealt with a lot of the same challenges, although he was much younger than I was. Through that discipleship process he turned toward God, married a godly woman, and began reaching others for Christ. That was in 1985.

Almost fifteen years later, I was on a men's retreat and asked a friend of mine, Rob, how he came to Christ. He pointed to the man sitting next to him, Tyler, and explained how he had met him through their business and Tyler had led him to the Lord. I exclaimed to Tyler, "That's spiritual reproduction! Rob is your spiritual son! That is two of the four generations described in 2 Timothy 2:2, which outlines four generations: Paul, Timothy, faithful men, and others."

Then Tyler excitedly said, "That was just the beginning, because Rob was doing consulting for a man named Stan, whom he led to the Lord and met with, who also became a disciple maker and through whom God reached his spiritual son Dave. And there are even others beyond these men."

Thrilled with the fact that I was staring at 2 Timothy 2:2— spiritual reproduction—right before my eyes, I asked Tyler how he came to Christ and he said his spiritual parent was a man in business at his office who was not only one of the best salesmen of his firm but was willing to meet with Tyler and help him with business. But this man's interest went way beyond business, and he led Tyler to the Lord. Then to my stunning shock and joy, Tyler said that the man's name was Charlie. It was at that moment I realized that this Charlie was the same man who was my spiritual son, with whom I had met fifteen years earlier. With tears of excitement I exclaimed, "You're my spiritual grandson, and Rob, you're my great-grandson!" We simply celebrated and marveled at what God had done through some very imperfect people who didn't always know what to do, didn't always show up, and weren't always faithful, but were willing to be available to God. As a result, He spiritually reproduced our lives in generations.

Sometime later I was talking to Charlie, and we had an opportunity to present this spiritual family at a large gathering, including my spiritual father, Jim Lyon. I asked Charlie how many people he and the others had impacted for Christ over the last fifteen years. He said probably over three hundred, to which I quickly countered, "How about 318?" He said, "Yes, that would not be an exaggeration."

You see, women and men, when you meet with a person and God uses your life to make not just a Christian, but a disciple maker, you are part of an eternally impacting explosion—God's explosion of changed lives, the impact of which you will only be able to fully understand when you are home with Him in heaven. Over the decades, as I have met with men each week, each month, and each year, I have prayed for God to make me a "318 men man" through the principles of discipleship. I am stunned that God has answered that prayer through just one of the men with whom I met almost twenty years ago.

AN INSIDE JOB

In a large city in the western United States, a small band of men was concerned about the spiritual welfare of a large company in their city. They were finding it harder and harder to gain access to corporations in order to reach businessmen for Christ because many companies now require ID cards, security control systems, and the like. As they prayed, a strategy began to emerge. One of the strategies was to pray for somebody "inside the walls" of the huge business complex downtown. Amidst the thousands of workers, they began to pray for somebody who would be part of their team and begin an outreach ministry inside that corporation.

Those six men, as a team, continued to pray. Rather than acting as Lone Rangers, they realized there would be more power if they banded together to talk to God about their concern. They prayed about their relationships, neighbors, friends, and co-workers, asking the Lord to choose somebody somewhere who would be able to find one man inside the walls who knew the Lord. Word went out, and eventually a friend at church introduced them to one man—a new believer who had recently begun attending church. Those six men met with that new Christian and told him they wanted to start a ministry inside the company.

Because of his invitation, several men were able to get inside the wall and they started to meet with the young Christian. Soon other Christians joined them, praying for non-Christians by name and encouraging one another to walk with Christ in their corporate responsibilities. After a short time, that group decided to have an open notice for a Bible study, and more Christians were added to their ranks. Then they decided to have an evangelistic Bible study, so they received some special training on how to do that. They were careful not to talk about "religious things," made sure not to lecture, and stayed away from divisive social issues like abortion. They just read and talked about God's Word.

They started small groups and put up notices for a Bible discussion, which was attended by increasing numbers of non-Christians. Many were hearing the gospel for the first time and some came to know Christ as Lord and Savior right there inside the walls of that corporation. Pretty soon there was an active Christian community within the walls, with men getting together for Bible studies, accountability meetings, and prayer. What God birthed through the efforts of those six men was an entire *team* inside the corporation. Where previously the few Christians did not know who their fellow believers were, there was now an outreach and discipleship team!

This is an actual description of what I've seen happen time after time through the efforts of determined Christians. When people get it in their minds that God has called them to make disciples and they get adequately trained to do so, incredible things can happen. They start to reach other people with the good news of Jesus Christ rather than keeping it to themselves. They are encouraged to band together as a team rather than trying to do it all on their own. They start to multiply their lives, helping others grow up in the Lord. Nothing makes a person feel more significant than knowing he is helping to change the world for the cause of Christ and the souls of men and women.

JOINING THE TEAM

Every boy wants to be on a team. About the time we reach our thirteenth birthdays, we begin to think that being a sports star is just about the most important thing in the world. Of course, very few ever become sports stars. Some are satisfied just to be on the field, most are happy standing around cheering, and a few won't even do that. But everybody wants to be part of a *team*. That feeling persists with men throughout all of life. As children we want to go fishing with friends or play ball with a buddy. In high school and college we want to belong to a group of people who will help us to be identified. As young men we long to be part of a group that accomplishes something important. In middle age we still have that desire to feel part of something greater than ourselves.

That desire for teamwork is often at odds with our culture, which teaches men to be tough loners in the mold of John Wayne or Clint Eastwood, showing little emotion and drawing close to few (if any) others. But part of man's nature is to work on a team, even though our selfishness and pride often create conflicts in teamwork. Christian men are no different from anyone else in that respect. We long to band together with other men and achieve something great for God. Too often our little idiosyncrasies and selfish desires keep us from that, yet I have found there are few things so fulfilling as working with a team of Christian men to change our world. When I pray together with my team, I know we have accomplished much more being together than we ever could have accomplished individually. There is just something about working together with other men that gives us a picture of what it must be like in heaven with all the saints working in unity. Women want to be on a team, too, though they usually think in terms of community, seeking the more intimate friendship side, as opposed to the "rah rah" of men's teams. Women today have never been more overworked and undervalued and yet more essential to the family and community of believers.

The Apostle Paul didn't work by himself. He was always with Barnabas, Silas, Timothy, Luke, John Mark, or any combination of men. He stayed in close contact with the congregation in Jerusalem and developed strong ties with the churches in Ephesus and Antioch. Paul made sure he was working with a team rather than alone; he was always discipling another man to help him so he could continue working with a team. Jesus did the same thing, working with a group of twelve men and preparing them for the day in which they would take over and be the leaders of the movement. We are to follow their example. See yourself as putting together a mature team with whom you can minister, and prepare them to do the same thing.

This can be done at any age. If you are young, look for a peer who needs to be discipled. If you are in middle age, look around for someone who needs some leadership. Many older men and women feel useless because they have retired, have been thrown out of business structures just because they are older, or the children have left the home. There has never been a time when older men and women have been more greatly needed, more in demand for meeting with the younger generation. Often the problem with older men, unlike older women, is that they don't connect to people relationally; they relate organizationally. Those born before the baby boom learned to know men through their businesses, where there were barriers to intimacy even if they met together socially. As soon as they leave their positions at work, they feel like they've lost their platforms as well. Even an old saint who has greatly influenced people for Christ in the past may somehow think he no longer has anything to say when he's out of business cards. However, older men have tremendous wisdom in the eyes of younger men who would give anything to meet with them one-on-one or in a group.

We need to impress upon our older men that they need to get started working with younger men. If you fit in the "older saints" category, look for a man in your church or neighborhood who is a believer but needs seasoning. Evaluate some of the men you know who do not have a ministry in their lives. Take the initiative: go to one of them, tell him you believe in him, and ask him if he would be interested in getting together occasionally to talk about the Lord. Perhaps starting a group in your home with your wife is a possibility—you've worked all your life to have time with your wife. Now turn it into a ministry.

When our children were young, Susy joined a women's Sunday school class of several dozen older women, most of whom were "empty nesters." Susy tried over and over to share the vision with these ladies of the critical role ministry could have in their lives, whether it was to disciple younger women or have Good News Clubs in their homes for neighborhood children. As valuable as women's Bible studies are, she was discouraged that so many women were taking their "twenty-second" in-depth Bible study yet still said they were unequipped to use what they had learned to minister to others. Sister, you can do it! If you are married, consider ministering as a couple, while still looking for the woman who needs your investment one-on-one. If you are single, ask the Lord for the spot He has prepared for you to minister. Remember Liane, a divorced mom, who discipled Susy and changed our lives forever.

We have friends who worked all their lives to have a vacation home in Arizona. They went off into retirement with a wonderful second home in the desert, but after a few short years they realized the six-month stay left them without long-term relationships in either their original hometown or in Arizona. They had retired early to minister to people, but without long-term relationships they weren't able to build into people's lives. They discussed it and decided ministry was more important than having a vacation home in Arizona. So they sold the retirement home and moved all the furniture back to the basement of their original home. Now their "Arizona Home" is in their basement—where they entertain a host of young couples from their community, their church, and his former profession. They are involved with Bible studies, marriage studies for couples and *Operation Timothy* and *Living Proof* groups; and they are beginning to see a cadre of young couples walk more closely together, more closely with the Lord, and more effectively with those who don't know Christ. Some of the young people they are discipling are now leading others to Christ, all because they were willing to commit to ministry.

WORKING TOGETHER

"And we proclaim Him, admonishing every man and teaching every man with all wisdom, that we may present every man complete in Christ. And for this purpose also I labor, striving according to His power, which mightily works within me" (Colossians 1:28-29). Paul understood he worked with a team of people to accomplish the Lord's will and knew why he was doing it. He wanted to win the world to Christ and was willing to work with others to see this goal achieved.

Sometimes it can seem as though people are the problem. Every time you want to accomplish something, somebody will be there to thwart you, criticize you, or stand in your way. But brother, *people are not the problem!* People are loved by God, valuable enough to die for, and the means by which He intends to get the gospel message out. When we start thinking people are the problem, we fall into Satan's trap of trying to divide God's people. "Our struggle is not against flesh and blood," Paul told the Christians at Ephesus, "but against the rulers, against the authorities, against the powers of this dark world and against the spiritual forces of evil in the heavenly realms" (Ephesians 6:12) (NIV). When you start thinking another person is the problem, remember the devil has deceived you into thinking that. As part of a team of Christians, you have tremendous power.

Encourage your disciples to be part of a church body that is ministering effectively. They need to feel part of a team. That team can be used by Christ dramatically to impact neighborhoods, colleagues in business, our country, and our world.

Pete is a friend who has a tremendous gift for proclaiming the gospel. He has traveled all over the world sharing his testimony and has had a number of opportunities to speak to large groups, yet he has never discipled anyone. Although he has had an effective ministry, Pete acknowledges something is missing from his life. I recently helped him clarify his problem. First, I asked Pete to take out a 3 x 5 card and write down the names of every person who knows Jesus Christ because of the influence of his life. Pete went right to work, scribbling down names on the card. Second, I asked him to turn the card over and write down the name of every person he is currently helping move toward maturity in Christ. Pete sat there a moment, then his face fell. There were no names to put on the list.

He can talk about meetings and all those who have checked a box on registration cards, but there is no one he can tell about with whom he has a personal relationship. Pete can talk numbers but he can't talk names. He is not alone in this predicament. It is easy for Christians to go out and speak to people about the gospel and never build relationships, yet if we do that, we have not really completed God's command in Matthew 28:19-20 to make disciples.

Instead of approaching ministry as part of a team so we can follow up and build into the lives of new believers, we too often leave the baby to survive on its own. We ought to be making disciples, not just decisions. We need to be a part of the process of growing new believers into maturity—helping spiritual infants become spiritual adults. This is best done in relationships, supported by teams of people. What is a church, if not a team of Christians seeking to help people move toward maturity? More than a preaching center, a church needs to be a spiritual school where we teach people to obey and a spiritual family where we offer a context for growth.

I'm not against speaking and proclaiming the gospel. I love to do it whenever I get the chance, but we need to keep that in context. Proclaiming decisions has to be matched by preparing disciples. Every great movement in the church has seen disciple making become as important as spiritual decision making. Our God is a God of order, so why would the Lord allow new spiritual babes to be born only to be neglected? Many would suffer great harm. Therefore it is imperative to begin seeing our churches as filled with teams of disciple makers, ready to help new Christians grow up in Christ.

My friend Pete's disappointment is that he doesn't know what might have become of his life if he had taken the time to follow up with some of those new converts. So he is now part of a team. He has found a team with which he feels comfortable—kindred spirits in leading souls out of darkness and into the light. He and his wife are involved with those couples in discipling others into maturity. They are still sharing Christ, but they are also building relationships with people who don't know Christ, cultivating them to a place where they are ready to hear the gospel, and then helping them mature in the Lord. The team is working directly with those who hear the gospel of Christ, explaining it to them in a one-on-one relationship and walking with them as spiritual parents.

As part of a team, Pete is the one who will probably always be most actively involved in inviting large numbers of people to various events and either speaking himself or getting others to speak. But that's his gifting; Pete is a born evangelist. He *ought* to be preaching the gospel; it is why the Lord made him the way He did. But, in addition, he has seen the value in his wife's inviting people over, using her gift of service to create a comfortable evening. Gloria's ability to follow up with couples and begin discipling them is almost uncanny. She seems to know exactly what they need. For several years now, Pete has been discipling one or two men a year and going very deep with a few. He sees the value in not just adding converts by proclamation but discipling them into maturity. He believes his ministry has a new depth now that he is seeing some real, long-lasting life changes.

All the parts of a body are essential. If one disciple is gifted in evangelism, another may be gifted in helps or hospitality. If one is gifted in wisdom, another may be gifted in mercy. All are necessary for a team of people to step in and complete a discipling process in the life of a believer. No matter what your gifts are, you don't have them all. By becoming part of a team, you link up with other gifted Christians to better minister to the world. You become more effective when all the parts work together. Offer encouragement and make your Timothy part of your team.

A HEART FOR PEOPLE

A lot of men and women, when they come to Christ, find they have lived a life viewing others as competitors. That sort of perspective causes everyone to be guarded and gets in the way of relationships. When they become Christians, they often retain that perspective and try to fit it into a Christian context. But it won't work. When you become a Christian, you have to establish a whole new way of seeing people.

Steve was a very self-focused man, though he had been walking with Christ for three years. When we met, he asked if I would disciple him; not too long afterwards he began to go with me on follow-up visits and hear about the other men I was discipling. He saw very quickly I had a deep focus on the real issues of men's lives and that I talked deeply with other men. That was a new thing for Steve, and he asked why I was different. "I gained that heart from the man who discipled me," I told him, "and he had gained it from the man who discipled him." After seeing men who cared for one another, Steve started to view people differently. He began to see his confrontational neighbor, his arrogant boss, and his floundering fellow-worker as people who had a need only Jesus Christ could fill. He started searching for ways to meet the needs he could, and to be available in a loving fashion.

As Steve's perspective changed, so did his heart. Rather than seeing men as competitors to be beaten, he began seeing them as souls to be loved. I watched Steve become a team player, a man who appreciated other Christian men for their different gifts. When you become a clean, available vessel for God to minister through, you can start to meet the needs of those around you. That's what it means to have a heart for people, and that's necessary if you are to be a disciple maker. It's what I call "seeing people with God's eyes"—not something that comes naturally.

We are naturally selfish, but when you see people with God's eyes, you learn to be less selfish. We are naturally most concerned with ourselves, but when you see people with God's eyes you become concerned about others. Christ didn't see people as competitors but as worthy individuals who needed God. That's why He reached out to them in love, offering healing, forgiveness, and purpose to their lives. Christ looked upon even the unlovely and offered them hope. At His death, He could look at the very men who were crucifying Him and say, "Father, forgive them" (Luke 23:34). Jesus saw people with God's eyes. He could look at an angry or evil man and see the possibility of goodness if only the man could meet God.

I long to have that sort of heart for people. Even though I've been a Christian for many years, I still struggle with seeing people with God's eyes. If a man cuts me off on the freeway or says something rude that upsets me, I still have a tendency to desire his destruction rather than his salvation. I can be like the Sons of Thunder, wanting to call down fire from heaven to destroy those who get in my way, rather than being like Jesus who was willing to forgive because He could see the great potential. So I pray every day for the Lord to fill my heart with love for others, that I'll view even the worst offender with God's eyes.

After my father's suicide, I was reflecting on the passage of Scripture that says God's desire is that none be lost, but that every man would come to know Him (2 Peter 3:9). That never happened with my dad. I had prayed for my father, shared the gospel with him, and done everything I could to help him embrace the truth. But he openly rejected Jesus Christ, and, excepting a last-moment miracle, I don't expect to see him in heaven. On the airplane coming back from his funeral, all I could remember was Romans 8:28: "God causes all things to work together for good to those who love God, to those who are called according to His purpose." At the time I was a self-centered, two-year-old Christian and just sat there, wondering how God was going to use this for good.

At the same time, the man who discipled me had begun to pray for me to develop a heart for men. Dr. Jim knew something wasn't right with me, for I didn't seem to care deeply about people. I had actually gone on a follow-up visit with Jim, led a man to the Lord by using the *Steps to Peace with God* tract, and walked out of his office yawning! Jim was ecstatic that another lost lamb had been found, but I was kind of ho-hum, thinking decisions for Christ were the intended outcome of an office call.

Jim could not understand why I wasn't excited because he was thrilled. That's the day I realized I wasn't excited because I was still focused on my own needs. Though I hate to admit it, I wasn't even very interested in what happened to the man I'd led to the Lord. So I began praying with Jim to gain a heart for people. I described to the Lord my tendency to be self-centered, my insensitivity to others, and my hard-driving, highly focused interest in success. To be honest, I didn't feel much of anything for anybody else. But as I prayed, the Lord changed me.

My father's death was a wake-up call. Here was somebody close to me I would never see again. I had shared the gospel and my faith with Dad countless times, but I was "only" his son—no businessman had ever told him about Christ. For two years as a new believer I had prayed that a peer of Dad's, a businessman, would talk with him—but none did. Now that opportunity was lost forever. I thought about all the men around me who were headed straight to hell and I came back from burying my dad with a newfound purpose in my life—and a heart to reach men. Today I have a burning passion inside my heart to reach men as I never have before. God turned the burner up on my fire the day I buried my father's body without any real hope of seeing him in heaven.

Two of the friends who inspired Susy and me with their heart for people are Dave and Judi Hill. Judi is the woman in Liane's neighborhood who reached out to her in her marriage crisis and led Liane to the Lord and discipled her the year before Liane met Susy at the baby shower. This was not a one-time event for Judi or Dave. Since coming to Christ in the early 70's, they have made discipleship their lifestyle.

A few years ago, some of the young people whom Dave and Judi had discipled decided they wanted to surprise them by a special afternoon of thanking the Lord for all they had done. They contacted all the people they knew whom Judi and Dave had impacted with their lives. Susy and I drove to Atlanta for the event with all of our children. Judi and Dave walked into the Fellowship Hall completely unaware of what had been planned and were greeted by about 350 cheering and tearful people. For several hours, testimonies were shared by person after person whose lives had been changed forever by Dave and Judi's investment in them. Susy says it was the closest thing to heaven she expects to experience on this earth.

The amazing thing was that, other than a few people like Susy and me who had not initially been reached by Dave and Judi, the people there were those who had been impacted directly by Dave and Judi, not all the people who had been influenced for Christ by those people. That multiplication effect would no doubt be in the tens of thousands.

But even more amazing to Susy, was getting to meet the person we had heard about for more than twenty years, the woman she alluded to in the Foreword. She went up to a woman who had flown down from Chicago for the event, and said, "Marilyn, you don't know me, but I have always wanted to meet you. Thank you for going next door and sharing over a cup of coffee with a young woman who was struggling with her husband and children. You led Judi to the Lord, she led Liane to the Lord, and Liane led me to the Lord. Without you, I would have long since been divorced and would not have any of my children. I owe everything to you."

Do you have a heart for the souls of men and women as Jim, Mary Gail, Marilyn, Dave, Judi, and Liane do? Do you keep in mind that those around you who don't know God are going to hell, to spend an eternity apart from everything that is good and holy? As I travel the country, I find too often that Christian men and women don't have a sense of urgency about their faith. They have forgotten "*now* is the day of salvation" (2 Corinthians 6:2, emphasis added) and are willing to put it off until some other day. If you need to develop a heart for souls, and if you need to begin seeing people with God's eyes, I urge you to get down on your knees and pray. Pray in repentance for your cold heart, and ask that

God fill you with love for others. Then pray by name for all those you know who do not love the Lord. Make a list of relatives, neighbors, coworkers, colleagues, partners, vendors, and those who work with your company in some way. Write down the names of everyone you encounter, ask the Lord who you should start talking to, and start praying for each by first name. God will help you see them as He sees them—valuable, worthwhile, loved, and in need of the Savior you know and love.

QUESTIONS FOR DISCUSSION

1. Do you believe the Lord Jesus has called you in Matthew 28:19-20 to disciple?

2. What, if anything, is keeping you from discipling another person?

3. As you look at the people in your life, whom do you think you could disciple?

4. How could you approach at least one person to begin the relationship?

5. What help could you offer him or her?

CHAPTER 17

Producing REPRODUCERS

*W*hen Chip MacGregor began his first pastorate, not a man in his church had been discipled. There were committees, programs, and all sorts of activities, but no one was helping the younger men of the church grow into maturity. I like Chip's approach: rather than announcing the establishment of a new program or putting an advertisement in the bulletin asking men to sign up, he simply started to pray. He prayed for God to send him ten men to disciple. Eventually, ten names came to him.

Chip approached each of those men and asked them to pray about becoming involved with him in a small group, talking about their spiritual walk, and getting serious about living for the Lord. He didn't press them for commitments; instead, he asked them to pray about it. In the meantime, he talked about the importance of discipleship from the pulpit and encouraged men and women to get involved in discipling relationships with other people. He also continued to pray that the Lord would make it clear to those men how much they needed to be discipled. None of them was ready to jump in initially. But each time Chip crossed paths with those guys, he would ask, "Hey, have you been praying about that discipleship group? You haven't? Well, how are you going to know God's will if you don't talk to Him?" Eventually, all ten men were praying.

Nine of them agreed that the Lord had directed them into a discipling relationship with Chip. Thus began a two-year commitment, in which those men met together to discuss the Bible, ministry, money, sex, and everything else men need to talk about. This group became serious about commitment, even arranging vacation schedules so no one could "disappear" for a summer. They went on work parties together, helping split wood and doing handyman projects for a local Christian camp. They held a couple's retreat together, just for the men and their wives. And they opened up their lives to the working of the Lord.

The results of those discipling relationships have been dramatic. Every one of those men has moved into leadership in a church. Every man is still walking close to the Lord, though the group ended many years ago. Several have become deeply involved in evangelism or short-term missions. But the real success is that most of those men are now discipling others. The discipling relationships produced reproducers, turning Timothys into Pauls. The only sad note to the whole story is the one man who refused the invitation to be discipled—the one who probably needed it the most. A man stuck in secret sin, he feared he would have to reveal himself to others, so he said no. But his sin caught up with him. He lost both his job and his wife before disappearing from the men and the faith. Had he been willing to be discipled, who knows what sort of spiritual growth he would have seen. Perhaps the accountability would have kept him from falling apart. Discipleship works. It is God's plan for changing the world.

LEARNING TO BE REAL

Discipling works because it forces people to get real. Rather than relying on the role models we see in movies or at home, discipling allows one man or woman to see how a mature man or woman lives and struggles with his faith. It allows a person to grow slowly, moving toward maturity over time, relying on the power of God and the encouragement of mature Christians. If you love God, have a heart for people, and are willing to be real with others, you can help shape people's lives. I say this knowing that many of the men and women reading this book are terrified of ever discipling someone. They fear their failures disqualify them for the role. But the real fear is probably more basic: they just don't know what to do.

Many men and women who have not been discipled will not disciple another because of the fear of failure, lack of training, or the absence of a clear plan. But I want to rid you of those excuses. Pray for God to send you a man if you are a man, and a woman if you are a woman. Look around and see whom you can help. Think about what that person needs. You don't have to be an expert in every subject; you just need to have a willingness to obey God.

If you are wondering what a discipling meeting looks like or what you will do when you get together, you are just like me when I was getting started. I really wasn't sure what to do, afraid the other man would show up for our breakfast meeting and I wouldn't have anything to say. To help you see the practical side of discipling, let me give you an outline of what one of my discipleship meetings looks like.

First, I try to schedule a meeting at a time that suits us both. Occasionally we'll have to make a few attempts before we discover the best time to meet. Second, I always try to pray just before the meeting, even if only for a minute while sitting in my car in the restaurant parking lot. I ask the Lord to make me sensitive and give me wisdom in our discussions. You see, I generally have an agenda for us to discuss but I also want to be aware of the other man's mood. If he has something weighing on his heart, like a bad marriage or trouble at work, I want to deal with that rather than force us into some half-hearted book study.

I try to break the meetings up into thirds. The first third is simply to have fun. We'll talk about last night's Braves game, I'll ask about his golf handicap, or we'll discuss the latest business news. I just want to spend some time having fun, letting him warm up to me and feel comfortable.

The next third is spent asking questions. Although women seem to be better at this, one problem men often have is that most of us live ego-driven lives. We're more accustomed to talking about ourselves than patiently listening to others, so I try to follow the model of Jesus and be a good listener. I usually begin very lightly, asking questions about his day, work, and family. Early in the relationship I ask some questions to get to know him: Where were you born? How did you meet your wife? Where do you live? What do you do? Where did you go to school? I particularly try to ask about things he has done well, things he knows a lot about, and things he's interested in so he'll get used to talking. Once we get to know one another, I'll start zeroing in on his struggles. Usually every man is struggling with at least one of the six issues mentioned earlier: his marriage, children, business, finances, spiritual walk, or health. I want to find out where his struggles are so we can begin talking about something important to him.

In the last third of our meeting, we move into our study. As I've said before, I like using the four-book *Operation Timothy* series (it also has an excellent leader's guide) because it gets into deep issues yet presents things in a clear format. My focus is never on simply answering all the questions, but on helping move the man toward Jesus Christ. We don't have to get through a chapter a day—as a matter of fact, we usually just get to part of one chapter. Sometimes we won't even use our books because there is a personal issue we want to deal with. But a study guide of some kind offers a general guideline, a path to follow as we walk the road toward maturity in Christ.

Of course, throughout our time together I share my life with him. I don't teach, and I try not to lecture; I attempt to answer his questions and reveal how I live my life. That's why social time spent together away from study time is so valuable. It allows your Timothy a chance to observe you in the real world, not the artificial realm of a church or a spiritual gathering.

Occasionally I'll simply ask, "How can I pray for you?" and that will get us going in a discussion. One morning last week I felt a man was holding back in our discussions, so I asked him if he needed prayer. Suddenly he choked up and said, "My son. Pray for my son." As I asked what I should pray for, he replied, "Pray that he would get his life straightened out." That led to more questions and the admission that the young man was running from the law while hiding in his father's house. As the discipler, I was able to talk with him frankly about the troubles of his boy and the potential trouble he could have if he were caught harboring a fugitive.

Going into the meeting, I had no inkling we were going to be discussing things like Christians and the legal system, but that's what was heavy on this brother's heart. Men and women are hurting out there. Unless we are willing to deal with the real issues of life, discipleship will be nothing but a spiritual game. If we stay on the surface, just discussing inter-esting theological ideas and passing out information, we'll never see a person change. So head toward each meeting with a general agenda in mind, but allow the Spirit to lead you down whatever path He chooses. Don't be surprised to find some incredible pain in the lives of those you are discipling. We live in a fallen world where Satan does his best to defeat and discourage us, so you can expect to face some terrible scenes. At the same time, take courage from the fact that an all-wise God is supporting you and His power is greater than the power trying to destroy the lives of men and women.

THE IMPORTANCE OF CHARACTER

You see, the goal of spiritual growth is to establish the character of Christ in our lives. That is a lifelong process. God wants your disciples to develop patience, love, humility, and a heart for others. Those aren't things they will *do*; those are things they will be. But it won't come fast or easy. A disci-pling relationship is simply the development of mature character in the life of another. Three elements shape a man or woman: character, competence, and community. As a discipler, you can influence all three of these elements.

The character of a person is revealed by his attitudes and actions. If you fail to shape a person's character, you fail to fully disciple him. I am a big fan of Scripture memory because I believe the Word of God has power to shape our lives. So when I'm discipling a man I like to work with him to memorize verses that speak to his needs. When we get into our study together, we often ask each other to quote the memory verse, just to hold each other accountable to complete our work. If he is committed to studying a chapter in the Bible, I'll ask various questions so we can discuss its meaning. I want to go over enough of the content to make sure we both understand the meaning, but it will quickly get boring if the meeting turns into an exam or a simple Q&A

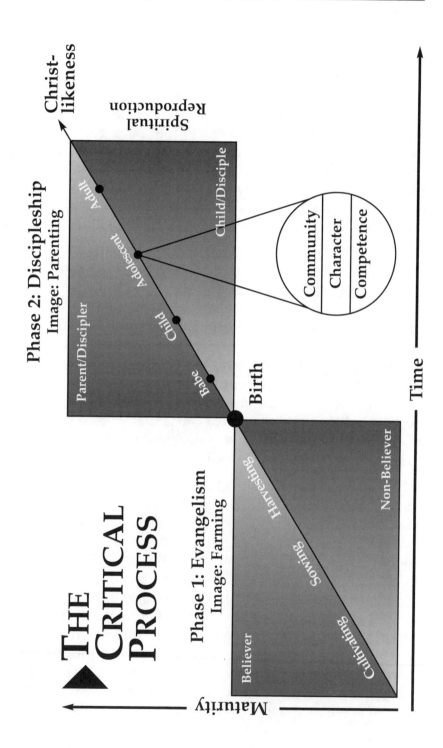

THE CRITICAL PROCESS

Phase 1: Evangelism
Image: Farming

Phase 2: Discipleship
Image: Parenting

Spiritual Reproduction

Christ-likeness

Maturity

Time

Birth

Non-Believer

Cultivating

Sowing

Harvesting

Believer

Babe

Child

Adolescent

Adult

Parent/Discipler

Child/Disciple

Community

Character

Competence

session. The goal of our discussions is to try routinely to turn the study material toward real life.

I ask questions like "In light of your answer to question three, are you viewing life any differently?" or "How should you, therefore, view the problem at work?" or "What do you think we should do in response to that passage?" I want to find a way to relate our studies to my Timothy's everyday life. One of my biggest struggles is that I can become program-focused, inwardly concerned that we're not making enough progress in the book, when the real issue is whether the Lord is working in our hearts to shape our lives.

When a man wants to talk about his problems, we focus on that. If he is going through marital difficulties or a job change, this becomes the focus of our time together. Often the material I'm taking him through can help walk the man through his problem by bringing the wisdom of God to bear on that need. We can deal with issues of forgiveness, faith, confession, relationships, quiet time, pain, and God's guidance as we get into the Word. But if we continue to approach a hurting man or woman with a cerebral approach to Bible study, we will never see change. Great content can actually drive him away. It's not just the content that is important but the character of the person we are trying to shape.

Remember we're not dealing with people who grew up responding to autocratic, top-down approaches to life. You used to be able to go into a group and say, "We have a need, and you have resources, so go meet the need." No more. The younger generation today will ask, "Why me? Why don't you go do it? I'm not interested any longer in being recruited to do your program." The old adage "Come join our mission" is dead. It needs to be replaced with, "Let us join you and be part of what God is doing so you can accomplish the mission God has given you." There has been a shift from content to character. This new generation is being reached by the advertising that proclaims, "Come and have it your own way." We need to serve men and women, understanding that they are felt-need driven, have less time, and have less margin. But they can be tremendously loyal once we break through the veneer of suspicion and lack of focus. If we come across with just content, we are going to drive people away. If we come across as servants, helping them change the world, we offer them the significance they desire.

Covering the study material in the book is, of course, vital. We need to be persistent in meeting regularly, working on the material, and holding each other accountable. But if a person is overwhelmed with problems, we may simply need to meet for a period of time to work through the problems. Once in a while you will meet someone who never seems to get out of trouble, always standing in the danger zone and hoping not to get hurt. If a person repeatedly fails to keep commitments, we need to evaluate whether his heart is really in being discipled. Pray for him, and don't give up too easily. Remember, the disciples all failed Jesus at one time or another. His willingness to forgive and move ahead brought them to maturity.

I think one of the best ways to minister to a person's character is through Scripture, so get your disciple reading the Bible right from the start. In *Operation Timothy* some great quotes start the study, like the story of W. C. Fields, seen reading the Bible on his deathbed and muttering, "I'm looking for loopholes." Perhaps with older Christians this would be blasphemy, but for modern, secular men or women who are not Bible-comfortable, it gives you a great opportunity to discuss another person's perspective. You have to ask questions and listen to his response.

Not long ago I was meeting with a man and discussing the issue of control. "Who is in control of your life?" I asked.

His reply: "I don't want to answer that question."

But I wasn't going to let him off the hook. This is a man struggling with the issue of total commitment, surrendering his life to God, so I asked him again, "Who is in control?"

"I don't know."

"Well, what does the Bible say?"

"The Bible says that God ought to be in control."

"Well, then," I said to him, "who is in control of *your* life?"

"I don't know."

"Okay," I tried, "then who do you *want* to be in control?"

He sat there for a few minutes, then said, "Well, I like to call the shots."

And with that answer, we were off and running, talking about the issues of control and surrender.

I met with another man who would not surrender control of his finances to the Lord. He wouldn't even let his *wife* know how much money he made. He did all of his accounting at the office, not even allowing his wife to look at their tax return. She didn't know how much he made, where it went, or to whom he gave it. In fact, his wife had to call his secretary to get money put into the checking account for groceries! In discipling this man, I was concerned not only for his spiritual life, but his marriage, his teenage daughter who was feeling controlled, and his spiritual future. A man's money often reveals a man's heart; this man had a heart for control!

I encouraged him to be more open with his finances. He agreed to sit down with his wife in a quiet spot and spend time talking about their finances. After he failed to do it four different times, I felt I had to force the issue: "Are you going to meet with your wife or are you not?" He reluctantly agreed to keep that commitment, as long as I was there. This led to some lengthy discussions about his attitudes, actions, and perspectives on money. We had to deal with anger and trust issues, but eventually we came to the point where the Lord took control of his finances. Here was a man who needed to be changed. It wasn't my job to change him, but the Lord used me as part of His plan to help instruct him, prod him, and eventually help shape his character.

That is one of the most important things we do as disciplers. Think through what is most important to the Lord and how God wants to use you in the process, then take the bold step of assisting men or women in their development before the Lord.

THE ISSUE OF COMPETENCE

One of the most easily neglected areas in discipling is establishing a feeling of competence. People don't want to bring it up because we're often willing to feign competence to look good, but a fully equipped disciple will have a sense of basic spiritual competence. A disciple needs to have strength in some areas of skill. He needs to feel he can study the Bible, pray, talk about the Lord, and explain the basics of the faith to others. Part of your role as discipler is to help him develop a feeling of competence in his role as "public Christian." You can help him develop the skills and knowledge he'll need to begin serving God and ministering to others. Helping him know and use his spiritual gifts is also important.

When I first became a Christian, I didn't think I had anything to offer anybody else. I didn't know my Bible, didn't understand theology, and was sure I'd never be able to explain my faith to another man. But gradually, over time, the man who discipled me helped me do all those things. While I'm no theologian and nobody is going to mistake me for a Bible expert, I've developed some level of competency in the Scripture. And though I might not preach like some of the famous evangelists, the Lord has allowed me to be able to speak about my faith to men all over the country, describing my spiritual pilgrimage from death to life. One of the reasons I'm in ministry now is because the spiritual parents I had around me encouraged and taught me how to do the things necessary to propagate the faith. Then the Lord began to use my spiritual gifts and natural abilities, and now I have a feeling of competence in the areas of evangelism and discipleship.

You can have the same influence in the life of another man or woman. Help him discover and use his spiritual gifts. Offer encouragement and guidance, and give him opportunities to grow. One of the biggest reasons men are not more involved with important ministries is because they secretly feel inadequate. So *help them know that they are adequate in the Lord Jesus.* Take them with you when you go talk to another person about Christ. Demonstrate how to talk naturally about the Lord. After they've had a chance to watch you a few times, delegate some of the responsibility to them so they can put into practice all the things they've been learning from you.

The Lord Jesus, in training the Twelve, sent them out to minister. His goal was to give them a taste of what their long-term calling would be. In doing so, He grew in them a feeling of competence, as evidenced by the encouraging report upon their return. The apostles were thrilled that the power of God was at work in them. Your disciples can experience the same joy. There is a wonderful feeling in knowing the Almighty God is at work through you. Build the feeling of competence in those you disciple and watch what the Lord accomplishes.

THE NECESSITY OF COMMUNITY

The third area I encourage every disciple maker to cover is the importance of being involved with a local church. Make sure the Timothys in your life have a secure place to worship God. They don't have to attend your church, but encourage that the church they attend be a Bible-preaching, God-exalting fellowship of believers. As new Christians, they also need to find a caring environment offering both accountability for themselves and an opportunity to exercise their gifts toward others.

I believe character is shaped within the context of community. We become like those around us. In Acts chapter 2 we see a flood of people joining the new church because they were attracted to its message, hope, and strength in God. People are attracted by the character of God, not just the skills of people. God works through our spiritual communities to shape us for His purposes.

Grant, a young man who came to Christ at a CBMC breakfast, really enjoyed our meetings together. He was reading his Bible, memorizing verses, and praying about the issues of his life. But one day he admitted to me something was missing: he felt as though he didn't belong. As we talked about it, he admitted he feared attending a local church since he had never been inside a church except for weddings and funerals. He didn't know the language, the culture, even what to wear. "For me, walking into a church is as foreign as some old saint walking into the local tavern," Grant admitted.

I was stunned. It had never occurred to me a believer would not feel comfortable in a sanctuary. Yet Grant clearly needed to join with a local body, to become part of a context that would assist his spiritual growth. After thinking it over, I said, "Grant, the Bible describes Christianity as being a fire. That means you are one of the hot coals in the fire, trying to reach out and bring light to a dark, cold world. But for a fire to work effectively, all the burning logs and hot coals need to be gathered together. If you pull one coal away from the rest of the fire, in a very short time it will cool off, then grow cold. But, almost like magic, if you keep all those hot coals together the fire continues to burn. In the same way, you need to be part of a local church and body of believers so you'll remain part of the fire. If you stay away, eventually your fire will go out." Understanding the illustration, Grant agreed to join us for worship.

The church is described in the Bible as the household of faith (Galatians 6:10). The people around you are members of the household and God can use them in great ways to mold

your character toward Christlikeness. Disciples rarely understand the significant impact the church has on their lives. As
C. S. Lewis put it, "You thought God was building a neat little
cottage; but God is building a palace that He intends to live
in Himself!" I'm not talking about joining a building or an
institution but a Christian community. A Christian
community is imperative for a believer. Like a hothouse
fosters growth in tender plants, a church assists in the
spiritual growth of babes in Christ.

HOW LONG WILL WE MEET?

Of course, meetings can take place anywhere and can last
for any length of time, but there are some guidelines I've
found that work well. I like to meet in the morning or at
lunchtime, usually in restaurants where we can talk and not
be rushed. More and more restaurants, however, are moving
away from having that "room in the back" so you can talk,
offering lazy table service where you can be comfortable
while talking through a Bible study. Thus, I'm finding that
brown-bag meetings in boardrooms or enclosed offices are a
nice alternative. It's effective because you can meet privately,
discussing the deep things that go on in people's lives. You
can also pray without interruption, it's less expensive, and
you can usually juggle things fifteen minutes one way or the
other with no problem.

I also find a Saturday morning meeting at home is a good
way to go, though you'd better check with your wife or
husband. I usually ask a man to meet with me once a week,
though we may get together socially also, and I find it very
difficult to accomplish much of anything in less than an hour.
It always takes a while to get people to open up, and about
the time you get them open it's usually time to quit. So be
wary of arranging for back-to-back discipleship meetings.
With travel time, a one-hour meeting probably means an
hour and 20 minutes if you are near your work.

Occasionally I find myself going overboard on meetings, trying to answer every question and deal with every issue. That causes the meeting to stretch into two or three hours, which always seems to keep us from meeting together the next week. Try to be disciplined and keep within the time frame of a businessman's day. Ask him up front how much time he has. Get agreement from him on how much time he'll spend, and then don't spend any more. And be sensitive— sometimes a man will get overextended and think it's his duty to spend time in a meeting at the expense of his business.

One thing that really needs to be clear is that these Timothy meetings are ordained by God. He puts them together, He breaks them up, and those involved must understand that a discipling relationship must be mutually beneficial. If the relationship doesn't work out and the two of you don't work well together, you need to allow your Timothy the freedom to meet with someone else. I've never understood why two people get along great even though they are very different, and it seems often if I have tried to "arrange" a relationship, it fails because of my inability to read people. Allow the Spirit to do His work, and God will make clear who should be together.

By the same token, the Lord will make clear when you should stop meeting together. With the men I disciple, I find we change the frequency of our meetings after a year or two, but the discipling relationship lasts forever. I have discipled some men with whom I still touch base every few months; others I call twice a year. We get together from time to time for "big events," but just as with adult children, a father does not spend as much time with his 32-year-old as he does with his 2-year-old.

THE SMALL GROUP

The Lord Jesus had twelve disciples, but He also developed a core group of three men with whom He spent the most time. Peter, James, and John seemed to be with Him for all the most important events of His ministry. That means Christ excluded some people at times, and He was not ashamed of that. Jesus wasn't trying to treat everyone equally. There were twelve men close to the Lord, but among that dozen it is clear three were closest to Him. Of those three, there was one, John, who was His closest friend.

As Jesus walked among the people, He touched everybody. Some drew close while others kept Him at arm's length. It will be the same for you. You will find there are a few with whom you have a natural affinity—draw close to them. Become a part of their lives. There will be others with whom you develop a warm friendship but not intimate bonding. That's okay. The same thing happened to Jesus Christ. The fact remains that there are people who need you and you can eternally impact their lives.

Where would Peter have been if Jesus hadn't drawn close to him? Simon Peter was an impetuous individual—somebody with whom I can identify! Jesus called him a "rock," but Peter denied Jesus three times on the day of Jesus' death. Later, Peter experienced a tremendous turnaround with the Lord, yet in Galatians we read he was once again having troubles because of prejudice and hypocrisy (Galatians 2:12-13). Peter, like us, remained a man in process. He discipled many, but never achieved perfection. None of us will in this world. If we could, Jesus would not have had to die for us. But Peter's imperfection didn't keep him from following Jesus' example of developing a small group of men to disciple. God continues to change the world through imperfect people who are wrapped around His perfect Son.

Paul's disciple Timothy would have been called a weakling in my neighborhood. He was raised by two women (2 Timothy 1:5), sickly (1 Timothy 5:23), often intimidated by others (1 Timothy 4:12-16), and in need of encouragement and leadership. (2 Timothy 1:8; 2:1-2) But Paul saw the true gem inside Timothy and helped mold him into a strong man of God. As a matter of fact, when Paul was in prison, he sent his letter to the Philippians along with the youthful Timothy. "I have no one else of kindred spirit," Paul said of his young charge, "who will genuinely be concerned for your welfare. For they all seek after their own interests, not those of Christ Jesus. But you know of his proven worth that he served with me in the furtherance of the gospel like a child serving his father" (Philippians 2:20-22). Many of us would not have selected Timothy to disciple, but Paul was willing to commit to a young man with a sensitive heart and a teachable spirit—even though he had a weak stomach!

Deuteronomy chapter 6 tells us we are to love the Lord with all our heart, all our mind, and all our soul, and we are to teach these things to our children. It goes on to say we are to do this as we get up in the morning, as we walk around during the day, and when we go to sleep at night (verses 5-7). In other words, the Lord is to be the normal topic of conversation. That suggests great relationships with our children, both natural and spiritual. Paul was willing to build into Timothy's life by sharing everything with him, showing him how God was an essential element of every part of Paul's life.

One of the problems we have today with discipling both our children and our spiritual children is that we are unwilling to make this sort of time commitment. People don't often seem to know how to carve out the time to disciple. They don't know how to hang out, how to share themselves, or sometimes, how to help. Men don't naturally think in terms of getting together and sharing their crafts or doing hobbies together like women do—that's just not a man's thing. For this reason, while most women are gifted in this area, some men really struggle with the issue of relationships. Learning how to build into the life of another will be an acquired skill.

This is why it is important for me to remember that one of the most productive things I have ever done with men is simply to go along and do things with them. I go to their jobs to see what they do for a living. I invite them to join my family for activities so they can see how I live. Many people have no idea how a Christian man treats his wife and children, how he spends his money, or what he does to maintain a vibrant spiritual life. That's the biblical admonition in Deuteronomy 6, as well as the model of Christ's life.

We are to be discipling men and women as they grow into Christlikeness. There is no greater spiritual impact you can make on the world than producing spiritual reproducers. The increase is not by addition, but by multiplication. If you reached out and lead one person to the Lord this year and disciple him into a reproducer, then next year the two of you reached two more, and this process continued, within about 33 years every man, woman, and child on earth would hear the gospel.

There is a biblical call to disciple people. Christ did it. Paul did it. Timothy did it. And the people they discipled continued to do it. We are to do it, too. If you want to be involved in the Great Commission, you need to begin a discipling relationship. If you want to have an eternal impact on the world, you need to begin producing reproducers.

QUESTIONS FOR DISCUSSION

1. Who led you to the Lord?

2. Who led that person to the Lord?

3. Whom have you led to the Lord?

4. How can you begin creating a spiritual family tree?

5. In what specific ways can you share your character, competence, and community with others?

CHAPTER 18

Becoming a Person of SIGNIFICANCE

$\mathscr{I}$t was one of those hot July days in the city of Atlanta. The children and I were on our way to the park, when we noticed a huge anthill in our driveway. I gathered around it with them, thinking this a perfect opportunity to teach them a very important military and biblical principle. "Kids," I said, "let's go kill some ants!"

So there we were in shorts and bare feet, smashing one red ant after another with our thumbs. There were squeals of glee from the kids, and they were having a great time for the first thirty seconds or so. But pretty soon the numbers of ants exceeded the numbers of thumbs, and that ant battalion started making great advances on the bare legs of the attackers. The squeals turned to howls, and within a minute our outnumbered force retreated in pain and defeat. As we huddled in the garage, all five children looked at me like I was a traitor.

"Kids," I told them, "we violated a basic principle of war, and when you do that you're bound to suffer—whether it's a military war or a spiritual war." Then I dried their tears and explained how the greatest military power in the world lost the Vietnam War because its leaders failed to find agreement on destroying the enemy's strength. Instead of barricading Haiphong Harbor, telling the Russians and Chinese their ships would be sunk if they dare resupply the North Vietnamese, and bombing strategic industrial targets, we just tried to knock out enemy units as we found them. A superior military force was defeated by a guerrilla enemy because we allowed them to choose the timing, method, and location of each battle. Of course, once they hit us we could respond in force, but their surprise attacks depleted our ranks and demoralized our troops. We waged a half-hearted war, and we lost.

The same thing happened when the British tried hunting down colonists in the thick forests of Virginia and Pennsylvania. Military history has proven that an army must be completely sold out on victory, or it will taste defeat. In the Gulf War American troops fought having learned that bitter lesson. General Colin Powell described for reporters the four stages of that war: Identify the enemy, find the enemy, cut off the enemy, and kill the enemy. That no-nonsense strategy allowed us to accomplish in one week in Kuwait what we could not accomplish in a decade in Vietnam. None of those four stages were done adequately in Southeast Asia. Whether or not you agree with American troops in Vietnam, we can probably all agree that the way in which we fought was a horrendous waste of young men and military equipment.

Yet that losing strategy is precisely the way most Christians fight the spiritual war. They fail to identify the enemy. They get angry with people who don't agree with them. They attack sinners as though they were the enemy, instead of seeing sinners as *victims* of the true enemy—Satan. They argue with the world over its goals and activities, in the expectation that changing the goal will somehow change the people. The cause of our nation's troubles is not pornography, gambling, abortion, or those who make a profit on evil. The cause of our trouble is that too many people don't know God. They are lost in sin, behaving exactly as lost sinners should be expected to behave, and our job is to lead them to the saving knowledge of Jesus Christ. I'm not against seeking righteousness in our schools and communities, supporting godly social causes, or voting for believers. But as my friend, former U.S. Senator Bill Armstrong says, "The only way to change America is to introduce people to Jesus Christ."

The answer to the world's problems is Jesus. The most effective way to change the world is to reach out to others with His saving message and reproduce your life in them. You can make an eternal impact in the lives of others as you allow God to use you for His purposes. If each of us struck out with the goal of winning and discipling one person into maturity this year, our world would be a different place within our lifetimes. Winning and discipling just one soul can make a difference for all time. Imagine if Chuck Colson had not been won to Christ—if he had learned to be a forger in prison, rather than an evangelist, the world would be a different place. If Dawson Trotman, founder of The Navigators, had pursued a career as a military officer instead of deciding to help believers become spiritually equipped, God's army would have far fewer soldiers. One life can make a significant difference in the economy of God. So if John Lennon, Hugh Hefner, and Timothy Leary had been brought to Christ, they might have reached thousands more. There are many worthy causes a believer can throw himself into. There are church committees, ministries, Bible studies, political rallies—but there is no other activity more significant than reaching out to another person and helping him grow up in Jesus Christ.

On the front lines in Vietnam, there were no debates about whose father was more prominent. I never heard an argument about race or national origin when we were facing the enemy. Nobody at the front lines complained about the beer being warm or the ice cream having melted. The men next to me were buddies, and we were willing to die to keep our friends alive. The same is true with Christians. Your wife becomes a source of joy when you sit with a man whose wife has run off with her boss. Your children become a blessing when you walk with a couple through their son's judicial arraignment. You have a new appreciation of your husband's diligence when you meet a woman under financial stress because her husband is lazy. The Word of God is no longer boring and repetitious, but the wellspring of life, like plasma to a wounded man or woman.

I once stood in a ditch in Southeast Asia, waiting for fresh recruits to show up and offer us some help. We had lost about one-third of our company that day, and I was glad to see Marine helicopters coming over the ridge, filled with new men. But the men inside had never been in war before. They showed up locked and loaded, and some began firing as soon as they charged out the door. I grabbed the Marine next to me and dove into a foxhole just to avoid being shot by our own troops! Those new recruits were eager, but they knew nothing about fighting an enemy. I had to help them learn who the enemy was, where he was, what to do to survive, and how to fight him. Over time those men learned to become good soldiers.

We're faced with the same challenge today. New Christians are excited about being in the kingdom, but they don't know who the enemy is, how to fight the spiritual battle, or how to walk in a way that honors God. They need somebody like you to help them discover how to survive. No matter what your giftedness is, you can have an eternal impact. The focus of my life is to finish well. I want to leave behind scores of disciple makers when I go to meet God—men who know that, despite my foibles, I was willing to share my life with them. Susy's goal is the same. The work of the gospel is expressed through our lives, no matter where we are, and we believe God is calling you and will empower you to mentor those with whom He brings you into contact. There is no perfect way to do it, but there is a perfect way to start: Look up to God and say, "Here am I. Send me."

QUESTIONS FOR DISCUSSION

1. What has been the best part of this book?

2. Having read it, how would you like your life to be different?

3. What are the top three goals you have set?

4. What lingering questions do you have?

5. What needs to be your first step to begin discipling another person?

A Note from
PHIL & SUSY

$\mathscr{I}$t is our privilege to serve you and the Lord in our common desire to be more Christ-like in our marriage, family, church, work, and in reaching others in a gentle and yet bold way with the love of Jesus Christ. God has called us to do this through Discipleship Network of America, a network of people committed to reaching and discipling others, serving pastors, church, denominational and parachurch leaders, men's ministries, the homeschool community, and individuals ministering in their homes and at work.

In all of our books (see Books by the Author on page 367), whether the focus is couples, men, family, or church, we address practical everyday needs, challenges, and pain with biblical answers. Because we have lived out His ministry first as a husband and wife and then as parents, our marriage and family have not only been the crucible for life change, but also the medium through which we transparently share life's joys, tears, failures, and blessings. We also share eternally significant relationships in a way that we trust will encourage, equip, and release you to more completely be one of His special and dear, life-changing disciples.

We are available for live seminars, retreats, church services, conferences, and outreaches to the uncommitted. We have also captured much of this in various video and audio series presented either individually, as a couple, or with our children who also share, transparently, the journey of our family.

Please consider us the friends next door or down the street who may be of some help or encouragement to you, your marriage, family, church, ministry, or work. We will co-labor with you as you answer God's call to see your life as a channel of His life-changing love and forgiveness in building disciples.

About the AUTHOR

$\mathcal{P}$hil Downer serves as President of Discipleship Network of America. DNA is a nationwide network of people committed to following Christ's example of winning and discipling others to become disciple makers. The spiritual reproductive ministry of DNA flows out of the lives of people focused on Christ in their work, marriage, family, neighborhood, and church.

Phil is a popular speaker at church and ministry conferences, retreats, and outreach meetings for men, couples, and families. His wife, Susy, and their six children sometimes speak with him. Phil has appeared on Focus on the Family, has spoken for Promise Keepers both in the United States, and Canada, and his daily radio program, "A Discipleship Moment" is currently airing on Truth Talk Live and the Moody Broadcasting Network. Phil and Susy coauthored *Optimize Your Marriage: Making an Eternal Impact on Family and Friends*, which was released in July of 2003. Besides the release of this second edition of *Eternal Impact: Investing in the Lives of Others*, Phil has written *A Father's Reward: Raising Your Children to Walk in the Truth*, and *Brave, Strong, and Tender in Everyday Spiritual Battles*—a book that details how this Vietnam veteran learned to transfer his leadership from the battlefield to his home, his law practice, and eventually to running a nationwide ministry. He and Susy are coauthors, with David and Teresa Ferguson, of *Unlimited Partnership: Building Intimacy & Teamwork Into Your Marriage*. Phil is also the author of *Just an Ordinary Man – The Principles of Godly Leadership* and editor and coauthor of *Effective Men's Ministry*.

A former machine gunner who served in Vietnam with the United States Marine Corps in 1967-68, Phil received a Bachelor of Business Administration from Southern Methodist University in 1972 and a Juris Doctor from Emory University School of Law in 1975. Phil was a successful lawyer before being led to Christ and discipled by fellow professionals. After leaving his position as a senior partner and member of the management team of a 50-attorney law firm, with offices in Atlanta, Washington, D.C., Dallas, and San Diego, he served as President of CBMC for a decade. Phil is on the Steering Committee of the National Coalition of Men's Ministries, a past elder of his church, and a member of CBMC.

Susy, also an attorney, graduated from Southern Methodist University and Emory Law School, and then served as Assistant Corporate Secretary and legal counsel for Delta Air Lines for 10 years. She resigned her position with Delta in 1985 in order to devote herself full time to their children, whom she has homeschooled throughout their education.

Phil and Susy have six children. Abigail, 24, graduated from Covenant College, passed the CPA exam, and is working as a tax accountant in Atlanta. Paul, 22, Managing Director of Eternal Impact Publishing, is a senior at Bryan College and will receive degrees in May of 2005 in Biblical Studies and Business Administration. Matthew, 20, is a sophomore at Harvard College, concentrating in Government. The twins, Anna and Joshua, 17, and Susanna, 11, are still being educated at home.

CONTACT THE AUTHOR

To discuss scheduling a church or ministry conference, retreat, or outreach meeting for men, couples or families, you may reach Phil Downer at 423.886.6362, email him at PhilDowner@DNAministries.org, or write him at 100 Downers Grove, Signal Mountain, TN 37377. For information about books, video or audio series, a calendar of events, references, and endorsements, or the Downer family, please refer to the DNA Ministries website www.DNAministries.org.

BOOKS BY THE AUTHOR

Eternal Impact
Investing in the Lives of Others

Phil details how we can leave a legacy that will endure forever – the lasting fruit of spiritual reproducers. This book offers men and women a realistic, step-by-step guide for building into people to become change agents in the world around them through discipleship. It includes instruction in finding a mentor and someone to disciple, living out your faith in the workplace and home, and learning to multiply your life by investing in the lives of others. Published in 1997 by Harvest House, among those who endorsed this book are

Dr. Joseph Stowell, Former President of Moody Bible Institute, Jim Peterson, author of *Evangelism as a Lifestyle*, Ronald Blue, President of Christian Financial Professionals Network and Founder of Ronald Blue & Co., Kay Arthur, Executive Director of Precept Ministries, Howard Hendricks, Distinguished Professor, Dallas Theological Seminary, and Dr. Glenn Wagner, pastor and former Vice President of Promise Keepers. The second edition was published by Eternal Impact Publishing in 2005. Each chapter includes small group discussion questions.

A Father's Reward
Raising Your Children to Walk in the Truth

As a father of six, Phil understands the challenge of raising godly children in an ungodly world. In this book he addresses such topics as how to build loving relationships with children, create great family memories, help children find God's wisdom in everyday situations, discipline your children biblically, conduct fun and effective family devotions, and prepare children to impact their world for Christ. Readers have consistently said *A Father's Reward* is the best resource available for discipling your children. Endorsers include Kay Arthur, Neil Anderson of Freedom in Christ Ministries, Steve Farrar, author and Director of Men's Leadership Ministries, Ron Blue, Steve Brown of Key Life Network, and Howard Hendricks. It was first published by Harvest House in 1998. Its second edition was published by Eternal Impact Publishing in 2004. Each chapter includes small group discussion questions.

Brave, Strong, and Tender
In Everyday Spiritual Battles

Like it or not, men today are in a war—and the stakes are eternal. These are times that demand courage, strength, and tenderness. In this book, Phil discusses how men can gain victory God's way over an undisciplined faith, fleshly attitudes, and the challenges of life. Focusing on how to be a man of courage, a loving leader, husband, and father, while developing an attitude of self-control and gentleness, every man who reads this book will be encouraged to find effective tools to accomplish positive life change. Phil also addresses how to establish relationships of accountability, maintain commitments, and understand God's desire to work through our family, work, church, and life. First published in 1996 by Multnomah Books, those who endorsed this book include Bruce Wilkinson, founder of Walk Thru the Bible Ministries, Bill Armstrong, former U.S. Senator and Businessman, Howard Hendricks, Patrick Morley, President of Man in the Mirror Ministries and author of *Man in the Mirror,* and Glenn Wagner. The second edition of *Brave, Strong, and Tender* was published by Eternal Impact Publishing in 2004. Each chapter includes small group discussion questions.

Optimize Your Marriage
Making an Eternal Impact on Family and Friends

Phil and Susy Downer share from their hearts and lives on creating a more joyful and intimate marriage and a lasting heritage of building Christ into your children. This book, released in 2003 by Christian Publications, includes a first-hand account of how God helped them overcome the selfishness, anger, and poor communication that nearly drove them to divorce court. Delve into *Optimize Your Marriage* for help in rebuilding relationships, overcoming past pain, operating your home in a loving and strategic way, finding the cornerstones of effective communication, building a great family team, and effectively reaching others for Christ. Among its endorsers are Patrick Morley, Howard Hendricks, Bill Armstrong, Dr. Bob Horner, Senior Pastor, Peachtree Corners Baptist Church, Don Mitchell, former executive with General Motors and Chairman of the Board of CBMC International,

and his wife, Nina, and Chris Van Brocklin, National Director
of Men's Ministry, Evangelical Free Church of America. Each
chapter is followed by questions for reflection.

Effective Men's Ministry
The Indispensable Toolkit For Your Church

Phil wrote two chapters and served as general editor of
this book, which addresses how to develop a thriving men's
ministry individually and in your church. This compre-
hensive handbook takes readers through the five stages of
building a powerful, life-changing men's ministry. Some of
the topics include teaching men to pray, becoming a spiritual
parent, encouraging vital relationships, unity in diversity,
becoming irresistible husbands, and holding successful
men's retreats. This book is endorsed by the National
Coalition of Men's Ministries. The foreword was written by
Pat Morley and includes twenty-five well-known authors
including Ed Cole, Rod Cooper, Steve Farrar, Jack Hayford,
Vince D'Acchioli and Steve Sonderman. It was published by
Zondervan in 2002.

Unlimited Partnership
Building Intimacy & Teamwork Into Your Marriage

Coauthored with Susy and David and Teresa Ferguson
and published in 1998 by Intimacy Press, this is a workbook
aimed at enriching marital relationships. The authors open
up their lives, marital struggles, problems, failures, and pain
to provide a resource for building a more joyful, intimate, and
cherishing marriage. This book offers insights into such
issues as constructive ways of overcoming conflict and poor
communication, the various aspects of true intimacy,
guarding marriages from affairs, establishing emotional
closeness, and identifying and overcoming baggage from

your family of origin. *Unlimited Partnership* is designed for a small group study or for a couple to go through together.

Just an Ordinary Man
The Principles of Godly Leadership

Ever feel ordinary, inadequate, or unappreciated? At one time or another, we all do. But these are exactly the moments that God wants to intervene by empowering and equipping us to become His representatives. From great struggles emerge great leaders. Phil describes the principles of godly leadership through the life of Gene Ast, who struggled with a difficult childhood, low self-esteem, and poor reading and writing skills. Yet, because of his relationship with God, this ordinary man extraordinarily changed his world. *Just an Ordinary Man* was released in 2003 by Eternal Impact Publishing. A study guide is available with discussion questions for each chapter.

Chip MacGregor assisted in the writing and editing of *Effective Men's Ministry* and the first editions of *Brave, Strong, and Tender*, *Eternal Impact*, and *A Father's Reward*. A former pastor and seminary professor, Chip is a literary agent and lives in Colorado Springs with his wife, Patti, and their three children. Chip can be reached at cmacgregor@alivecom.com.

Ken Walker assisted in the writing and editing of *Just an Ordinary Man* and *Optimize Your Marriage*. He is a freelance writer. He and his wife, Janet, have four children, seven grandchildren, and four great-grandchildren They currently are residing in Lexington, Kentucky. Ken can be reached at kenwalker33@cs.com.

All books can be ordered at www.DNAministries.org.

Other Helpful
RESOURCES

CharacterLink: www.characterlink.com, 888.330.8678. CharacterLink offers outstanding computer protection from pornographic and other objectionable Internet sites.

Child Evangelism Fellowship (CEF): www.cefonline.com, 800.300.4033. CEF provides excellent training materials for evangelizing and discipling children, in addition to setting up a Good News Club in your home.

CBMC: www.cbmc.com, 800.566.2262. The mission of CBMC is to present Jesus Christ as Savior and Lord to business and professional men and to develop them to carry out the Great

Commission. CBMC publishes both Operation Timothy discipleship material and the Living Proof video series, *Lifestyle
Evangelism* and *Lifestyle Discipleship*.

Christian Financial Professionals Network: www.cfpn.org,
404.497.7680. Ron Blue is encouraging and training Christian
financial professionals around the world to lead their clients
towards the life-changing principles of Biblical stewardship.

Crown Ministries: www.crown.org, 800.722.1976. The purpose
of Crown Ministries is to teach God's people financial principles.
They have wonderful resources for adults and children.

Discipleship Journal Bible Reading Plan and **Topical
Memory System**: www.navpress.com, 800.366.7788. Various
plans for reading the Bible through in a year are offered in
addition to Bible memory systems.

Discipleship Network of America: www.DNAministries.org,
423.886.6362. Founded by Phil Downer, DNA's vision is to win
and disciple people to become disciple makers. Phil speaks at
church and ministry conferences, retreats, and outreach
meetings for men, couples, and families, in addition to offering
print, audio, and video resources.

Family Life: www.familylife.com, 800.358.6329. Family Life
has a goal of saving marriages and families and provides
excellent resources to support its vision.

Focus on the Family: www.family.org, 800.232.6459. Focus on
the Family has an outstanding breadth of resources to assist in
every kind of family issue.

God's World News: www.gwnews.com, 800.951.5437. God's
World weekly newspapers for children and World Magazine
for adults assists in the development of a biblical worldview for
all aspects of life.